AD

CODE RED
Conversations and Solutions for an Educational System in Crisis

"*Code Red: Conversations and Solutions for an Educational System in Crisis* is a must read for public and private school educators, administrators, education faculty, parents and anyone interested in improving the state of education in the 21st century. The book serves as a guide to current issues and challenges in education, including such salient topics as school violence, teacher retention, educator burnout, and inclusivity. I highly recommend the book for those interested in exploring the issues and possible solutions concerning educational systems which are in conflict and crisis today!"

—*Jerry Aldridge,*
Professor Emeritus of Education, The University of Alabama at Birmingham and author of numerous books, including co-author of A Turning Point in Education: A Time for Resistance, Reflection and Change *(with James Kirylo)*

"*Code Red: Conversations and Solutions for an Educational System in Crisis* is a must read for all educators, community leaders, School Board members, and education policy makers. This book will help every reader understand what the experience of school is like in the second decade of the 21st Century for students, teachers, and principals. It is an honest portrayal of the myriad ways that schools and the policies and procedures which govern schools are broken and breaking those who work within schools. But it also provides a portrait of the possible and gives us hope. From my experience working with schools and school leaders, hope is in short supply. These short engaging essays, readable, compelling and accessible to all knowledge and experience levels, are a first start."

—*Elizabeth Altieri PhD,*
Professor School of Teacher Education and Leadership and Co-Director, Virginia Inclusive Practices Center at Radford University

"*Code Red: Conversations and Solutions for an Educational System in Crisis* is a must read for all Americans. As the 'Introduction' asserts, we are all responsible for the education of our children. Schools are microcosms of society at large, therefore any dilemma or crisis that influences society also affects schools. In both arenas, we must critically analyze our current practices to plan how we move forward. As someone who both teaches high school and trains future teachers, I recognize the influence of standardized testing, technology, social and mainstream media, political involvement, parental disengagement, and many of the other challenges mentioned in the book. This book shines a light on many issues that society is not talking about and how those issues affect the reality of our current educational system. Indeed, it is a Code Red."

—Vincent W. Youngbauer PhD,
Bibb County School District, Georgia

CODE RED

CODE RED

Conversations and Solutions
for an Educational System in Crisis

EDITED BY
JOSEPH R. JONES, ANNA DUNLAP
HIGGINS-HARRELL, AND JULIE A. LITTLE

Copyright © 2024 | Myers Education Press, LLC

Published by Myers Education Press, LLC
P.O. Box 424
Gorham, ME 04038

All rights reserved. No part of this book may be reprinted or reproduced in any form or by any electronic, mechanical, or other means, now known or hereafter invented, including photocopying, recording, and information storage and retrieval, without permission in writing from the publisher.

> **Myers Education Press** is an academic publisher specializing in books, e-books, and digital content in the field of education. All of our books are subjected to a rigorous peer review process and produced in compliance with the standards of the Council on Library and Information Resources.

Library of Congress Cataloging-in-Publication Data available from Library of Congress.

13-digit ISBN 978-1-9755-0641-4 (paperback)
13-digit ISBN 978-1-9755-0642-1 (library networkable e-edition)
13-digit ISBN 978-1-9755-0643-8 (consumer e-edition)

Printed in the United States of America.

All first editions printed on acid-free paper that meets the American National Standards Institute Z39-48 standard.

Books published by Myers Education Press may be purchased at special quantity discount rates for groups, workshops, training organizations, and classroom usage. Please call our customer service department at 1-800-232-0223 for details.

Cover design by Teresa Lagrange

Visit us on the web at www.myersedpress.com to browse our complete list of titles.

CONTENTS

Introduction
by Anna Dunlap Higgins-Harrell — xi

Part I

Chapter 1
Code Red *by Joseph R. Jones* — 1

Chapter 2
"We Don't Talk about Bruno:" Seeing the Needs of Our Neurodivergent Students and Their Families *by Lindsay Tisdale Harrell* — 5

Chapter 3
Trauma-Informed Colleagues *by Jennifer Medgull* — 9

Chapter 4
Paper and Pencil, The Building Blocks of Learning *by Rebecca Doyle* — 15

Chapter 5
Speaking a Truth: Interview with a Veteran Educator
by Joseph R. Jones — 19

Chapter 6
Teachers Have Lost Their Voices *by Michael Jeffcoat* — 29

Chapter 7
A Voice from the Field *by Anna Dunlap Higgins-Harrell* — 33

Chapter 8
Technology and Its Effects on Student Behavior *by Jadziah Ogletree* — 39

Chapter 9
From Chemist to Educator: Navigating an Unconventional Path to Education Innovation *by Tenecia Powe* — 43

Chapter 10
No Longer Part of the Problem *by Jessica Traylor* — 49

Chapter 11
Nobility and Salaries: A Reciprocity of Value *by Joseph R. Jones* — 53

Chapter 12
So, You're a New Teacher: Bless Your Heart! *by Julie Little and Randall Brookins* — 57

Part II

Chapter 13
Creating Professional Learning Opportunities for Our Teachers
by Noah Lawton Harrell — 69

Chapter 14
Tough Customers *by Emily Salmon* — 75

Chapter 15
If You Watch Sports, Then You Want Instructional Coaches
by Jennifer Medgull — 87

Chapter 16
All In and Burned Out: Why Principals Are Leaving
by Adam Dovico — 93

Chapter 17
Instruction, Identity, and Inclusivity: What Can Teacher Preparation Programs Learn from Gay Male Teachers in the South?
by Joseph R. Jones — 105

Chapter 18
Superhumans: Student Teachers in a Time of Crisis *by Erinn Bentley* — 125

Chapter 19
Promoting Student Engagement and Enhancing Outcomes Through Community Involvement *by Noah Lawton Harrell* — 135

Contents

Chapter 20
Pressing Issues and Contemporary Concerns *by Fran Dundore*   139

Chapter 21
Violence in Schools *by Forrest R. Parker III*   151

Chapter 22
Recruiting Teacher Candidates from Marginalized Groups
by Stephen Raynie   175

Chapter 23
From Great Challenge Comes Great Gain: Promoting Collaborative Planning in K-12 Schools *by Noah Lawton Harrell*   191

Chapter 24
Schools in Crisis: The Importance of Social-Emotional Learning in the Lives of Rural Middle School Students *by Kraig Howell*   197

Chapter 25
The Unique Needs of Generation Z in the Educational Work Environment *by Nila Burt and Joseph R. Jones*   219

About the Authors   243

Index   247

INTRODUCTION

Anna Dunlap Higgins-Harrell

"I am a firm believer in the people. If given the truth, they can be depended on to meet any national crisis. The great point is to bring them the real facts." Abraham Lincoln

"Code Red" is K-12 administration lingo at some school systems for a lock down initiated when there's a potential school shooting. As faculty teaching in an initial certification program, we never want our student teachers to hear any such codes called. Sadly, we know that they probably will. They'll probably also experience aggression by "lawnmower parents" and deal with acts of hatred and intolerance perpetrated right in their own classrooms. They'll at times feel unheard and unseen, disrespected, and unappreciated by students, guardians, and administration. If forced into remote instruction by another shelter-in-place order, they may also feel they're teaching into the void. They may be blamed for what the public sees as "failing schools." Shouldn't we protect our pre-service students from such horrors? Shouldn't we show them only pictures of children "crisscross applesauce" on the floor, "catching a bubble," and looking up lovingly at their teacher offering bits of wisdom?

The editors of this edition are the teachers, advisors, mentors, college supervisors, and friends of first-year college students beginning their fledging path towards the education major, program students navigating degree requirements, entrenched majors walking the hallways of practicum teaching, and newly minted teachers grinding it out in the field. We're also relatives, neighbors, and life-long friends of devoted administrators, staunch school board members, committed central office personnel, and veteran teachers. Like Lincoln, we believe in the people and their ability to deal with the truths of K-12 education: some moments are catching-bubble-sweetness, some moments are harrowing and demoralizing. One of our purposes in bringing together these essays is to prepare students in initial certification programs for the field of teaching. We believe it is a field in crisis. We know that there are voices crying, "Code Red;" teachers, school personnel, and community members who want what is broken to be fixed. And that leads to another of our purposes: we hope this book will also cast a wide net to anyone connected with K-12 schooling. We want the words of our collected authors to be catalysts generating productive conversations about what needs addressing in the American education system.

What needs addressing? As defined by *Webster-Merriam*, the term crisis signifies "an unstable or crucial time or state of affairs in which a decisive change is impending," especially "one with the distinct possibility of a highly undesirable outcome;" it's a time when "a situation has reached a critical phase"(n.d.). *Cambridge Dictionary* defines crisis as "a time of great disagreement, confusion, or suffering," "an extremely difficult or dangerous point in a situation," "a time of intense difficulty, trouble, or danger"(n.d.).

Is this an unstable, decisive moment in K-12 schooling? Are we at a critical phase? Is there a great amount of disagreement? Is American education in crisis? Some will say that "crisis" is a bit exaggerated. Authors in this edition—and students they represent—say otherwise. For us, the system is bleeding, cancerous, in turmoil. Teachers are underpaid, devalued, exhausted, voiceless, abused. Students are committing suicide; political discourse is wrestling control from teachers in certain states. Neurodivergent students are being pushed aside. The altruistic profession of teaching is reduced to factory work. Teachers—especially those in their first five years of service—are leaving the profession at staggering rates. The profession itself is at risk of becoming obsolete. Alarms are going off, triggering Code Red for this book's authors.

And we, editors of this edition, believe our voices should be heard, that our stories and lived experiences should be part of the curriculum of initial certification programs in America. We also want the voices of hope to be heard, those who see the situation as it is, but who also see a way forward. The adage is true: the answer to any problem resides with those who own the problem. We cannot solve any problem without owning that it exists, and all of America owns the education of our children. This is our rationale,

Introduction   xiii

then, to bring forward voices of truth so that the people are better prepared for whatever Code Red develops.

How We Organized This Book

Just recently, one of us conducted two pre-service teaching observations, one on either side of a K-5 hallway. On one side, the veteran teacher functioning as the clinical supervisor bemoaned the current situation in education, counting down the months, days, even minutes until her escape from what she sees is a sinking ship. On the other side, a veteran teacher with over 30 years in the system, with systems in place (ones foreign to her only a few years ago): calming classical music played quietly in the background while children completed math problems on Chromebooks; then it was time for a "brain break," where all the children quickly shut down computers and headed to the dance floor.

The teacher, the most excited hoofer on the parquet floor, shouted out nuggets to me from her recent forays into brain science and behavioral studies. "We're resetting our neural circuitry! We go all out for good behavior outcomes!" For this seasoned educator, the truth is: students are always changing, so teachers must change with them. With enough care and professional development, she stressed, all those affiliated with K-12 schooling can see ways to solving today's educational issues.

This duality—the one teacher defeated, the other dancing—spoke to us about the collection of essays gathered here. We understand too well the feelings of defeat one teacher has, yet we hold out hope with the other teacher determined to learn new ways to deal with new realities. Thus, was born our book structure and organization.

Part One, "Code Red," is dedicated to the defeated, to those bent low, to those counting down the days. Essays in this section of the book are honest, naked, raw. We want to value and document voices of hard truths: of dealing with calloused administrators and colleagues who won't talk about certain realities. We want to capture the roar of those watching students being bullied, the cries of those counting suicides. Writers in this section share, confess, vent. These authors bemoan situations that seem unbearable, behaviors that leave educators exhausted. Readers will hear trauma, defeat, concern, even bitterness. For these authors, alarms are indeed ringing. And we hear you. It is Code Red.

Part Two, "The Way Forward," offers possible solutions, new ways of viewing current issues and working to resolve them. Our writers argue for relational administration, instructional coaching, and professional learning to retain the ranks of teachers already in the field. They urge us to tap into the "unseen and grossly underpaid" numbers of paraprofessionals to fill positions bleeding dry. They assert the importance of community involvement with local schools. They explain how powerhouse vice-principals and principals who are "all in" can endure without burning out.

No one author claims to have the one answer. These authors know situations in education are complex, with multiple crisis situations occurring all at once. As these essays suggest, what might be the most critical need at a rural middle school may not be for an urban high school. One truth that will arise from reading this edition is, all proffered solutions are student-centered and hope-filled. As our authors demonstrate, we already have in place most of what we need to solve issues: teachers (pre-service and in the field), school staff and administration, and community members who care.

That care can be seen in both parts of this book, especially in the great diversity of our authors. In the ranks of our writers are those whose voices represent pre-service teachers, paraprofessionals, veteran teaches, teachers-turned-administrators, central office personnel, vice principals, principals, coordinators of innovation and design, offices of curriculum and instruction, a Governor's Office, instructional coaches, teacher preparation faculty, and deans of initial certification programs. They hail from rural areas and urban settings, and everywhere in between. The coming chapters also showcase a great variety of personalities: the reasoned and seasoned voice of qualitative research and data analysis, the rich velvet of personal narratives, the urgent pleas of persuasion, and the lyrical songs of vignette and poetry.

Overall, we believe our text will benefit readers nationwide by giving them what Honest Abe called, "the real facts" and trusting them to meet this national crisis. We show: here are ways in which Code Red is truly alarming; here are some possible solutions. We believe our book will especially benefit pre-service teachers. As one of our authors says of her own pre-service and newly minted teachers, they're the future, the superheroes for future children in their care. In our own pre-service classrooms at a small state college, we ensure that future teachers can design instruction and plan lessons, ignite young minds, effectively deliver content, engage through differentiated strategies, and assess with purpose and fairness. We also want to ensure they hear the many voices of K-12 American educators, each sharing their lived experiences.

And what of our two clinical supervisors, the ones on either side of the hallway who inspired our two-part structure? What of them? With the one, we listened, truly listened; with the other, we danced like fools.

References

Cambridge Dictionary (n.d.). Crisis. In *Cambridge Dictionary*. Retrieved October 30, 2023 from: www.dictionary.cambridge.org/us/dictionary/english/crisis

Merriam-Webster. (n.d.). Crisis. In *Merriam-Webster.com dictionary*. Retrieved October 30, 2023 from: www.merriam-webster.com/dictionary/crisis

PART I

CHAPTER 1

Code Red

JOSEPH R. JONES

When this book was being written, I was teaching a dual enrollment English course at a local high school. During one of our class discussions, Adam, an 11th grade student, asked, "Did you have school shootings when you were in high school?" I responded, "No, we didn't. Why are you asking?" He recounted the following saga.

> Yesterday, we had a school shooter drill. That's what we call it. The teachers call it a Code Red drill. We all know what Code Red means. It means one day someone is going to walk in with a gun and kill our friends and our teachers and maybe us. We all know. The intercom sounded. Dr. Lewis announced, "Teachers we are in a lock down. Code Red." Ms. Johnson walked to the door, and unrolled a piece of fabric to cover the window. We all sat in the corner of the room. Kayla screamed, "Is this for real? Or another drill?" Ms. Johnson responded, "It's a drill. Be quiet and do what we're supposed to do." We all do what we're supposed to do, but what if it really happens? Won't the shooter know what we're supposed to do? They go to school here. They'll know we're all in the corner. It doesn't make any sense to me. We're all sitting in the corner waiting for one of our classmates to take free shots at us.

Adam's words became too real for me in that moment. As we all sat and listened to his experience from the previous day, I began reflecting on my personal experiences with school shootings.

A few years ago, I left higher education and returned to the high school classroom as a special education teacher in a co-taught English classroom. At the beginning of the year, all faculty and staff had to endure "Stop the Bleed" training led by our school resource officer. I sat in a plastic blue chair in the nursing vocational classroom believing this would be another horrendous professional development session.

The principal gave brief remarks and introduced the school's resource officer. The officer stood up, and walked to the center of the classroom uttering, "It's not if it happens, but when it happens. You'll have to step over your student who's definitely dying to go and help another student before he or she bleeds out." His words still resonate in my mind whenever there's a shooting at any school, even on a college campus. I left the training that day traumatized by the experience.

The next academic year, I walked out of my high school classroom to watch some of my students working on an assignment in the hallway. Suddenly, a young female ran around the corner from the cafeteria screaming, "He has a gun." Immediately, I ordered every student to enter my classroom. The young girl joined them. I opened my neighbor's classroom door and told her to lock her door. I walked back into my room and watched my class huddled in the corner out of sight from the door. I followed all procedures. I stood between the door and a mass of silent weeping.

I watched the students as they frantically texted parents. They hugged each other. It didn't matter that differences existed just a few moments before. These students all came together to emotionally support each other, the only beautiful aspect of this experience.

The outside wall of my classroom was full of floor-to-ceiling windows overlooking the front of the building. I stood across from the windows and watched a swam of police cars racing into the school parking lot. The lights and sirens were overbearing. As I stood there, I realized how helpless I was. I was attempting to mask my own fear by faking bravery and protection, but in the moment, I realized there was nothing I could do. I had no method of breaking the windows. I had no method of protecting these students should the shooter crack the glass in the door. We were all trapped.

We were in lockdown for over an hour. The gun was a pellet gun, which the student had aimed at another student in the cafeteria. From a distance, it did appear to be a real gun. The student was punished appropriately, but scars that he caused are permanently in our lives, especially mine.

I returned to higher education after that year with a new addition to the ways I'd prepare future teachers to enter the profession. In my Foundations of Education courses, we discuss the true possibilities of a school shooting. I recount the experience above; we reflect on my reactions and possible other reactions. In my Secondary Methods courses, we engage in similar discussions. Additionally, in all my classes, we discuss the importance of relational pedagogy and its impact on students' beliefs of belonging to a community. We discuss the power of creating safe and affirming classrooms for all students. Relationships matter in the schooling process.

As I pen these words, I realize there's a strong possibility of another school shooting within the next few weeks. Students are in crisis, believing this action is the best method to address their moments of crisis. However, the crisis extends beyond the student pulling the trigger into a broader crisis within teacher preparation. To my knowledge, I am one of the few faculty members who discusses this topic with my future teachers. When I asked colleagues around the country, there were only two other teacher preparation faculty who discussed the possibility of school shootings with their teacher candidates.

School shootings have increased dramatically since Columbine, with no indication shootings will begin decreasing. Thus, as teacher preparation faculty, we must engage in these difficult conversations with our students. The moment a shooter enters the building should not be the first time our teacher candidates have reflected on the real possibility of such an action happening in their schools. The school resource officer should not be the only individual preparing teachers in the event of a school shooting. More teacher preparation faculty must add this topic to their teacher preparation curriculum.

The school resource officer's words still haunt me. I hope none of my teacher candidates ever have to step over their dying students to stop another student from bleeding out. I hope effective changes will end these incidents, but until then, teacher preparation programs must end our own crisis of silence.

CHAPTER 2

"We Don't Talk about Bruno:"
Seeing the Needs of Our Neurodivergent Students and Their Families

Lindsay Tisdale Harrell

My absolute favorite films are produced by Walt Disney Animation Studios; not only because of their feel-good messages and catchy songs. I love the creative ways this movie giant is beginning to portray marginalized identities. Dory (*Finding Nemo*, 2003) and her loss of short-term memory, and Elsa (*Frozen*, 2013) with her disability "encoded as magical ice powers," are far cries from Dopey (*Snow White and the Seven Dwarfs*, 1937).

Recently, I was drawn to the character and storyline of Bruno (*Encanto*, 2021), who thinks differently from others and is shunned because of that "disability." But by movie's end, Bruno's precognition "ability" ignites the healing of intergenerational trauma that informs the movie's storyline. Finally, everyone could talk about Bruno. He's seen and better understood.

My own mindset as a teacher was shaped by my childhood struggles as a learner. I was neurodivergent and didn't seem to process like the other kids. In fact, I didn't learn to read until I was in third grade. Because of my impulsive energy, I was also constantly in trouble. My parents worked hard with me at home, but learning was such a struggle for me. And what of my teachers? They couldn't clearly see me. I was the kid who couldn't sit still, who couldn't learn. I was certainly never the teacher's "pet." Looking back, I know I even made teaching difficult for many of my teachers. I was the kid they may not have wanted to talk about.

It was my second-grade teacher who truly saw me and my potential. She was determined to talk about me to school personnel to get what I needed to succeed academically. She also dutifully collected the data needed to have me tested. Throughout the rest of elementary school and middle school, I had an Individualized Education Program (IEP) and received small group services to help me catch up to my peers. I remember vividly that one day when the light bulb came on: because someone saw me, I could now see my educational world clearly, and I discovered a passion for learning. It took one dedicated teacher to see me, to see that there was something more to the little girl who was always in trouble. It took one dedicated teacher who determined she'd talk about me and my struggles. Her determined acknowledgement changed my life—and it continues to affect the way I teach in my own classroom.

Every year, I request the principal and administrators for students who struggle, who are "hard" to teach, who aren't talked about (at least not in productive ways). Each year, I request the children who have been or will eventually be identified as our Exceptional Student Education (ESE) students. My words to my principal are, "These are my people, I see them, and I know them because I was just like them." Every year I make it my mission to see my students, to find them where they are, and to help them move mountains because I know that one day their lightbulbs will come on too. And, I am determined to talk about them to those who can help me with that mission.

This past year was one of the most challenging I've ever had as an educator. In my fourth-grade classroom of almost 30 students, I had five students with major behavioral issues that not only set off each other but others in the room as well. "That's fine," I said to my colleagues, "we can do this!" In response to my optimism and hope for the new year, I heard, "Oh dear, you have Bruno" (renamed for his privacy and my love of that Disney character). Even my administrators had only negative things to say; he had a behavior record that was five miles long, he was terrible, and his mom is "difficult." When it came to saying anything productive, it seemed that the policy was "We don't talk about Bruno."

My heart broke when I heard all these negative comments because I knew those behaviors spoke to something that needed to be identified. Those other teachers and administrators were not fully seeing this child. I determined that I would. So, I worked very hard to build a relationship with him, and I made sure to communicate with his mom. I let her know all the positives I saw in him, sprinkling in the struggles we were working through, so she wasn't overwhelmed.

After working with Bruno and trying different behavioral approaches, I realized there were deeper issues that could only be addressed through Multi-tiered System of Supports (MTSS), a data-driven tiered system of supports relying on assessments to identify students who seem to be at risk, whether academically or behaviorally. Why had other teachers before me not seen this in Bruno? But I knew the answer to that question; it was because he was "hard"–he was a behavioral problem most teachers just wanted to get rid of, not talk about, and to move on from.

I called Bruno's mom for a conference with me and my co-teacher. As soon as she walked into the classroom, my heart hurt for her. She was on edge and exhausted, she was fearful, and she looked defeated. The first thing I did was talk about Bruno, beginning with everything I honestly loved about the boy. He had a caring heart and could sense when people were hurting, he had a curious mind, and loved to build and create. I told her that, yes, we had a long way to go but that he was not a "bad kid." That I'd do everything I could to support him—and to support her. His mom started crying. She said that previous teachers had said nothing but bad things about Bruno, or worse, never talked about him. She said she knew how difficult he was and that he shows unruly behavior at home just like he does at school. Mom shared how she had tried everything she could think of to help him, that she felt in her gut something had to be "wrong," but no one would listen to her. She shared she even hated coming to the school because she felt like everyone was judging her. I looked at her and said, "I hear you, and I see what you're doing, and I will do everything I can to support Bruno."

Halfway through the year, after collecting data and advocating for Bruno, I finally received news he qualified for special education services under Emotional Behavior Disorder (EBD). Things were still difficult. I knew we had a long way to go, but now we had a plan. Now, teachers, staff, and administration could talk about Bruno and how to best address his learning needs. At the end of the year, his mom told me how much I'd changed her son's life, and hers as well. She thanked me for everything I did to support them; she told me she'd always be grateful for the love and support I gave her son.

My journey as a struggling learner led me here, to becoming a teacher who can see beyond the exterior of a student's persona, who wants to talk about the student so that I can help the student. My experiences with my own mom, struggling to help me at home, opened my eyes to the hopelessness some parents feel when they interact with teachers and schools. I am the teacher that I am today because someone saw me and saw something more than just a child struggling with behavioral issues. My experience with Bruno and his mom helped me realize how important it is to see and listen not only to our students–but to their parents as well.

I know how important communication is; parents and guardians want what's best for their children. Even though communication with parents and guardians can be challenging, we cannot stubbornly declare, "We don't talk about Bruno." When families, teachers, and school personnel work together to openly talk about the needs of students, a foundation can be laid to enable that child who thinks differently to grow and flourish.

References

Hand, D., Morey, L., Jackson, W., Sharpsteen, B., Cottrell, W., & Pearce, P. (Directors). (1937). *Snowwhite and the Seven Dwarf*s [Film] Walt Disney Productions.

Howard, B., & Bush, J. (Directors). (2021). *Encanto* [Film]. Walt Disney Animation Studios.

Lee, J., & Buck, C. (Directors). (2013). *Frozen* [Film]. Walt Disney Pictures.

Stanton, A. (Director). (2003). Finding Nemo [Film]. Pixar.

CHAPTER 3

Trauma-Informed Colleagues

JENNIFER MEDGULL

IF YOU'VE BEEN IN education or education courses for any length of time, you may have come across the term *trauma-informed teaching*. Without getting too technical, this is an approach to teaching that acknowledges the past and present experiences of the particular students in the classroom and asks what it means to teach the students who have had or are having traumatic experiences. It's a very important conversation to have among colleagues and school leaders because it affects decisions about instructional literature, classroom management, homework philosophy, cooperative learning groups, and more. There are good resources out there for learning about how trauma in a student's life affects their learning abilities.

I was in a district training for *trauma-informed teaching* a few years ago. About one hundred teachers were in a large room watching videos that aimed to teach us about traumas our students may have experienced. Across the room, a teacher watched intently and started to sink deeper and deeper into her seat. Eventually, she got her phone out and started to disengage from the videos. I wondered if anyone leading this professional learning session noticed that the cues described on the screen were the same cues this teacher was exhibiting.

Body language and diverting attention are two of the ways students let us know they're too triggered to learn the academic content we teach. When we moved into groups to discuss the videos, I made my way to that teacher I'd been watching. As we shuffled our belongings around the room, I attempted a casual conversation about the videos. She told me that she was watching her life on the screen. It was too much, she said, to watch that in a professional setting with no warning about the topic of the day. Teachers need administrators and colleagues to be just as careful with them and their traumas as they're expected to be with students.

I'm not aware of training workshops or conversations that address the effects of trauma on teachers. Just as instructional literature should be chosen carefully for students, professional learning materials should be chosen carefully for teacher training too. If my colleague knew she might see videos reminding her of her childhood experiences, she might have been in a better position to learn that day. And even if she wasn't able to learn, she might have been given a voice to add to the conversation about ways in which her own life experiences affected her teaching.

Just like students are not blank slates when they come to our classrooms to learn math or literature or science or social studies or art, or another language, teachers are not blank slates when they come to the classroom either.

A middle school girl had her head down in class one day. Her teacher asked what was wrong, the student said she didn't feel well. The teacher offered to let her parents know she was not feeling well, but the student said her father wouldn't come pick her up. The teacher was immediately transported back to a high school experience of her own when her father wouldn't pick her up from school when she was sick. The teacher let her colleagues know what the girl said, and confided she simply couldn't contact the parents herself because she didn't know what she might say. A colleague called the parent who, as predicted by the student, refused to pick her up from school. Teachers need administrators and colleagues who will get involved to help out when a situation triggers traumatic memories for an adult.

Let's be slow to point these colleagues to therapy as a solution to keep their lifetime experiences from showing up in professional settings. While therapy is an appropriate step for managing such experiences, no therapy can undo that experience. Therapy helps us cope with our realities, but it doesn't change anything that has already happened. In both stories above, professional settings brought out compassion from traumatized teachers. We cannot say that we want to eliminate that compassion. Teachers do need emotional support at critical moments. A caring colleague or administrator might ask them later if they've sought therapy to deal with their traumas.

Other traumatic experiences teachers bring to the classroom may be more recent or even occurring at the current time in their personal lives. For example, a principal called teachers to individual meetings with those who had missed more than five school days in the year. He informed them their attendance was a problem, that it needed to improve. One of the teachers he called in had kept it private she had a chronic illness exacerbated by stress, with medical episodes making it impossible to come to work at times. She knew she'd missed many days, but she attempted to come in whenever possible. A colleague approached the principal to let him know about the medical diagnosis.

Another episode happened at school because the teacher tried to push through the episode to come in after the meeting with the principal about attendance. The teacher had to be picked up from work by a friend; she couldn't walk to the car on her own. The principal walked into the parking lot as she was being helped out to the car. It was only then, when he saw the degree of assistance required, that he reassured the teacher she should take care of herself and not worry about having to leave. Teachers need administrators and colleagues who will not make assumptions about their work ethic when attendance is a problem. (It must be said here that sharing a colleague's medical diagnosis with the principal is not appropriate, but helping them share what is necessary can be empowering.)

A brand-new school opened, with lots of discussions to create the kind of culture that would make teachers want to work there. A department chair was determined to gather input from department members before most decisions were to be made, regularly reminding the team of the importance of work-life balance. The team looked out for each other with administrators and parents when needed. One day, the department chair discovered devastating information that would destroy her marriage. She sent word to her team that she would be late to work. When she arrived, there were lesson plans made, copies of handouts on her desk, and candy lying on top of it all with a note from her colleagues. She had worked to create that culture without knowing it would serve her in a traumatic season later in her life. Teachers need colleagues and administrators who will step in when life outside of school is unbearable. This is the ultimate example of collegial teamwork balancing unexpected professional-personal demands.

"Trauma-informed" is not just for how we work with students. Teachers have life events that can be traumatic as well. Administrators won't always know what's going on with a teacher, but a colleague might see something and be able to help.

Teachers can help each other in so many ways. First, we can listen. Telling a story can help us understand each other better, and it can be a small piece of the healing process. Second, we can empower each other. When a colleague tells us they cannot engage in a particular situation, it validates their experience when we believe them and help them navigate getting around it whenever possible. Third, we can respect what a colleague describes as effects of a traumatic experience whether we understand it or think we might respond differently. We are not required to choose a colleague as a life-long friend after we know they're experiencing or have experienced trauma, but we can seek to mitigate the effects of that trauma on students and on our school environment.

Students bring all of their life experiences to class with them each day. We're learning that welcoming those students with those experiences can be challenging, but rewarding. It can certainly change their lives when their traumas are respected and they're supported in their learning activities along with their traumas. The same is true for teachers. Teachers who have experienced trauma might not need as much training in trauma-informed teaching, but they might need training in self-regulation or stress management to support their teaching duties along with their personal traumas.

What if we differentiated professional development training based on the strengths and needs of teachers and their personal experiences?

Trends in education currently include using data to inform instruction. There are also trends to consider the life of students outside of the classroom and how their life activities affect learning. Those two trends may be difficult to hold in tension because the first tends toward reducing students to numbers and spreadsheets, while the second embraces their whole life experiences. Teachers would be the ones to lead conversations in how to do both; it may be that teachers with traumatic experiences can help us best with those challenges.

For administrators and veteran teachers reading this, we must consider the trends established in education training regarding first-year teachers. If they have the hardest classes to teach or the greatest number of preps, aren't we setting them up for a traumatic first year? Instead of thinking about the next generation of teachers as people who need to "pay their dues" we experience in our first years, what if we handled them with care and did everything we could to make their first year a positive experience? What if veteran teachers taught the difficult classes? What if we focused on strengths new teachers bring to the classroom and ask them to share their best work with colleagues? Maybe first-year teacher experiences in our schools wouldn't have to be the worst year of their careers. Maybe our schools would be inspiring places they'll want to work in for a long time. Maybe they'd work hard to develop teaching skills our students need, to learn from their teachers—this demonstrating a proven and positive instructional strategy.

CHAPTER 4

Paper and Pencil, The Building Blocks of Learning

Rebecca Doyle

Times are changing and schools are changing with them. Schools have transitioned from chalkboards to whiteboards to smart boards and now Chromebooks. In the past, schools used textbooks, notebooks, paper, pencils, books, and classroom materials that in some classrooms have all been exchanged for a single Chromebook for each student. Classrooms have evolved from a place where students can be creative while learning new information to nothing more than a business office where children engage with keyboards and screens. On the surface, many do not see this as a problem within the educational system. Parents see children coming home with grades through a website or app, administrators see high- or low-test scores, and students are advancing grade levels. However, if one examines a little deeper, one will see a system that's broken.

First, I want to begin my argument by discussing the pros and cons of Chromebooks and how the reading/writing levels of early elementary students are being impacted. While the Chromebook can be a great tool or resource, I do not support it being the sole focus of classroom pedagogy. Paper and pencil are the building blocks of the American education system. Students learn more from writing on paper than they will from typing on a keyboard or watching a video. I'm not suggesting technology is bad, because when used in moderation it can function as an educational support tool, but teachers and schools that have transitioned to a fully technological classroom creates a learning environment that limits social interactions between students, while diminishing writing skills, reading skills, and basic education building blocks.

As a student teacher, I'm able to experience a new world in the classroom where I can learn and grow as a new teacher from multiple schools and districts. During my first year as a teacher candidate, I witnessed first graders in a Title 1 school who had little expectations from parents and society. They had Chromebooks, but they were used as an extra resource, not as the main instructional tool. The students still read books where they had to turn the pages and could feel the texture of the paper between their fingers. The school focused on writing with paper and pencil instead of typing. Students learned to sound out letters and to recognize the letter shape by truly writing, instead of memorizing a key placement and letting autocorrect correct spelling errors. I had one student who started the year unable to spell his name; every day he practiced his writing skills in a small group using pen and paper. By Christmas break, he not only could write his name but was writing sentences with few spelling errors. He showed incredible growth and improvement, and he built a strong base for the rest of his educational journey and life.

In a different non-Title 1 school, I worked with a second grader. While he was able to write his name and put the letters in the correct order, he'd write them out of order using finger spacing for letter spacing. His reading level after Christmas break was on a kindergarten level, and by the end of the year, he showed very little growth. The pedagogy in his classroom relied on the Chromebook. All writing assignments were completed in Google slides. Reading was completed through articles embedded in slides or a separate webpage, and autocorrect made his writing and words coherent. He was very smart and was able to easily memorize key locations instead of letter shapes, but he was unable to use many reading assistance guides because the screen made it difficult to add help. I sat with him and worked on reading in a one-on-one setting. I listened as he sounded out every letter sound to every word, and struggled with every sight word, never showing improvement, even with my assistance. He stated one day that he was always going to be stupid, and he did not care, which broke my heart. I began working with him on his writing. We started using pencil and paper to start to learn the basic letters and writing skills, but he already decided he didn't want to learn and was going to be stupid. Sadly, he moved into third grade without making adequate progress. I believe he's going to struggle because he's missing basic building skills, and he'll always be behind in school because of learning loss. He's going to miss many crucial parts of his education simply because his teachers and schools decided the Chromebook was the only method to learn, not realizing that paper will always be the building block for education.

I want to dive more deeply into some of the pros and cons of Chromebook use in the elementary classroom. To start with the pros, a Chromebook can be used to help differentiate assignments for students who may require specific assistance such as read-aloud text or larger fonts. Another pro is that the Chromebook can allow students to break up into smaller groups during work sessions and work more independently; it can also allow teachers a way to be in more than one place at a time by recording videos for students to follow along with during lessons. Lastly, the Chromebook allows teachers and students a platform to continue their education if there's another pandemic or some kind of national disaster that causes schools to shut down.

Conversely, there are cons for just relying on the Chromebook. Many young students miss developing foundational writing skills when the classroom is solely focused on Chromebook use. Students start to learn to memorize key placements instead of letter sounds, digraphs, and letter shapes (when writing with pencils and paper). Students will also struggle with spelling since autocorrect will change errors to the correct spelling; thus, students will soon become reliant on technology instead of learning to be self-sufficient. Students will also become dependent on the text being read to them instead of reading it themselves. Lastly, when a classroom relies solely on Chromebooks, students become disengaged and can easily become distracted or off task without the teacher knowing. This means students may look as if they're engaged but, are actively playing a game on the Chromebook and missing valuable information.

The use of a Chromebook in the classroom teaches students that instead of reading to find answers and text evidence, they can simply conduct a Google search and get an instant result. According to an article in the *Washington Post* (2012), a fourth-grade student told her parent "she had a horrible day. She had forgotten her Chromebook at home and complained that the teacher made her read books to find the answers" (Strauss, 2012, para. 1). This action upset the student because she had to work so much harder to find answers rather than just getting them instantly. The use of Chromebooks is continuing to worsen the attitude of many young children because it creates the belief that everything in life should be instant and easy. The Chromebook can cause delays in brain development and functions. The more time a student spends staring at a screen instead of using cognitive functioning skills such as writing, handling manipulatives, and printing on paper, the less the brain has developed during crucial times of the child's life. The more time a child spends staring at a screen, the more they're missing key brain developments, social skills, and overall human development at a young age. Perhaps unsurprisingly, paper and pencil truly are essential building blocks of the learning process.

References

Strauss, V. (2012, Nov. 29). Time to Remove New Technology from Elementary School. *Washington Post.* https://www.washingtonpost.com/education/2021/11/29/remove-technology-from-elementary-school/

CHAPTER 5

Speaking a Truth:
Interview with a Veteran Educator

Joseph R. Jones

Sarah has been an educator for 25 years. She started her career as an English teacher, which she did for 10 years. Afterwards, Sarah transitioned into school administration as an assistant principal at a high school. Presently, she is a high school principal. She has earned four degrees, which include a doctorate in educational leadership. In this interview, Sarah shares her unfiltered beliefs about the schooling process.

On a warm spring Saturday morning, Sarah and I were discussing the editors' plans for *Code Red* when Sarah expressed an overwhelming desire to participate. I invited her to write a chapter, but she did not feel comfortable because of the political forces surrounding her current district. As we chatted about her district, we decided on an interview format because her contributions to this text are too valuable to omit. Sarah offers an interesting perspective to the schooling process. In this interview, she speaks candidly about students, special education, faculty, and standardized testing. It is a raw discussion of her realities of a veteran career in P-12 education.

Joseph: You and I have talked a lot about some of the things that you've experienced throughout your career. I want to spend some time speaking with you about your views as a veteran teacher and a veteran administrator. Let's begin discussing students. How do you view students in schools, especially high school?

Sarah: I don't want to call it the popular thing of the day but whether it's bullying or anxiety or ADHD. I know that sounds so horrible. I think they're all real things, but kids are very smart, and they'll say "that's my crisis" to avoid traditional or social situations that they don't like. Right now, I think students have learned to say that their social or emotional experiences are hard, so they can avoid going to class or going to an activity they don't want to do. But, I think teenagers have been teenagers forever. I do see the whole COVID and social media thing as an exponential growth of stress in the last three years, but it's still teenagers avoiding uncomfortable situations, or things that they're not secure with, which they don't do as well as adults. If that makes sense. I never want to seem like I don't think those things are serious or real, but I think that teenagers, if they believe they can get out of something by saying something about their emotional or mental health, they will. The use of it has increased in the last few years since COVID.

Joseph: Are you saying that kids are making up a diagnosis just to get out of work? Or are they using a real diagnosis as a way to get out of work?

Sarah: I think kids are very bright, and they watch a lot of social media, which makes their dialogue on point as in what they need to say. But I'd be very cautious to be judgmental and say that a kid didn't have those feelings because let's be real; your hormones are crazy and teenagers are teenagers. I'm sure you can remember. I can remember being a teenager and where emotions are so heightened, but they're really playing into what they see on social media. I mean the counselor can barely move because of all the traffic they get with students and their anxiety and all those types of things, which wasn't the case five years ago. Students were not running to the counselor's office to discuss their emotional or mental health.

Joseph: I think back on my K through 12 teaching experience, and the counselor was the cushiest job in the building. I mean kids didn't seem to have these problems. If they did, they hid them, and so the counselor was mainly there for college admissions or to do the testing that was going on for the school.

Sarah: Where you are as a counselor determines how hard you work. Obviously, a counselor's job at an affluent class high school is very different than a counselor's job at a Title 1 socioeconomically disadvantaged school. The job is very different, and I think today's students are influencing the role of a counselor.

Joseph: I recognize that in my college classroom. Students have become manipulative. I teach an English 1101 course. Students keep using Google

Docs to submit their papers, even though I told them not to do it. It turns out they do that because I don't have permission to view their documents, and it gives them a few more days to complete the assignment.

Sarah: They're smart, and they manipulate the system. I attended a conference recently and one of the biggest conversations was about young children and how different they are in this current generation. We discussed what their motivations are and how they're different, and the struggles teachers face in meeting those needs because we don't understand their motivating sources. They're not motivated by money. They're not motivated by grades. They're motivated by attention and affirmation.

Joseph: That's absolutely correct. I see that in my freshman students in my English courses and my foundations courses because I don't give grades, and that doesn't drive them crazy as it did to my students a decade ago.

Sarah: That would have driven me crazy as a student, but the young people are saying "I want you to give me immediate feedback." It's just different with this generation, and schools are not prepared because we're doing the same things we did 20 years ago.

Joseph: I think it's fascinating. What are your experiences with special education?

Sarah: Most schools are sitting at 24%-25% of their student populations in special education.

Joseph: Is that a lot?

Sarah: Oh yeah. The school I was in as an AP had 12%-13% and that was equal to 200 kids. 504 plans are important, especially in the school I am in now. Military families have figured out that if you get a child in a district that doesn't have all the support services, the military will not move you to those unpleasant places. People are trying very hard to get their children 504 plans.

Joseph: Wow.

Sarah: Then, if I get my child an IEP (Individualized Education Plan) or 504, they can be tardy; they can get out of class when they want; they can have extended time on tests, but the crisis is we don't have the teachers to support them, and it becomes a legal issue. It's not that teachers don't want to do right by children. We literally can't find the teachers because parents are suing special education teachers, and advocates are making a fortune. People are making fortunes on the backs of these people by suing school systems. This is just my daily experience as an educator and being in the meetings with advocates. It's become a profitable service, and the school systems can't keep up with it. At the school I was at previously, out of the hundred teachers in the building, 24 of them were special education teachers, so you're talking about a fourth of your staff is in special education.

Joseph: That's a lot. I was a SPED teacher, and I discovered from my experience that a number of parents want their child labeled with special needs because of government support. The head of the SPED department at central office affirmed that for me.

Sarah: Yes, every additional service, occupational therapy, speech therapy, every service you have, if you're getting state support, the state gives you more money. That's my understanding also. For the small district where I am, meeting specialized needs is traumatic. Every parent wants the best for their child. I know that every time I talk to a parent, this is the child that they would go get in front of a car for and die. Every parent wants the best for their kids. I think they need all the services, but at the same time, I think the state or the nation doesn't do well by them. But, if we can use some common sense, we could serve the children better. I think that we have lost some common sense. 504s which were originally designed for kids who had cancer or broke a leg, or some short-term disability has become just the alternate special education route. A parent can ask for a 504, and they don't really have to have any documentation or testing. They just ask for it and get it.

Joseph: Oh, wow.

Sarah: I mean there's a committee. It's a committee decision, but teachers are afraid to say no. I mean I could go on and on forever, but it almost takes away from the children who really need the service because now we have to find a new SPED teacher or overload a current SPED teacher for all of the new 504s.

Joseph: You're right. Let's talk about testing because I want to know your thoughts. I quit teaching for the first time in 2002 to complete my doctoral program, which was before No Child Left Behind. What are your thoughts about testing?

Sarah: They are mixed. I would say pre-administration it just made me mad. I would argue that you gave me a degree in this field. I am a professional. I test my children, and I assess my children. You need to take my word for it because I'm a professional just like a doctor giving a diagnosis. I think this child has earned A, B, or C. He has learned the standard or hasn't learned the standard, but post-administration it's not so awful. There are different teachers who have different strengths and maybe a standardized test really does assess a student's knowledge of the standards. It's a mix, and that's why I'm on the fence about it. I do wish I had the idealism of myself as a young teacher, but as an administrator, I've seen some great teachers, and I'd take their assessments in a minute. But, I have also seen teachers who for whatever life circumstances are causing them to put their job second, could use some standardized testing to make sure students are learning the material.

Joseph: How do you think it impacts students and student achievement?

Sarah: We know what percentage of the test is factored into the student's final grade. If I were a teacher and I knew that exam was 10% of my student's grade, then I'd make sure their grade, whatever I had to do, would have the buffer of that test. But, I'd be interested in how well they performed to be able to maybe teach those standards. It's very different in the last few years than it was before. Everyone just knows that this is what we have to do. This is what gives your school a good state accountability score. If we know what subjects we're going to need to do well in, then we're going to put our best teachers in those subjects, and we're going to encourage our students and incentivize them to do well in those classes. We're going to play whatever game we need to play. We're going to do what we need to do. For example, in the school I am in now, they take geometry in 9th grade and algebra in 10th grade. Why would we do that? A more mature child will make better test scores.

Joseph: So, it's manipulating the system?

Sarah: Of course, all districts do it because those state scores are connected to property values which impact property taxes and school funding. It's all connected.

Joseph: Wow. I've never thought of it like that.

Sarah: Take Algebra I for example. Across the state, all of your brightest kids are taking Algebra I in middle school where most of those scores don't get counted for high school. So, high schools are now begging that honors kids in middle school, whatever school they're assigned to, will get those algebra scores counted to their state accountability score because it will raise the score. It's a game of numbers because parents come from out of town, and they look at the schools and want to know who has the best test scores. The school I'm in now has a big transient population. It's a huge struggle for us on how to best serve these children, and at the same time, make the school work.

Joseph: Wow, speaking of manipulation what are your thoughts about grading? I remember when I went back, we were told in our district that we could not assign a zero. The grade had to be a 50. I've learned a lot of districts have this rule. What are your thoughts?

Sarah: It's hard for me to answer that. As a human being, I absolutely believe you get what you deserve. You do nothing, you should get a zero; but there are many, many superintendents and many, many book writers and many, many people who disagree with me. At the same time, I think I'm looking at my staff and saying if you give them lower than a 60, they cant recover, and they'll be a behavior problem for your class all year long. It's a hard thing, but at the same time I really don't understand. In the past two years, I have had children I've never seen before do absolutely nothing, literally nothing; not like the days of old where kids would do nothing because they're going to school to eat because they're hungry. These are wealthy kids doing absolutely nothing. I don't know. It's a struggle. With my age and all that plays into it, I don't like seeing everybody get credit for doing nothing. As a human being I also have to think that there should be some grace given to special circumstances. I don't know what the solution is. I really don't.

Joseph: What are your thoughts about amnesty projects? As a college professor, I had a kid come up to me. He didn't turn anything in, and he was failing. He came up and said, "Dr. Jones, I know I haven't done anything all semester, so can I have my amnesty project?" I looked at him. I was like, dude what are you talking about? He said, "Well in high school they gave me an amnesty project. I did the project and it made up for all the work that I didn't turn in."

Sarah: It's like every summer school in the whole world. We let kids make up a course in two weeks. I'm just going be honest. No, I don't like that. I don't think that's how real life works, but school districts are pressured to do it because failure rates mean a lot. We pressure our teachers to do it. You call it amnesty projects; we call it credit recovery. We're all pressured, whatever you name it, to do it, but the truth is, the real world doesn't give you those kinds of chances. I believe if a kid's dad dies or he has a disease, those things yeah are okay; but if he's not doing his work and just being a lazy person, give the zero. I hate it for you, and no, you can't go to summer school if you make less than a 60. You have not done any work. In high school nowadays, in a regular class, you have to do almost nothing. Teachers aren't even giving homework anymore. It's astounding; it's just one way high schools are screwing up kids for college and real life.

Joseph: Why does this happen?

Sarah: Because the state is telling the district that we're not going to fund you appropriately if you don't pass kids. It's a horrible circle, but I don't believe people at the state level think they're really doing anything wrong. I don't think anybody is sitting there with bad intentions. I think it's a lack of awareness. Those people are so disconnected from the realities of schools.

Joseph: Exactly.

Sarah: They haven't had homework, and they haven't had full essays. They've had paragraphs at a time, and we're sending them to you as a professor having only read parts of novels during class together. They don't ever have to read at home. It's all bizarre to me.

Joseph: Or, they come to my class having never read Shakespeare.

Sarah: Shakespeare is no longer required in high school, which is ridiculous to me. These are epic failures of the school system. What are we robbing children of because we want to increase the test score?

Joseph: As an administrator, which you've done for a number of years, tell me about your faculty experiences, of hiring faculty and working with faculty. What do you want to share with me?

Sarah: I've loved almost every faculty member with whom I ever worked, with the exception of a few; and the few I have not liked were dishonest human beings. It was not about their teaching; it was about their integrity as a human. I think almost everyone who goes into teaching goes into it with a pretty pure heart because no one's fooled. Most people want to be a good teacher, and not everyone's going to be because you have to be an actor, and they dont realize that. They don't realize that there are two types of people who go into teaching: the ones who were really good students and the ones who were horrible students and want to be good teachers. There's no one in the middle, and if you're the person who's a great student, you're shocked and astounded that kids don't go home and do their homework. But, we need all types of teachers to make a school work. We need teachers who will tell students some truth and tell them that their grandmother would be embarrassed of them. We need a teacher who's going to say "You're not up to par, and you have earned an F in my class. I know it's the first F you've ever made but suck it up." It takes all of those teachers to make a school work. I have another administrator in my school who doesn't have grace. She's brilliant, and she makes a lot of things work. She's way smarter than me in this community, but she has so little grace, and she doesn't understand why you have to have all of these different people to make a high school work. There's a teacher in our building who this administrator doesn't like, but this teacher makes all the pep rallies and parades and all of that work. It takes a whole bunch of people to make education work. It takes the coach that's going to work a million hours but might be the most horrible teacher in the world. I think until a person enters administration you don't understand the big picture.

Joseph: I can see that. Tell me about this generation of students who are becoming teachers.

Sarah: I have a fairly young teacher whose parents were teachers, and she's an honors English teacher. She's doing a great job. She's a good solid teacher, and she's happy and loves to teach. But, there's a brand new teacher at the school who told me, "Hey I just had a baby." I called him three days later to say, "Where have you been?" He says, "Oh, I don't have any days, so I just asked my buddies to cover my classes." He was so unaware of procedure and didn't care to even read it. They're also quitting left and right saying, if I don't like this school, I'll leave. This is happening across the state.

Joseph: Do they realize their teaching certificate can be revoked by the state for breaking contract?

Sarah: They don't care, and there's a teacher shortage. They know they'll find someplace that will take them. I was told by a young professor at a conference recently that this generation doesn't care. They just want to be needed and to be important. I don't know maybe that's it, but maybe they're living in their parents' basement. I don't know, because I know rent is no joke. I don't know how they're making it financially. I don't know how people can simply quit a job.

Joseph: So, they're quitting mid-year?

Sarah: They are quitting whenever, and I recently released two coaches from their contract. One just said, "OK, I quit being a para-pro. I was here to coach." I mean at $14.00 an hour, I might quit too because you can work at McDonald's and not have nearly the stress, but not the benefits.

Joseph: That's crazy to me.

Sarah: I also have been on tribunal boards in my previous district, and teachers are being physically abused. I've had my nose broken by a child.

Joseph: Wow.

Sarah: It's a different job. There are all those memes and TikTok videos that joke about teaching, but there's a level of reality in them. Recently, I had to go to a school and deal with parents who were upset because a bus driver turned a whole bus load of kids around and drove them back to the school because they were acting so badly. Teachers don't want to deal with them.

Joseph: It's so very different from when I taught.

Sarah: It's different. I've even had a friend tell me that I needed to run the school more like a business; you all keep running them like educators. No, we don't. It's not a business; it's a ministry.

Joseph: Take that a little further, what do you mean by that?

Sarah: Well, it's a ministry with me. I go and buy candy every week, so I have candy in my office. If people want to come by and talk to me, I want to be there for them. The teachers who are most successful really love their children, and they get past how children behave. Children are naughty, and they're self-serving just like we were. But great teachers move beyond the child's behavior and see the child, the human who made a mistake just like the teacher has done. I really don't think children have changed that much.

Joseph: I agree with that, so what's the future look like? How can we do better?

Sarah: We need to change, because the old way of doing school is not going to work any longer. I'll give my superintendent this credit. She and I don't agree on everything, but she hit it on the nail. She says we're going to have to become more flexible and change who we are. Children can put their phones over a math problem and have all the steps read out to them. We're going to have to become more creative and engaging, and I believe online and virtual classes are necessary for a whole lot of kids. We have to differentiate learning for all students. My husband's brilliant, and he can build an entire house. The other day, I wanted him to do something that

I had to give him a measurement for, and I measured something wrong. I have a doctorate. He views tasks in a different way. He would not have been successful in an online format, and I would have said "This is the best thing because I can knock it out in a few hours." We're going to have to offer different formats for all of our different types of learners.

Joseph: You are right, that's the reality.

Sarah: I also think we need to be in a place where we can speak some real truth.

Joseph: OK, what do you mean by that?

Sarah: We are being so awful to children and to their parents to not tell them the truth. We should tell kids in high school the truth. I will look at a parent and say your child is not going to that college because the average GPA is 4.2 and your child has a 2.5. Your child is going to have to pick a reasonable college. Why we don't tell the truth is beyond me, but nobody wants to tell children and parents the truth. I mean nobody wants conflict, and everybody's baby is brilliant. But, that's the American way. We're so self-serving because if the kid can do AP classes it does us well at the educational level to tell them to do AP classes and less well to do dual enrollment. AP classes help with the state scores, and AP will help students if they want to go to Harvard and Yale. Otherwise, high schools are lying because they're saying, "If you take AP classes, it will be accepted." It's actually the college that decides whether it's accepted. Dual enrollment is always accepted, but that's a truth that we are not telling. It's just one example.

Joseph: You are right.

Sarah: To have a student graduate from high school and also graduate with an associate degree is fantastic. That's a great financial situation for them because the state pays for all of their dual enrollment courses, but that does not benefit the high school because it looks better for the high school to have more kids enrolled in AP courses.

Joseph: I agree with you that we need to speak some more truth to parents and to the broader community especially if that truth helps students become more successful. You are right. The way we have done school for generations is not going to work any longer. Thank you for spending this time with me. I appreciate your contribution to the book.

Sarah: Maybe this book is the beginning of speaking the truth about education; thank you for doing this. Good luck.

CHAPTER 6

Teachers Have Lost Their Voices

Michael Jeffcoat

The cancer has spread throughout your body. If we do not start treatment, you will only have a few months to live. Your child is not progressing the way he should academically. We must begin interventions to increase his chance to succeed. When a licensed medical professional informs you of data results and statistical future, you believe them. When a licensed educator reveals to you the growth or lack thereof about your student, you blame the educators.

Teachers are licensed, educated individuals who have lost their voices in society today. We have embarked on a time when teachers are at fault, students are blameless, and parents are uninvolved. The educational system has become a political tool to launch individuals into positions of power. The state and federal governments have been dictating and mandating the requirements of teachers without the knowledge of trained, licensed educators. Although some people think teachers are leaving the profession because they despise their jobs, others, like me, understand that teachers have left the field because they have lost their voices because of governmental mandates, parental attitudes, and a lack of support from administrators, parents, and the community.

Our nation is in a dangerous teacher shortage. In fall 2022, the federal data report indicated "45% of public schools had at least one teacher vacancy" (Turner & Cohen, 2023, para. 1). With over 90,000 public schools in America, nearly 41,000 teaching vacancies are available. There are many speculations as to why we are experiencing a drastic teacher shortage within the last decade, and one reason involves requirements placed by governing officials. Laws and mandates are drafted and created by political figures with limited consultations from educators. Teachers want a voice in making state and federal mandates when it corresponds to educational laws. It must supersede voting for elected officials. Teachers know how to teach. They spent years in college perfecting their craft, learning diverse techniques, and empowering themselves with educational knowledge. So why do elected officials have the authority to dictate how and what educators are to teach, what schools need, and how students should behave? As Carlisle (2022) stated, "Clearly, there is a disconnect between elected officials' perception of what schools need and what teachers say are the most pressing issues" (p.4). Teachers want to build relationships with their students, have autonomy in classrooms, and teach material that creates successful future citizens. However, even state standards are maximized to the point where it is nearly impossible to teach them all in one year.

While political mandates are one huge reason for teacher shortages, parental obscurities also determine why teachers feel they have no voices. One can ask almost any teacher if they want parents involved in their students' education, and most teachers would prefer parental presence in the educational world. The detrimental truth is that parents have a much larger voice than they previously had, which sounds great in theory. The reality is that parents exalt themselves in the community as dictating what their children learn, how they are reprimanded, and they refuse to adhere to state and district policy. As educators, we want parents to be involved in the classroom, but they should never have the power to infiltrate the autonomy of a teacher's class unless ethical codes are violated. Parents sue schools, contact local leaders, and blast teachers on social media like corrupted pariahs. An American Psychological Association survey of "14,966 educators found that 33% of U.S. teachers have experienced at least one instance of verbal harassment or violent threats from students during the pandemic. Another 29% have experienced it from parents" (Salai, 2022, para. 3). Teachers should never have to acquiesce to such violent work conditions. Parents should have a right to dictate what their children learn and endure. If you are against certain reading material, health mandates such as masks, or even behavior protocols, then it is your right to homeschool or to pay for private schools to teach your children. The problem is: administration and district officials have bowed to parental voices in fear of harassment, lawsuits, and job security.

Currently, teachers are desperate for administrative, parental, and community support. This support system combined could alter the future of teacher retention. The reality is school administrators adhere to the voice of the public and street committees instead of their teachers. Talley (2016) noted, "These specific elements were: lack of support with student discipline, not being able to trust the administration to be fair, lack of administrative consistency, lack of respect shown by the administration, lack of modeling by administration" (p. iii). Problem behaviors in classrooms should be dealt with as a team. Parents should be involved but instead, simply blame teachers and other students. There are administrative teams who take an active role regarding behavior in the classroom, but so many melt to parental wishes and fault the teacher for the circumstances. Parents can request class transfers based on the premise that the teacher does not like their student and in most cases, it is granted. Teachers are verbally abused, disrespected, and devalued by students and parents alike. This lack of support contributes to why teachers are dropping the profession altogether.

The teaching profession is in a deficit. It is proven that the system is "bleeding existing teachers faster than it can replace them" (Hanks et al., 2020, p. 115.). Veteran teachers are quitting. Younger teachers realize it is not worth the stress or abuse to continue. Many states ignore legislative requirements and hire unequipped individuals to teach in classrooms because the demand for teachers has skyrocketed. Teachers are exhausted by poor work conditions; such conditions include, challenges with student motivation and discipline, insufficient planning time, inadequate facilities and resources, inadequate support from school administration, large class sizes, low salaries, expanding work roles, teacher morale, and stress. Teachers want their voices back. They are tired, overworked, stressed, and feel powerless. The listening world needs to support our teachers because if things do not change, the teaching profession will become obsolete.

References

Carlisle, G. (2022, October 5). Teachers can positively impact education policy, we just have to use our teacher voice. *EdSurge.com*. www.edsurge.com/news/2022-03-24-teachers-can-positively-impact-education-policy-we-just-have-to-use-our-teacher-voice

Hanks, J. H., Ferrin, S. E., Davies, R. S., Christensen, S. S., & Harris, S. P. (2021). Law and policy impacts on teacher attrition in public education: Data suggesting a new focus beyond silver bullets of targeted STEM and other salary increases. *Brigham Young University Education & Law Journal, 2020* (2), 115–46. https://scholarsarchive.byu.edu/byu_elj/vol2020/iss2/3

Salai, S. (2022, March 18). Teachers report increased threats from students, parents that's driving the educators to quit. *Washington Times*. www.washingtontimes.com/news/2022/mar/18/teachers-report-increased-threats-students-parents/

Talley, P. (2017). *Through the Lens of Novice Teachers: A Lack of Administrative Support and Its Influence on Self-Efficacy and Teacher Retention Issues* (ERIC No. ED578812) [Doctoral Dissertation, The University of Southern Mississippi]. ProQuest LLC

Turner, C., & Cohen, N. (2023, March 23). 6 things to know about U.S. teacher shortages and how to solve them. *NPR*. www.npr.org/2023/03/23/1164800932/teacher-shortages-schools-explainer#:~:text=As%20of%20October%202022%2C%20after,behind%20these%20local%20teacher%20shortages

CHAPTER 7

A Voice from the Field

Anna Dunlap Higgins-Harrell

Recently, we sat down with one of our adjunct faculty, Amy Morgan. She worked for 17 years at a nearby middle school but found herself so burnt out that she moved to the local elementary school. Our education majors love Amy's classes, especially because she is currently working in the field. Since she literally runs from one educational setting to another, Amy has little time for writing chapters, but we value her voice and wanted it documented in this text: it is a voice from the field, one that should be heard for her lived experiences. She is frustrated; she is crying "Code Red." Since she has so little time, we simply sat down with her and listened. What follows, not in any certain order, are her thoughts about the most pressing issues in K-12 schooling.

Parental Involvement, or a Lack Thereof

I work in a small county school system that has four schools: primary, elementary, middle, and high. Most everyone knows each other, and many teachers have been employed in this county for most of their careers. Existing teachers taught the parents of the younger students coming through the system. A community member not directly linked to one of the schools might think that these parents are involved in their family's education, but I know differently. I see parents that care about communicating during the good times but are never to be found during the challenging times of their children. Students that struggle with academics are some of the same students that are part of behavioral issues. In our Title 1 school, there are very few parents who even showed an interest in starting a parent and teacher association (PTA). Parents would not even come out and support Curriculum Night with their students or attend meetings for behavior or academic challenges that a student was experiencing. When I taught at the middle school, I even had parents block my phone number—after they hung up on me a few times. I called too many times, and the parents were not going to help with the student's success.

Changes in Students

Sometimes I ask myself, "Who are our students post-pandemic?" The mental health of both elementary and secondary school students has steadily declined over the last few years. I've seen confusion, depression, anxiety; I hear about suicide. I argue that social media and internet hype have played a huge role in children trying to fit in and be validated by and with their friends. Even parents are caught in the social media and internet web.

Vaping at school? Don't get me started! A fifth grader brings weed to school and lights up in the restroom while others are in the restroom with him. No concern for any consequences. Is he reaching out for help? Does he want to get caught? Does he want his parents to notice him?

Where Are the Answers?

The disrespect of students towards the teacher/teacher's aide in the classroom is rampant! Some parents tell their children that if they ask the teacher three (or whatever number they pick) times to do something, like go to the bathroom, and the teacher tells them no, get up and go anyway. As if the parent is degrading the teacher's judgment in the classroom. Parents do not always think the teacher is doing what is best for those involved. Another common complaint from parents and students is that when their seat gets changed or they no longer sit where they want to, the teacher is picking on them or calling them out in front of their classmates. Total disrespect.

Worse, I don't see any intrinsic desire to learn. Maybe it stems from the lack of parent involvement? Students of all academic levels are not concerned about low scores or low grades. Social media, games, and TicTok have taken over our children's lives. The motivator for students now is to be socially accepted, not well-rounded individuals that know random knowledge. Many (young) parents do not know how to teach students how to fulfill themselves without technology. Intrinsic desires are instilled in people at a young age, but the desire to do well and surpass your own learning has become too much work. The school system cannot teach everything to students to become well-rounded citizens. The school only has eight hours each day to teach. Intrinsic learning is like a seed planted, and it must be watered in order for the student to know that there is more than social media and internet browsing in life. That's the parents. Oh, I guess I rounded back to the first issue.

Required Standardized Testing

When standardized testing became a requirement in 2002, the idea was to keep all teachers and schools accountable for teaching the same thing. Our education system has standardized education, but no one has mandated our children to naturally be standardized. It is understandable to have accountability in all areas of the school system, but is this what is best for our children? It does keep teachers in each state accountable to teach what is mandated, but understand that teachers MUST have a plethora of teaching methods to reach every learner during the school year. Then the students are placed in a silent setting, no hands-on, no interaction with the teacher, and no tools or manipulatives to answer the question. In addition to that, they are timed!

Teachers are teaching research-based learning. New ways to reach students are developed and researched around the clock. New curriculum (in math) is focused on student-led, center-based learning. Differentiated instruction is being implemented each day, while preparing these students to pass the standardized test at the end of the year.

Administration

What can I say? It's like that old poem about the girl with the curl on her forehead: when they are good, they are really, really good, and when they are bad, they are horrid, bad. When an administrator has never been in the classroom, lacks good communication skills, and falls back on their word (especially regarding discipline), chaos has trumped school classrooms.

In order for administration to understand the ins and outs of the daily classroom, the experience of being in the classroom should be mandatory. If not, have confidence in the staff! You have to report what really happens in the classroom. Consider the mix of students in one classroom. Are there strong conflicting personalities? Are skill levels of students common or are there drastic differences in skill levels? Basically, is this a mix that can be taught? If not, listen to the teacher, the professional, and hear out their concerns in the classroom.

Really, teachers and administration have the same duties: teachers put the student first, and administration put the teacher and the climate of the school first. So, listen to us. For example, administration should tweak in members of a class within the first couple of weeks. Discipline is a huge problem when creating each class, especially in a small community where there is only one hallway per grade level. There was a class that was predominantly boys. The boy-to-girl ratio was 18:8. The mix of these boys was horrendous.

Many of these boys could not leave the room as it was an ESE (Exceptional Student Education) classroom. After many student referrals and teacher discussions with administration, three boys were separated, and the problems in the classroom lessened. They did not go away, but the classroom was better. Teachers must fight for this relief. The class is unproductive when the class has a bad mix of students.

Don't get me started on dress code. I mean, seriously. Teachers are in a battlefield on a daily basis. As trivial as dress code may sound, it is something that is important to the teachers and staff. The article of clothing in question is jeans. Jeans dressed up or with sneakers do not make me teach better or worse. Wearing jeans or not allows me to be an individual. It allows a teacher to relate to students more, work in comfortable attire, be an individual, and have some freedom. Teachers are real people and students need to see that. Clothes do not make a person a professional; it is the job a person does and how well they perform. Can't administration at least let us wear jeans?

For the editors, this teacher's voice is raw because she cares. She is frustrated because she feels unheard and disrespected—by students, families, and administrators. Despite the alarm in her voice (perhaps because of it), we hear in her comments great care for the students. Look back at her comments about standardized testing and the relational pedagogy behind her desire to wear jeans. She wants to see and treat students as the unique individuals that they are, and she wants to be seen and treated as the professional that she is. Her exasperation with the system shows. That vexation comes from feeling that the system doesn't allow her to teach to the best of her ability. Her most heroic efforts—continually trying to get parents involved, so much so that she gets her phone number blocked—speak to truths that we think future teachers should hear.

CHAPTER 8

Technology and Its Effects on Student Behavior

Jadziah Ogletree

If you walked into most classrooms in my state, you would see that every student has a Chromebook. This is because technology has become a vital aspect of the educational system. Even though this technology has proven to be useful, it has a negative impact on student behavior. As a student teacher, I am gaining knowledge and experience from multiple schools and districts. I view issues in the classroom differently than someone who has been working in the educational system for years. One issue that I have seen in numerous classrooms is the negative effects, both emotionally and behaviorally, that technology has on students.

During my first year as a student teacher, I was placed in a first-grade classroom at a Title 1 school. In this classroom, every student had a Chromebook, and the Chromebook was used in every subject. Among the students, we had one little boy who would react negatively if he was asked to put the Chromebook away. He would often scream and cry when it was time to put the computer up to transition to another subject or activity. These outbursts resulted in him hitting and screaming at other classmates when they were asked to place the Chromebooks in the charging cart. During my observations, I noticed that he was extremely zoned into his computer when the students were allowed to use the Chromebooks. It was very hard to capture his attention from the computer because he often sat with his face only six to eight inches from the screen.

This problem followed me into a second-grade classroom I was placed in, during the spring semester of my first year in the teacher education program. The school I was in was also a Title 1 school, and I saw that this school used Chromebooks for every subject as well. In this classroom, we had a female student who would act out when it was time to put the Chromebooks away. She would ignore the teacher when she told the students to place the Chromebooks in their desks. She would also kick, stomp, and cuss at other students when they asked her to put her Chromebook away. After my first year as a student teacher, I felt that technology has a negative impact on student behavior and emotional development.

Students in the classroom react negatively to the removal of technology because they are addicted to the stimulation that technological devices give them. Students today have grown up with tons of technology at their fingertips, and are often given a cell phone or iPad from a very young age. Students have begun to rely on technology for everything, and when teachers take the devices from them, they often react with anger. Due to this reaction, I believe that technology has a negative impact on students' emotional and behavioral development. According to Kenley and Zeligner (2017), "behavioral effects include irritability, inability to calm down, tantrums, distractibility, and aggression, especially after lengthy periods of time spent interacting with screens. On a more serious behavioral spectrum, many children show symptoms of depression, anxiety, impulsivity, as well as other mood and conduct disorders" (p. 25). Technology impacts emotional development, as Thomas Kersting (2016) argues, "emotional intelligence is the ability to use, understand, and manage emotions in a productive, healthy way. It is what helps us communicate effectively, empathize with others, and overcome life's challenges" (p. 63). Additionally, "In order to develop strong EQ, the front part of the brain—the prefrontal cortex—must have a healthy development. Research is validating how chronic screen exposure negatively affects this development by weakening the neural circuits that send messages to the prefrontal cortex. The prefrontal cortex controls executive functioning, facilitating skills such as decision-making and regulating impulse control. Children with lower EQs experience anxiety, depression, and lack resilience. Consequently, there is an overall sense of helplessness or fear of failure" (Kersting, 2016, p. 63).

This research, coupled with my experiences in the classroom, leads me to believe technology has a negative impact on students, emotionally and behaviorally. I believe that this problem will continue to worsen if changes are not made soon. If students today are behaving this way, imagine what classrooms will look like 10-20 years in the future. This is a serious problem that needs to be addressed before it becomes unmanageable.

References

Kenley, H., & Zelinger, L. (2017). *Power down & parent up!: Cyber bullying, screen dependence & raising tech-healthy children*. Loving Healing Press.

Kersting, T. (2016). *Disconnected: How to reconnect our digitally distracted kids*. CreateSpace Independent Publishing.

CHAPTER 9

From Chemist to Educator:

Navigating an Unconventional Path to Education Innovation

Tenecia Powe

Becoming an educator happened to me most unexpectedly. As a child, I always found myself teaching my stuffed animals and imaginary friends. Eventually, I graduated to teaching my baby sister how to read and write, stepping into the role of a teacher's helper. However, the thought of becoming a teacher never crossed my mind. Teaching? No, I was destined for something different. My parents and grandparents had grand visions of me becoming a doctor, a lawyer, or something that would yield substantial wealth. That's what they told me. So, I embarked on my journey to college, majoring in chemistry, and ultimately becoming an R&D chemist. But to be honest, I loathed it. While I cherished the camaraderie with my colleagues and the knowledge I gained, the monotonous solitude of the laboratory left me feeling unfulfilled. I felt like I wasn't making a meaningful impact on the world.

During this period, a local school district garnered considerable attention due to the risk of losing its accreditation. I mistakenly attributed this crisis to a lack of qualified, dedicated teachers. Little did I know, it wasn't about the teachers; it was the toxic school board at play. Nonetheless, this misunderstanding led me to take a drastic step. I enrolled in their Teacher Alternative Preparation Program (TAPP) and began my journey as a high school science teacher. It was a life-altering decision.

At the age of 25, pregnant and newly appointed as a teacher, I received just two weeks of training, a stack of textbooks, and the keys to a trailer classroom. I soon realized that not only was I responsible for supplies, but also for mastering the content and pacing. Moreover, I found myself in an entirely unfamiliar environment where the students' upbringing was vastly different from my own. As a Black woman in a STEM field, I was a minority in every educational setting I had encountered, from rural Alabama high schools and colleges to suburban Maryland middle and elementary schools. None of these experiences could have prepared me for the challenges of a metropolitan Atlanta high school, especially after the upheaval of Hurricane Katrina.

My small trailer classroom was filled with students, each with distinct personalities. There were gang members, older students who had been in high school for five years, and even some with ankle monitors. Yes, ankle monitors! We had immigrant students, as well as gay, transgender, and non-binary students. I had no prior experience with such diverse populations, but these students became my purpose. I quickly learned to manage the classroom with just a glance. I also discovered that while I had a passion for chemistry, not all my students would become chemists. However, they would all become global citizens, and it became my mission to expose them to the skills they needed for success. I taught a student how to sign a paycheck and write checks. I assisted others with job applications and setting realistic expectations. I loved and supported them regardless of their gender or sexual orientation. I became that teacher—the one who embraced all students, including those often labeled as "problem" kids. I cherished the gifted, the troubled, the struggling, the nerds, and the jocks—all of them were "my kids." I became their voice when they faced challenges with other teachers and helped them find their voices when advocating for themselves. My perspective shifted as I began to view social issues through different lenses, shedding my previous religious conservatism and embracing liberal advocacy for all marginalized communities, not just those that resembled me.

As I progressed in my career, I transitioned into roles such as a digital learning specialist and eventually the Coordinator of Innovation and Redesign for a different, large urban district. Being a catalyst for change is no easy task. Education remains deeply rooted in an agrarian culture, adhering to an agrarian calendar. We still expect students to sit in rows and complete assignments based on rote memorization. However, in today's globalized world, this approach is no longer acceptable. As I passionately advocated for the future-proofing of our students, I encountered several obstacles. School leaders who excelled with previous generations struggled to adapt to the needs of Generation Z and Generation Alpha. Moreover, education has become entangled in the web of politics. Superintendents and school board members often viewed their positions as stepping stones to larger political careers. Lastly, parents seemed to perceive themselves as adversaries rather than partners with the school system. Each of these factors contributed to a crisis marked by teacher attrition and college students pursuing alternative careers.

A New Generation of Learners

Understanding differences between the newest generations, or somewhat misunderstanding these generations seems to be at the heart of the education crisis today. Veteran teachers and leaders yearn for a return to the educational practices of their youth, while our current generation craves instant gratification. Memorizing facts that can easily be found on smartphones is no longer relevant. What holds greater importance is teaching our students how to analyze and process information. Our students must possess the skills to discern fake news from someone else's biased narratives. Assignments that can be copied and pasted from Google or ChatGPT miss the opportunity to leverage these tools for analysis and creation. The challenge lies in breaking free from the habits of traditional teaching and adapting to the preferences of Generation Z and Generation Alpha, who thrive on "edutainment." Whether it's right or wrong remains a debate, but what's certain is that we must change to meet their needs, not our own.

Another critical consideration is the significant amount of missed classroom time during the pandemic. Many students, including my child, left traditional school settings, some not returning for 18 months. For adolescents during development, this hiatus posed a substantial challenge. Moreover, the pandemic brought with it isolation and loss, transforming schools into not just centers of academic learning, but also hubs for socialization and mental health support. Mandatory reporters could no longer identify signs of abuse, depression, and anxiety in students visible only through screens. Likewise, educators themselves experienced trauma and loss, impeding their ability to operate as they did before the pandemic. This peculiar struggle has led to teacher attrition and disruptions in the academic environment, making learning an uphill battle for all.

Politicizing School Leadership

Politics and education have become inseparable. Books are banned, teachers are instructed to present distorted narratives, and transgender students face discrimination. The influence of political agendas has permeated every facet of education. The only place politics rightfully belongs is in civics and history classes. The divisive rhetoric has placed teachers in a precarious position, making it challenging for them to fulfill their roles without fear of reprimand or termination. This situation raises critical questions such as: how can a Black, gay, or transgender person feel comfortable under such requirements? How can anyone who advocates for marginalized communities accept these mandates? The current state of affairs in education deeply concerns me, as education is the cornerstone of our growth as human beings. Education enables us to learn from our past mistakes and strive for a better future. However, when we are teaching fallacies such as the benefits of slavery, how can we possibly convey the long-term effects of slavery on Black Americans?

Another significant issue is the prevalence of personal agendas within our education systems. Superintendents and school board members engage in battles driven by their agendas, often using their positions as stepping stones to larger careers. While personal growth and ambitious goals are commendable, students should not suffer. I have witnessed innovative and effective superintendents lose their jobs because their new ideas made some uncomfortable. Innovation is imperative for progress, yet innovators are being replaced with old-school educators who undo the transformational changes introduced by their predecessors. The idea of "bringing back old-school teaching" is touted by some, but it is essential to recognize that old-school teaching methods were ineffective even before, during that time.

I have had the privilege of observing numerous board meetings in various districts. Regrettably, most of those making decisions have not set foot in a classroom for over two decades. How can they possibly understand what works in today's educational landscape? Have they engaged with the various stakeholders who truly matter? Have they sought input from the students themselves? Far too often, decisions are made for and imposed upon students. It's time to involve them in the design process, listen to their perspectives, and understand what works for them now. For instance, some parents oppose asynchronous learning, even in small doses, but many students relish the freedom to choose when and where they learn. This ties into another significant problem in education today—we've been told to differentiate for years, yet we fail to differentiate based on the lessons learned during COVID-19. It's unreasonable to expect "normal" to be the same now when we've discovered numerous effective ways to reach students.

Parents Versus the School

Lastly, the role of parents in education is fraught with challenges. Some parents are not involved enough, while others are overly intrusive. As a self-professed helicopter parent, I understand the concerns and the need for support. However, it's the "lawnmower parents" who make life miserable for schools. In one instance within my district, a school had to search for yet another front office secretary because parents had treated the staff so poorly that they resigned. Parents express dissatisfaction because they want more say in some areas but less in others that are deemed important. During my tenure as an education technology specialist, I received emails from parents insisting that I find a way to prevent their children from using computers at home. I was bewildered—shouldn't parents have control at home?

In my current role as a Coordinator of Innovation and Redesign, we employ the liberatory design framework to identify and address needs. In line with this approach, conducting empathy interviews is a pivotal part of my work. Unfortunately, one recent interview began on a sour note, as the parent was defensive and questioned why she had been chosen for feedback. After explaining my selection process, she expressed a complete lack of trust in the district, alleging that we had ruined her children's education. Her perception is her reality, and delving into her grievances revealed that they were all rooted in the school's failure to operate as it had in the past. The concepts of equity and the necessity for innovation seemed beyond her grasp. In her privileged world, she could afford far more amenities than others. She displayed a lack of concern for the fact that school decisions aim to serve the greater good of all.

Conclusion: My Truth

I do not possess the ultimate solution to the ongoing crisis in education, but I can identify some of the root causes, which I confront daily. Many days, I find myself in tears, yearning to do what's best for children while my hands are tied by politics. Implementing meaningful changes takes time, and patience is a rarity. The average tenure of a superintendent in my school district is a mere three years—how can we bring about genuine systemic change in such a short span? I embarked on the path of teaching with a genuine desire to change the world, yet now, I often find myself cast as the scapegoat for everything that's amiss in education. It breaks my heart daily. I contemplate leaving, but I am aware that the crisis will only persist or worsen if educators who genuinely care about children and seek their best interests continue to depart. Money is not the answer; many teachers have left despite bonuses and raises. They yearn for flexibility, balance, fewer mandates, and less political interferences. They crave respect from the community they work tirelessly to serve. We must find a solution swiftly, or we risk ending up with what nobody desires—overcrowded classrooms, virtual teaching, and teachers who view students as numbers rather than unique individuals.

CHAPTER 10

No Longer Part of the Problem

Jessica Traylor

This is the story of why I chose to take a $30,000 pay cut. A few years ago, I made the decision that I would no longer be a school psychologist in a rural school district. This was something I had considered for a while, but I was reluctant to make the change. Beyond the fact that I would be losing a significant portion of my income, I would also be losing my position in the organization. As a long-time employee, I had gained the respect of most of the teachers and administrators in the district. Because of a series of events, I was finally uncomfortable enough to make the change.

At the time of my "big change," I had been a school psychologist for approximately 10 years, had been teaching as an adjunct for two colleges, and was doing contract psychological evaluations for another local school district. I was working too much, but I thought I had to because my husband was out of work for a few years and we were struggling to pay the bills. He had recently gotten a job making much less than we were accustomed to, so the financial burden was real. Regardless of this reality, I put a lot of pressure on myself to close this gap. I had been working at this pace for three years at that time. Of course, something like this can only last for so long, but I was determined to keep going.

In addition to working multiple jobs, I was also continuing to pursue my own professional development. That year, I chose to present my dissertation research at a local conference. My presentation went well. It was probably the best presentation I have ever delivered. I still remember the feeling of floating out of the room and calling my best friend. Later that afternoon,

I attended other conference sessions. The last session of the day was about mental health for school administrators. Most people had already left the conference. No one would care if I stayed or went home early, but something in me convinced me that I needed to be in that room.

The presenter showed slide after slide of youth mental health statistics from the previous year. The data were presented by county. On each slide, the students in my county were the highest: depression, self-harm, suicidal thoughts, and suicide attempts. We were winning the wrong race. I found myself crying, in a conference, in the room with local principals and district leaders. I couldn't help it. I raised my hand and explained to the presenter that those were my kids. His kind response was, "I know."

I made a decision at that moment, one that would change the course of my future. I decided I could no longer be part of the problem. There were plenty of solutions to this, and I was going to be a driving force in changing the direction for my local students. With the presenter's permission, I reorganized his presentation, adding the results from focus groups with students and teachers. I presented this information to all teachers at all of the schools in my district. I offered to present to the Board of Education, but they were not interested. That should have been a warning sign. Next, I presented that same information, with the addition of recently gathered teacher mental health data, to local organizations. I talked to the Rotary Club, Family Connection Collaborative, Board of Commissioners, and a local church. I presented this information to anyone who would listen. I was in the newspaper multiple times that spring. My call to action was this: do something now!

Next, I found a program that could have been very beneficial. I called the representative, set up a meeting with district leaders, and even put together a budget. After pretending to be interested, the district decided to invest in more computers. Needless to say, I was hurt. The teachers were motivated. The community wanted to help. Most of the principals were on board. There was one principal who did not want to give up a portion of his budget for the program. So, because he is friends with the superintendent, the program was not pursued.

This is where I made a series of immature decisions. At this time, I was writing a blog on a fairly regular basis. Normally, I would write about mental health topics like stress management, values assessment, and other positive growth topics. After my efforts were blocked, I started writing blogs with titles like Speaking my Truth and Do We Have to Play the Game? I was also sharing youth mental health articles on Facebook with comments like, "our district is doing the bare minimum to address mental health," and thanking all of the principals, except one, for their willingness to acquire more mental health support for our students.

As you can imagine, this didn't go well. I was called into the superintendent's office. Remember that guy who was friends with the principal who didn't want to give up his budget and was blatantly left off of the Facebook thank you post? I learned the hard way that offending the superintendent's buddy is not a good career move. After thirty minutes of him treating me like I was trying to destroy his school system, I was asked if I had anything to say. No. I was crying too hard to say anything.

I was very hurt. This guy did not, and probably still does not, know more than five teachers in the district. The students wouldn't recognize him if they saw him at a school function. But here he was, berating me, the person who grew up in this county and had served faithfully for over a decade. It was as if none of that mattered. The only thing that seemed to matter was the public persona of his friend. Later, I sent an email to the three people who were in the room that day and expressed my concerns about the way I was treated. The superintendent's response to me was that this matter was closed. I could take up any further concerns with my supervisor. I was fairly certain I was going to resign when I left crying, but that email cleared up any doubt I had. I started packing my office that day.

I remember crying for the next two weeks. I couldn't even run a meeting, which was inconvenient because the spring is very busy for most school psychologists. Everyone tried to console me and remind me that "that's just how he is." None of that mattered. What mattered to me was that he was the leader of the district. He set the tone for the entire organization. That was the problem. I knew I was leaving because I could no longer be part of the problem.

Fortunately, I was simultaneously becoming more involved with college activities beyond teaching my two evening classes. While attending a Challenge Course facilitator training, I learned that the college would soon have a full-time professor position posted. I knew that if I chose to teach college that I would be taking a huge pay cut. At that point, I didn't care about the money. I wanted to be somewhere that would allow me to be part of the solution to the mental health crisis facing our youth. Now, I am able to reach future teachers and human service workers while they are still in school. I'm also able to support young adults through a challenging transition to college.

Looking back, this transition could have been much less traumatic if I had listened to my intuition and made the change earlier. There were warning signs that I was unhappy with the current administration. I could have also slowed down enough to allow the school system to catch up to my level of knowledge and passion about youth mental health. Overall, I learned that rushing a major change is not necessarily the best practice for all involved. I may not agree with or respect the superintendent, but he was the leader of the organization. His choices set the tone and direction for the district. While a small group of people could have eventually made a change from the ground up, having the support of the leadership would have made it easier.

CHAPTER 11

Nobility and Salaries:
A Reciprocity of Value

JOSEPH R. JONES

THE BROADER RESPECT FOR the teaching profession is eroding. In our society, teaching maintains no social capital, and often is associated with negative social stigmas. This is evident in how one can become a teacher. In my state, if one has a four-year degree outside of education, they can accept a teaching position and have three years to complete a certification program. I admit these policies exist because of a critical need to fill teaching positions. Teacher attrition is incredibly high, and fewer individuals are entering the profession. That being said, with a PhD, I cannot accept a job as a nurse and have three years to gain credentials, even though America needs more nurses. Conversely, individuals are allowed into schools yearly to teach our children without learning the complex learning theories that are necessary for effective pedagogy. In doing so, we allow an engineer to teach mathematics or a journalist to teach English, because the social status of teaching has diminished the importance and the nobility of the teaching profession.

Moreover, the teaching profession does not maintain any social capital within our society. A few years ago, I sat at a restaurant bar with friends-a prominent couple within my state. As we were discussing the minutiae of our day, another politically prominent couple walked over to my friends. One of my friends asked the couple, "Do you know Dr. Jones? He is a high school teacher here, but he was an Associate Dean at the university. He is writing a new book." Her words immediately shocked me and reminded me of the social stigma of P-12 teaching. She chose not to end her introduction with, "He is a high school teacher here." Rather, she believed teaching high school lacked the social status that their friends would respect; therefore, she ended her introduction with an academic profession, one that their friends would respect.

I engaged appropriately with the new couple answering their questions about my academic pedigree and my research agenda. However, I was never asked a question about my high school classroom nor my beliefs about our schooling process. This experience revealed to me the dire state of the teaching profession by illuminating the need to begin addressing the social stigma attached to the teaching profession because the stigma diminishes the nobility.

The lack of nobility in the teaching profession is also directly connected to teaching salaries. A few years ago, I left higher education and returned to the secondary classroom. I accepted my new job as a high school teacher in a large suburban district. Seth, a colleague in the district, was in his second year of teaching. He owed student loans, a car payment, car insurance, and other traditional expenditures. For perspective, his rent was $850 which was close to the average one-bedroom rent for our area. His car payment was $350 and his car insurance was $133. Student loans cost him $200 per month. He did not have cable. His cell phone plan was still part of a shared plan with his parents, and his home utilities averaged $300 per month. He chose the highest deductible for his health insurance because it was the cheapest, and he was relatively healthy. He lived paycheck to paycheck. In fact, Seth, like most of the other early career teachers in our district worked a part-time job.

During a separate conversation with two other teachers in our conference room, we began discussing unwanted expenses, specifically auto repairs. One of the teachers mentioned she had to pay a car repair for her son, which left her with $16 in the bank. Another teacher responded, "I have less than $50, but I have a full tank of gas."

At the time, a teacher in this district with a bachelor's degree and one to three years of teaching experience earned $38,000 annually. Today, the salary has increased by $7,000 because the state increased teacher salaries during election years. I should also note that average rent in the area has increased to $1250 for a one-bedroom apartment, which nearly depletes the actual rise in earnings.

In this state, teachers are paid according to their highest earned degree within their discipline and their years of experience. When I returned to the classroom, the district determined my salary using all of my years in the secondary classroom and all of my years in higher education; thus, my salary offered an acceptable level of comfort that Seth and other new teachers could not experience. In fact, my salary was higher as a high school teacher (190-day contract) than my earnings as an associate dean at a state university for the same ten-month contract.

I recognized that I existed within a level of economic privilege, but I wanted to experience, as authentically as possible, a new teacher's financial realities. Thus, I vowed to live on the same monthly salary that a new teacher would earn. Each month, I utilized only the monthly earnings of a new teacher, and I placed the additional funds into another account.

I cancelled my cable subscription, and I purchased a television antenna. I changed my traditional choice in bourbon to a less expensive one within my budget. My financial life changed dramatically, and for the first few months, I simply survived. I bought groceries differently, and I only bought new clothing when it was absolutely necessary. I started preparing meals at home, which was antithetical to my normal lifestyle. At the end of each month, I maintained $100 in my checking account, without placing money in investments or saving accounts for retirement or for emergencies.

During the third month of my experience, I incurred an unexpected medical expense which impacted my ability to pay utilities. The lack of funds snowballed, and on March 28 of that year, the electricity to my house was disconnected. After work, I walked into my dark house. At the time, I drove an SUV that carried the same electrical outlet located within a house. I used an extension cord to provide some electricity to meet my very basic needs, but the next morning my power was restored. Unlike Seth and other new teachers, I maintained some financial privilege.

In this situation, I was only creating a simulation of what a majority of new teachers endure as real-life experiences, but this experience did offer me a small glimpse into the lives of new teachers. It was annoying having to use my cell phone as a hot spot, so that I could respond to emails and other internet necessities. The television antenna was an inconvenience. The experience was irritating but it was not stressful, which was contrary to Seth's and others normalcy.

I mention teaching salaries and my experience because I believe teaching salaries are directly related to the nobility of teaching. There is a reciprocal relationship between teaching salaries and society's beliefs concerning the teaching profession. Until a majority of society values the teaching profession, salaries will continue to be low, especially for beginning and mid-level teachers. I do acknowledge that my state pays teachers one of the highest amounts in the southeastern United States. In fact, if I worked in other southern US states, my salary would have been $15,000 to $35,000 less than what I earned in my state, but that salary is premised upon advanced degrees.

P-12 schooling is in a state of turmoil. Teachers are leaving the profession at an alarming rate. Fewer undergraduate students are majoring in teacher education. Recently, I conducted an antidotal poll asking parents if they wanted their children to become teachers. Out of 50 parents, 40 of them did not want their children to choose a career in education. Of those 40 parents, 15 were educators, a fact that alarmed me. The teaching profession is in a downward spiraling crisis. I posit the correction is to increase the nobility of teaching, beginning with teacher salaries.

CHAPTER 12

So, You're a New Teacher:
Bless Your Heart!

Julie Little and Randall Brookins

Starting a career as a new teacher is exciting and maybe a bit daunting. You've completed the coursework and the practicum hours, passed the licensure exam, and gone through several job interviews. You've envisioned a Pinterest-worthy classroom and created your Amazon wish list. Now reality sets in; you are going to be responsible for a classroom full of students. There is always a learning curve as you familiarize yourself with your new environment because every school system, and each school within a system, runs differently. You need to take what you've learned in your teacher preparation program and make it work for your teaching style and your new school's expectations. In this chapter, we help you navigate the first years of teaching by offering observations and practical advice from two seasoned teachers who have been there and thrived.

Parent Communication

One of the first tasks of the school year will be to introduce yourself to the parents and welcome them. Always begin the year with an optimistic letter to the parents about your general plans for the school year and how happy you are that their family will be a part of your classroom community. It is best for the letter to be sent before the first day of school (it can relieve some anxieties of the parent or child and create excitement about the school year) or at least within the first couple of days. Most schools also begin the year with an Open House, and it may be the only time you talk to some parents in person, so it is important to be positive and ensure them that their child is in good hands and will have an amazing year. After this initial meeting, it is a good idea to follow up within the first few weeks of school and send a positive note to every parent/guardian about their child. If you reach out in this way, and later need to contact the parent about a behavioral issue or bad grade, you have already established a rapport and it will be easier to give them more challenging news.

There will be numerous occasions throughout the school year when you need to contact parents. Regardless of the method of communication, make sure that you lead with a pleasant greeting and something positive about the child (no matter how difficult that may seem at the time). Ask the parent for suggestions for helping their child (after all, they know their child best). Assure them that you are a team, and you want to work together in the best interests of the child. End your communication by thanking them for their time and support.

If the parent contacts you, never send a quick response to something that angers or offends you. Go back and reread an email or text later before responding. Even if the parent is out of line, ALWAYS take the high road. Emails and texts are today's paper trails and will always be your proof that you have maintained professional communication with parents. Often parents will realize in time that they were out of line, and if you have treated them fairly, they will have more respect for you.

If a parent asks for an in-person meeting, never meet with them alone. You should always have another person in the room especially if the topic might be contentious. Remember, everyone has a different parenting style and even if you blatantly disagree with their choices, it is not our place to judge. ALWAYS, ALWAYS let the parents know that you see something good in their child. When you balance all negative feedback with something good, parents will trust what you say because they see that you genuinely care for their child.

Relational Pedagogy:
Building Relationships with Students and Managing Behavior

There is much discourse about classroom management and how to keep students not only engaged, but also about teaching and learning. Classroom management takes precedence over curriculum at the beginning of the school year! Your school will probably have a Positive Behavioral Interventions and Supports (PBIS) plan or schoolwide behavioral expectations. These should be presented in positive ways that teach students what are expected, instead of telling them they are wrong. For example, rules should read "walk in the hallway" instead of "no running." You set the climate in your classroom, so keep it positive: let your students know that you care about them and want to get to know them. Ask them about their interests, how they spend their afternoons and weekends, etc. Building these positive relationships goes a long way in preventing negative behavior. Be mindful of your word choices and tone, and make sure you are communicating as positively as possible.

You also need to take time to establish procedures–it buys you lots of teaching time for the rest of the year if students do not have to constantly ask for directions. Students need to know where supplies are kept, how to ask to go to the bathroom, where to turn in assignments, etc. These procedures should be practiced extensively at the beginning of the year and again after breaks for all age levels (middle school students are notorious for forgetting how to open their lockers after breaks). It is also helpful to give the students jobs or responsibilities so that they have some ownership in how the class functions.

No matter how well your class is structured, there will always be challenging students, and they are well-known throughout the school. Teachers see their names on detention/ISS lists, we hear their names called to the office, etc. If possible, you need to build relationships with these students before they ever enter your classroom.

Julie's Story

One year, a 7th grader was always in trouble (cursing at teachers, fighting, skipping school, etc.). I learned she would be in my connection class the next nine weeks. When I found this out, I immediately started talking to her in the hallway between classes. I let her know that she would be in my class, I asked how she was, inquired about her interests, etc. I knew from teaching in a small town, and from her records, that she had a difficult home life.

My goal in making small talk with her was to let her know that I cared and was not judging her based on her discipline record or grades. After a while she started seeking me out in the hallway to say "hi." She also complained about other teachers, sometimes legitimately and sometimes not. I saw this as an opportunity to help her deal with her frustrations and to explain to her why teachers did certain things (like assign homework or not allow outbursts in class). By the time she was actually in my class, I honestly never had a moment of trouble with her. These short conversations were just a small part of my day, but they let this student know that my classroom was a safe place for her.

Randall's Story

Another student, Becca, suffered from anxiety that often affected her ability to fully engage in class activities. I worked to build a rapport with her and introduced her to a couple of teachers in the next grade, knowing that establishing an early relationship for her would result in a better emotional and academic experience during the next school year.

In order to track student emotions and interests, you can do check-ins through journal writing, class discussions, group activities, or individual activities. To build that trust for them to provide accurate information during these activities, it is important for the teacher to model and share their feelings as well. Many students will feel a sense of importance, well-being, and connection knowing facts about you and what your interests are outside of the classroom. Establishing that familiarity allows a student to see you as more than a teacher and that they can positively influence your day.

Just as communication with parents/guardians should always include something positive, make sure that you balance your communications to students as well. When giving feedback or redirection to students, balance what they can do better with what they are already doing well. When they know that you also see the good in them, they will trust you even more and most often are more willing to work hard to make progress in their areas of need.

One thing that teachers never have enough time to do is visit one another's classrooms. This is a great way to share ideas for seating arrangements, wall displays, organization, scheduling, and to experience the classroom climate.

Julie's Story

One year the principal asked that teachers visit classrooms monthly during their planning period (that's another issue!), just for a quick observation. These were supposed to be friendly, benign walkthroughs to gather information. My first visit at the beginning of the year was to a 6th grade English/Language Arts classroom. The teacher was near retirement and had a reputation for being very strict with students; her advice for new teachers was not to smile until Christmas break (seriously!). Upon entering the classroom, the largest bulletin board directly across from the door was adorned with "How to get detention" and "How to get ISS." I am not making this up! Imagine being a new 6th grader: navigating a new environment, trying to operate a combination locker, and dealing with the insecurities of adolescence. My summation was that students would respond in one of two ways.

- "Let's test her" (student sees this as a challenge).

- "I'm too scared to even speak in her class" (student shuts down).

Neither of these options is ideal. We need to welcome students with positivity and let them know that our classrooms are safe spaces for them. Classroom rules and routines need to be displayed in a way that encourages participation and success and not rooted in negativity.

Collaborating with Colleagues

Collaborating with colleagues can be one of the best things about your teaching experience, and also one of the worst. Most of us do not have the option of teaching without collaborating with a teaching partner or a grade level team. Keep in mind that no two teachers teach exactly the same way. You have to be open to trying lessons differently.

Randall's Story

Whenever I collaborated with another teacher, I always learned something new, and it affected my approach to some degree in future lessons.

When you are willing to try another person's idea, they will be more likely to reciprocate. If your lesson changes through collaboration with your colleagues, do not take the change as a personal slight or failed idea. This was a difficult lesson learned for me as I was once paired with a teaching partner who not only had an opposing teaching style, but also a different philosophy of education. The compromises were sometimes difficult, and I often had to "take the high road." In the end, we were respected and heralded as one of the best teaching partnerships by peers, administrators, parents, and students. In these situations, lead with positivity and always assume good intentions.

No matter where you work or what you do, there will always be negativity and the infamous rumor mill. Participation in this element of a school will never result in anything positive and almost always results in disrupting or tearing down the community. The more you can work from a positive perspective, the more people and students will be drawn to you, and the more your colleagues, especially administrators, will trust and respect you.

- Be friendly to everyone (even those whom you do not particularly like or whom you share interests with).

- Break rooms and lounges are notorious for gossip and negativity. Physically remove yourself from an environment that is negative and from discussions that are unproductive.

- Always assume the best. It is often difficult to discern a person's intention via writing, like texts, emails, or social media. Never respond immediately to a message that you perceive as negative. Even if it turns out that person was angry when the message was written and intended it to be negative or confrontational, cooling off time for both sides will result in a better outcome. A negative response from you will create a "paper trail" that will be difficult for you to defend.

- If an interaction with a colleague or parent turns uncomfortably negative, seek mediation from an administrator. Most good administrators will be happy to help you through a tough situation.

Interacting with Administrators

Like them or not, administrators are always going to have some authority over you. You have to figure out what style of communication they prefer, and just as you do with students and parents, you must meet them where they are. Always assume goodwill when dealing with your superiors. Just as they do not have first-hand knowledge of what you are going through personally and professionally, you do not know what they are going through either. You should try to handle issues with students, parents, and colleagues on your own before going to an administrator. Administrators deal with numerous matters on a daily basis, so the more you show that you can manage situations that arise, the more willing they will be to support you when something unmanageable comes along. You will have good and bad administrators (just like with any job), and you will learn important lessons from them all.

Taking Care of Yourself

When you are tired, rest. Taking care of yourself is one the best things you can do for yourself and for your students. If you can show up at your best each day, you will enjoy teaching and your students will enjoy learning. All well and good, but how do you take care of yourself?

- Set boundaries–with your students, with the parents, with co-workers, and with administrators. You don't have to answer every email immediately.

- Take breaks. Take personal days and sick days when you need them. Come in late or leave early on occasion, with permission of course.

- Eat. Keep snacks for yourself at school. Plan your meals ahead of time and make it a habit to eat healthy foods at school.

- Talk to a trusted friend.

- Do not feel obligated to take work home. Make it a rare occasion that you take work home unless it is a project that you are passionate about and the work at home will bring you joy.

- Find a balance. You will work with teachers who pride themselves on being the first one in the building and the last one to leave. There will also be those who walk in as the bell rings and leave with the buses. Don't be either of those. One teacher chose one day per week to work late. She saved anything that she couldn't finish during the normal workday and completed it on this planned day. Find what works for you.

- There are pros and cons to sharing cell phone numbers between teachers and parents, and you must weigh what is best for you. Of course, you should always follow your school's policy.

- It's okay to say "no" your first year because you need to focus on acclimating to your new environment and teaching preparations.
  - No coaching.
  - No club sponsorship.
  - No graduate school (not just yet; definitely do this after the first year!).
  - No grade level/ content chair position.
  - No new certifications.

Professional Development

Randall's Story

Early in my career I worked for a school system that supported consistent, quality professional development. There were yearly classes that all teachers were required to take and financial assistance for additional classes and conferences that teachers wanted to attend. Some systems value professional development more than others, and some just do not have the financial resources to support any extra professional development for teachers. If you are fortunate enough to teach in a system that aligns with your curriculum beliefs, you will likely have ample opportunity for relevant professional development.

The school system that best supported my professional development had each teacher meet with the curriculum specialist at the end of each school year to reflect on what went well and what did not. From that reflection, teachers were required to write at least two goals for the following school year, one of which had to be a professional opportunity that would support teacher growth. I found that balance and trust in me as an educator to be very empowering. Set your yearly goals early on to address what you want to learn or improve and try to steer your professional development toward supporting and accomplishing those goals.

Regardless of how your school system deals with professional development, always take advantage of the opportunity to attend classes and conferences. Even when opportunities that are presented seem not relevant or interesting, try them anyway! Seeing different perspectives, curriculums, and programs can often facilitate growth in your philosophies and teaching practices.

What Else? Random Nuggets

- Be open to change and know that it is inevitable.

- Be careful on social media. Because teachers are often well-known in most communities, you must always maintain a level of professionalism that others are not necessarily bound by. Anything that you post can and most likely will live on forever on the world wide web. Be a good role model, especially within the community in which you teach.

- Every few years, reflect on your teaching experience and consider a change. Burnout can occur if you stay in the same school, school system, grade level, or subject too long. Changing one or two of these elements can result in a much more fulfilling career in education.

- Do not hesitate to ask for help if you need it. We should all be working together for our students.

- Know that you will get sick so that you are not discouraged (new school with new kids and lots of germs; it's inevitable).

- Lead with kindness.

The first year of teaching is an adventure. It is exhilarating and exhausting. You will feel heroic and helpless. You will laugh and cry. And it will all be worth it. Enjoy!

PART II

CHAPTER 13

Creating Professional Learning Opportunities for Our Teachers

Noah Lawton Harrell

Our society is data-driven. You see it in all walks of life, from sports to the world of business. Education is no different. I am a firm believer in using data to encourage student and teacher growth, which means that I need to be a firm believer in data-driven professional learning opportunities for the teachers in my building. As educators, we often think of any professional learning as professional development. However, there is a distinction between the two.

There is a useful distinction between traditional "professional development" and "professional learning;" both are intended to result in system-wide changes in student outcomes. Professional development, which "happens to" teachers, is often associated with one-time workshops, seminars, or lectures, and typically a one-size-fits all approach. In contrast, professional learning, when designed well, is typically interactive, sustained, and customized to teachers' needs. It encourages teachers to take responsibility for their own learning and to practice what they are learning in their own teaching contexts (Scherff, 2018).

Being able to see these differences is key to being able to grow in the profession. Professional development is what we often pursue in order to enhance our vitae or move up to the next pay grade. Professional learning is life-long learning, and urgently needed in K-12 American schooling.

Professional learning engages learners in the following ways:

- is tied to specific content and standards;

- incorporates active learning;

- is job-embedded;

- is collaborative;

- provides models;

- includes coaching;

- is sustained and continuous; and

- is aligned with school goals, standards and assessments, and other professional learning activities (Archibald et al., 2011; Darling-Hammond et al., 2017; Labone & Long, 2016).

And professional learning is what I want for teachers under my care. However, I have to tread softly. Teachers often get a bad taste in their mouths when it comes to professional development. It is usually a one-time deal and in their minds, a "waste" of time. It was for me when I was a teacher. If we look at professional learning as an ongoing process, teachers will not be as easily dismissive of the practice. Making sure that leadership in the building is looking at what makes effective professional learning is essential for growth in a building.

In education, you can find data, mountains of data. Data can range from behavioral data to testing data to demographic data. All these different data points can lead to different conclusions regarding what type of development should take place. Making sure that teachers know how to use data is key. Thus, with so many types of data points available, teachers can easily feel overwhelmed or even intimidated. Working with data is not what teachers do every day, as it is with administration. The truth is that the use of data is no longer a choice for schools and school districts. We all must accustom ourselves to data, recognize that data analysis is not going away any time soon, and be open to learning how to understand data; doing so will help all of us see the benefits of data, including how to analyze and apply data carefully.

According to *Contemporary Issues in Technology and Teacher Education (CITE)* (n.d.), issues exist for data relevance primarily for three reasons: "timely availability of data, accessibility of data, and teacher understanding of how to use the data for classroom instruction or differentiated instruction" (para. 5). As far as timelines go, it is an issue due to the fact that test results come after the group of students have moved on to the next grade or level. Even when data is around, often teachers are not sure how to access the data. Teachers can have issues, such as the lack of training or they are not given the access to the data because only administration has it. The last part of this is: even if teachers have access to data, they often wonder what they are supposed to do with it. In most schools, teachers have not had the training to use data successfully in classes. Setting up professional development—or, more preferably, professional learning—is key for teachers to be able to learn how to use data given to them.

With issues that have surfaced at my school regarding the use of data, I wanted to help come up with some professional learning opportunities for the teachers in my building. Along with other members of the administrative team, I began by looking at two different types of data; we then created professional learning opportunities to address those data points. The first was dealing with common formative assessments (CFAs) that our county has created for several academic courses.

My field of expertise is in social studies, so I decided to sit down and create professional learning communities (PLCs) for both World History and US History. These PLCs would meet weekly to discuss CFA results and how to better instruct students who needed remediation. The CFAs are only five questions, but they are given weekly. The data is never too much and is directed toward standards that the teacher was covering for the week. These weekly PLCs were an opportunity for teachers to unpack the data and discuss instruction that was taking place in class. If one teacher had a successful lesson or activity, they were able to share it with the group.

The second type of data I wanted to unpack with more teachers was behavioral data. This year at my school we have had a large number of referrals. I led a professional development session I created with our administrative team that had discussed the data and some solutions for teachers. The data showed that many referrals come from tardiness. During a design team meeting, we were able to bring up the data and come up with possible solutions to help with this issue. This led to a teacher idea that was reviewed by the administrative team. After discussing solutions, I was able to present the plan to staff and discuss the data behind it. This professional development session also gave me the opportunity to discuss other behavioral issues in the building and to engage in meaningful conversations on how to address those concerns. After the session was over, I was able to create a PLC focused on behavioral issues in our building. The solution to help with tardiness in the building helped cut down significantly the number of referrals.

As a teacher of over 14 years, I always dreaded attending professional development; when I added to my teaching responsibilities of being a coach, that dread became outright angry aversion. I hated waiting till after the end of course assessments to receive the data, and I certainly felt too busy to discuss data. I felt like "PD" was a waste of time. I could be prepping for class, grading exams, or guiding athletes through their workouts. As an administrator who's done more research into the issues surrounding data, I now see the ways in which I could have used data more effectively in my past classrooms. My hope with the PLCs is that other teachers will make better use of data than I did as a teacher. Doing so will help teachers and students, and that is what I am all about.

References

Archibald, S., Coggshall, J. E., Croft, A., & Coe, L. (2011). *High-quality professional development for all teachers: Effectively allocating resources* NCCTQ. Educational Testing Services. www.ets.org/research/policy_research_reports/publications/report/2011/indc.html

Darling-Hammond, L., Hyler, M. E., & Gardner, M. (2016). *Effective teacher professional development*. Learning Policy Institute. https://files.eric.ed.gov/fulltext/ED606743.pdf

Gates, S. (2018, October 18). Benefits of collaboration. *NEA Today*. https://www.

nea.org/professional-excellence/student-engagement/tools-tips/benefits-collaboration

Labone, E., & Long, J. (2016). Features of effective professional learning: A case study of the implementation of a system-based professional learning model. *Professional Development in Education*, 42(2), 54-77. https://eric.ed.gov/?id=EJ1082693

Scherff, L. (2018, January 4). *Distinguishing professional learning from professional development. Institute of Education Sciences*. Regional Educational Laboratory Program (REL). https://ies.ed.gov/ncee/edlabs/regions/pacific/blogs/blog2_DistinguishingProfLearning.asp

Schifter, C. C., Natarajan, U., Ketelhut, D. J., & Kirchgessner, A. (n.d.). Data-driven decision making: Facilitating teacher use of student data to inform classroom instruction. *CITE Journal*. https://citejournal.org/volume-14/issue-4-14/science/data-driven-decision-making-facilitating-teacher-use-of-student-data-to-inform-classroom-instruction/

CHAPTER 14

Tough Customers

Emily Salmon

When I was a student teacher in 1989, I could not have imagined the technological tools and tasks essential to every aspect of my day—shared folders, contact logs, online professional learning, assessment data, and learning management systems. Beyond the technology revolution, there are other surprising differences: 504 plans and SST meetings; tiered interventions; competing with residual earbud pounding; having to *earn* respect; bold eye rolling. Students of the 21st century are tough customers.

Were those simpler times, *better* times? In some ways, yes. There was little pressure beyond preparation, delivery, grading, and communicating possible failures. There was no data to disaggregate. There actually wasn't any real accessible data. You might listen to what other teachers said about your roster (ill-advised). But there was definitely less busyness around our tasks. As English teachers, we were working for increased skills with language. Thirty-plus years later, our goal remains largely the same.

I was fortunate to teach a variety of students in my student teaching experience, so there were relatively few surprises when I got "my own" classroom. Remarkably, I remember several of my students from my first teaching job (high school English), and I clearly remember Ricky. Ricky almost never spoke to me nor spoke during class. He was never off task. He was not social. He worked; he wrote things on his paper. As I assessed more of his work, I realized that when answering comprehension questions, he copied words located near the words in the questions. Though copied from the text, his answers made little sense. I realized then that Ricky couldn't read. It was unfathomable to me that a high school student could not read, but this shocking revelation was ultimately the only explanation for Ricky's work. I was perplexed; how could I help him? When I questioned my more experienced colleagues about Ricky, the general response was it's too late for him; we were not trained to teach students HOW to read. Even if we were, how and when would that happen? It wouldn't be the last time I felt helpless as a teacher.

The middle 15 years of my career were spent in the school media center. Here I observed the ever-increasing pressure to utilize data and willingly did my part to develop and maintain a literacy community. Not long after re-entering the classroom, I was presented with a challenge: would I teach a 9th grade reading class the next school year? I was still "new" faculty and did feel passionate about literacy so, ok, I'll do it. That was seven years ago and since that time I've been on an unexpected journey. It turns out there is plenty to learn even after 20-plus years in education.

I have been teaching a developing reading class for 9th graders using Read180 (a blended learning program by Houghton Mifflin Harcourt) since 2017. What can be done for students (like Ricky) whose needs stretch far beyond the scope of the high school English classroom? While this reading course has not been my first teaching experience with struggling students, it is the first time I have taught struggling readers contained in one classroom. I can assure you this is a DIFFERENT experience altogether. It's unlikely that you will teach this type of a course, but you will certainly have students in your classes who are not reading on grade level. The focus of this chapter is sharing what I've learned in reading class.

By the time students enter high school, their data stack is 9 years high. You may teach 50–150 students per semester; will you have time to research their strengths and weaknesses? There's so much data that analyzing student history adequately can overwhelm any teacher. I've known teachers who feel compelled to data dive BEFORE they ever meet the students. I believe it can be more impactful, however, to meet the students first before forming opinions, assess some work, and then analyze the most relevant data.

By the time students enter high school, they have had 9 years of school "experience" behind them. The fact that you are reading this–an academic text for pre-service teachers–suggests that those years have been at least moderately successful. I was very good at school, and I have the trophies and certificates to prove it. I was so good that at 8-years-old, I had a classroom set up in the kitchen of our small home. I graduated at the top of my high school class. Then, in spite of some monumental challenges, I finished my undergraduate degree and went on to earn two graduate degrees. I love school! It holds great memories of competence and affirmation.

One of the first surprising things about my reading class was the surly attitude of most of the students. I mean, teenagers don't typically love school, I get it. But . . . this was something else. I was probably well into the first semester when I realized that for most of these students, school was a place where they felt like a failure. And someone made them go EVERY DAY and stay ALL DAY. I shouldn't have been surprised that not caring and not trying are coping mechanisms, protective mechanisms for never showing how frustrating the situation is. "Other kids who are successful will assume my failure is the result of not caring which is far better than failing because I'm unable." During that first year of the reading class, I progressed from frustration to curiosity to compassion. I met their frustration with compassion. Additionally, I exposed my own insecurities about utilizing Read180 (all new to me) and communicated that "we" were going to work together and figure it all out. The result was more trust and less resistance.

In order for educators to broaden perspectives on students' school experiences, we should consider current educational trends, most notably the current emphasis on standardized test achievements. Once administrators realized the stakes, the pressure was on to identify students who were not performing adequately. Differentiate to get the best results. "Differentiation" communicates support for students who need it; accelerate/challenge those who are ready. It's an impactful strategy! But struggling students have been sorted into the "needs help" group repeatedly by the time they enter high school. It's no surprise that their confidence and self-image have suffered. I'm not suggesting that differentiation is not an effective practice. These struggling readers most likely have benefitted from differentiated classrooms. But there seems to be a cumulative effect on sorting and labeling them.

How can we measure the effect of previous school experiences? Ask your students. While teaching 8th grade ELA, I pulled a sentence completion activity for the first day of school. Honestly, I needed something simple to collect information and affirm that I wanted to build a relationship with them. The activity was one page with about 20 statements to be completed. (I did not create the original but I have made it my own and usually adjust a few things each year.) Some examples from the activity include the following.

My teacher last year would say that I am_____.
Most people at school don't know that _____.
I like working in groups when _____.
I do my best work when _____.
My best year in school was _____ because _____.

These simple statements yield remarkable feedback from students. Initially, you get a sense of their performance habits by noting the time they invest sharing this information with you. Handwriting and volume reveal (to some degree) skill level. The most revealing information collected from this "first day" assignment is how students reflect on strengths and weaknesses and what school memories–IF ANY–they choose to share.

Over the years, certain responses have been repeated: a desire to make good grades, fears of being wrong or not knowing the answers, especially when working in groups. Memorable classroom responses were based on comfort and relationships, not surprising answers from children. But many of these 9th graders (and perhaps for several years before 9th grade) *behave* as if their academic performances do not matter to them. In fact, there is a notion that bad behavior is what has CAUSED the reading deficit. That may be true sometimes, but it's likely that the reading deficit has preceded the bad behavior.

So, what are some identifying traits of struggling readers? I mentioned that by 9th grade, students have plenty of experience coping in school. They are children and have used accessible strategies to get through it. Not all of these students will behave the same. I've found it interesting, in fact, to learn that there are a variety of behaviors students display in order to get through the school day. Observation, skills assessment, and past data *combined* can help teachers determine reading level, motivation, and performance habits.

Some students with developing skills will behave like Ricky; they are never a problem, and they don't ask questions. They may be very respectful, always following directions. They may also work very hard and feel unaccustomed to attention from their teacher. They are willing to move forward with support and understanding.

Some struggling students crave attention–often negative attention. Most teachers AND administrators are very familiar with low-achieving students due to behaviors such as avoidance (skipping class, refusing to work) and resistance to discipline. I am no expert on the spectrum of psychology associated with these behaviors. But after seven years, certain "truths" have emerged regarding low-achieving students with accompanying disciplinary issues listed here.

1. Frustration: Expect these students to have a low tolerance for task difficulty, complicated directions, other students' comments, and physical discomfort.

2. Poor executive function: You will notice difficulty finding or organizing papers, resistance to changes in schedule or structure, and low stamina with multi-step instructions.

3. Lack of respect for authority: Being "sent to the office" is not a new experience and while other students may feel intimidated by this, students with a history of behavioral problems might not be affected; being dismissed from class may even be their goal.

I've described three common types of behavior but there exists a wide range. These students are just as complex as any other and getting to know their layers will inform your approach to supporting them. What follows are pedagogical and cultural strategies for addressing these students' needs in your classroom. Two notes to keep in mind: one, there's some overlap between culture and pedagogy; and two, these are sound strategies for working with just about any type of student. (I teach AP Literature and Honors as well as reading support, and frequently use these same strategies with all my students.)

Pedagogical Strategies

1. Implement structure and routine. Discuss it frequently. Change it when needed.

These students are not as adaptive as more accomplished students; keep things predictable. Share daily agendas on a smartboard, LMS, white board, whatever, but keep it in the same place. I use thematic warm-ups like "Motivate Monday" and "What's Up Wednesday" which allows me to adjust the content and stick to the routine. An example for "What's Up Wednesday" would be reading a nonfiction article about a current unit. This structure also helps when you are absent, a situation that can really upset both the students and the sub. You may even quiz them on these routines at the beginning of school.

2. When giving directions, repeat them and always provide time to clarify language.

Don't be surprised WHEN some of the students are stuck because they have not followed directions. I like to put directions in a checklist format so that when I'm helping them, we can examine which specific item is unclear or has been skipped. Also, be mindful of the vocabulary within the directions. My students have frequently mentioned problems with directions in their other academic classes; if they don't understand directions, it is likely they will not attempt the task. If you have already repeated directions, see if another student can help. This builds confidence in the "helper" and will likely provide needed clarity.

3. Provide models frequently.

One of the best features of Read180 are "frames" used to support writing. Developing students will typically struggle at the beginning of a writing task; provide examples and allow them to copy the examples. You may do this by providing a "fill in the blank" topic sentence and then share one or three ways to complete the sentence. You can do the same for conclusions or any other portion of a writing task. Whenever possible, share student writing models as teacher models can be intimidating.

4. Scaffold new or frustrating tasks.

Like models, scaffolding inspires confidence. There are times when students have not NEEDED the scaffolding but they were more motivated because of it. It communicates that you are supporting them and can affirm that they are ready for less support. An example of scaffolding a difficult task: teaching theme statements. I show a short video (created for a younger audience), write the steps from the video in guided notes format, then practice writing a theme statement. After assessing the practice, I show students various levels of mastery, emphasizing that some have mastered the skill and some have not mastered it YET.

5. Break down heavier assignments like projects. Give grades for completing steps and weigh practice in more equal proportion to assessment.

A bit like number 4 above, but correlated to grades. My school system has set weights for "assessments" and "practices" but I am able to fiddle with the "multiplier." Over the years, I have found that appropriate "weight" of practice in the gradebook adds value to practice. And if they are practicing, assessment grades will most certainly improve. I have found that my struggling readers are very aware of their grades and notice when I enter grades. Use this attention to your/their advantage by regularly providing opportunities for high practice grades.

6. Favor dropping low grades over re-takes and re-submissions.

Stamina is a big issue for struggling students. Even if you offer re-takes and re-do's, few will typically follow through with those tasks. Replace old, low grades with "new" work that addresses similar standards. Then use the comments section in your grading program to note the improvement. Example: "Grade replaced based on improved skill level."

7. Vocabulary and more vocabulary.

It's no surprise that vocabulary is a big issue for this population. Weave vocabulary into all aspects of the course. As stated previously, don't underestimate the importance of vocabulary when giving directions. Frequently confirm that students understand vocabulary. You really can't "over-do" vocabulary. I typically add more vocabulary to any provided list for novels, stories, etc. Additionally, if teachers from other subjects wish to support your students, vocabulary support is usually one of the most impactful ways to differentiate other subjects.

8. It's ok to change direction.

There will be frustrating days, for you and for them. When you greet your students, forget all about it. You might be in the middle of a unit and realize it just isn't working. You can conclude the unit sooner or add something to it. Be flexible about adjusting content. It's ok if they don't study five *Odyssey* chapters. These adjustments ultimately communicate that you care and this affirmation will be more helpful to them than locking into planned units of study.

Cultural Strategies

1. Implement structure and routine. Discuss it frequently. Change it when needed.

I know I already added this one in Pedagogical Strategies above, but I feel compelled to add it here too, since structure contributes to the culture of your classroom. Routine speaks to organization and predictability, providing safety for students who feel uncomfortable at school.

2. Establish a "family" community. Speak of it often.

Yes, I say out loud, "We are a family in here." I realized the power of this concept when I taught middle school. Why not use it in high school? There will be students who don't like each other, but use those situations to say "We didn't choose to be here together, but let's make the best of it. School is hard enough–let's support each other." This family theme can lighten the mood and even though students may balk, they will appreciate that you want to protect their environment. You will probably have to specify early on that words like "stupid" or "dumb" are not acceptable. These kids are acutely aware of their labels (either official or not). Forbidding such negative statements affirms that you are committed to a positive environment.

3. Check your belief. Start **new** each day.

This strategy has to happen within YOU. After so many years, I have a firm foundation for my belief that all students can grow and even exceed their own beliefs. This can be challenging as a new teacher, especially when working with struggling students. But do whatever you need to do (talk to yourself, read affirming/inspirational statements, study scripture) to breathe belief into your classroom. After a difficult day you may need to make seating adjustments or email a parent/administrator, but still approach the next day as Brand New. Suggested mindset: What will we accomplish today?

4. Read the room. Be flexible about responding to class needs.

I mentioned this under "Pedagogical Strategies" but you may also need to be flexible about things like bathroom policies, late work, or school events (examples are homecoming week or a fight during lunch). Responding to needs/events affirms that you are paying attention to the students.

5. Be honest/transparent.

I admit that early in my Read180 teaching experience I was extremely uncomfortable discussing things like low Lexile scores. But guess what? They ALREADY know. Pretending that a problem isn't a problem is dismissive. Focus on the opportunity you have to frame discussions with a positive mindset. "I can see you're frustrated that your score did not improve more. Do you feel that you could have prepared differently? I know you will get there–stick with me. Keep going." Model a growth mindset.

6. Utilize small groups for conferencing.

I used to think I had to completely isolate a student to discuss their progress. It's really unnecessary. Once you have established a safe, family environment, you will see how well students handle small group conferences. You can look at the gradebook, review writing feedback (that the student might NOT have read) or review goal status.

7. Never demand sharing or performance. Request, then praise loudly.

Never require students to read aloud. (Nearly every struggling student probably has experienced unforgettable read aloud failure.) Ask for their participation and then no matter the outcome, praise the attempt. Use the "family" concept to forbid negative responses to attempts. This applies to sharing ideas, sharing answers, etc. Providing a safe environment of sharing will enrich the classroom and emphasize that students share many of the same struggles.

8. Acknowledge all successes.

While these students will soak up positive statements, they will not be impressed by vague praise. Be specific so that they know they have succeeded, even if it's just one question on a handout. Examples: "I liked how responsible you were after returning to school from OSS" or "I know it's been tough getting through this poetry unit–it's not your favorite but you have gotten everything completed."

Is it possible for these struggling students to survive? Improve? Absolutely, yes. And although I cannot give a simple answer as to HOW this can be accomplished, I can endorse these strategies that have consistently yielded positive results. All are deliberate, intentional. And all require belief in the students' ability to grow and participate.

A few years ago, I taught Evan in American Literature. For the first nine weeks of the course, he did no work. Nothing. Because college football season was getting interesting, I included a football article in our "What's Up Wednesday" warm-up. Even though I had never talked to Evan AND had assumed that he was completely resistant to doing ANY work, I was surprised when he approached me at the end of class. He said he would do his work every day IF we could read material like the football article. I couldn't give up Emerson for NCAA football, but something monumental had happened: lines of communication opened up and I was able to get Evan to participate. He shared with me that he was determined to graduate high school, even though the work was so hard for him. He didn't pass my class but learned by participating and eventually passed the course. Evan and I got a photo at his graduation; he was about to turn 21.

Evan had struggled quietly for his entire school career. He visited my Read180 class one day and noticing our work, he asked, "What kind of class is this?" I explained it was for strengthening reading skills. He said with envy, "I wish I had had a class like THIS."

I could also tell you about Brendan, a baseball player who cried when his Lexile score did not improve. Or Landon who used to work on his computer under a table. Alyssa set a goal to graduate early. Mattie made it through my course and decided to take an Honors class the next year (and passed!). Kamari almost cried when we took a photo together at his graduation. Not all of them succeeded. Some shattered growth goals while others made only small gains. But without question, these "tough customers" have enriched my career. I have worked harder than I did in those early days, but I do believe that the returns have also been greater. I hope they know. I hope you will invest in students who think they're not valued.

CHAPTER 15

If You Watch Sports, Then You Want Instructional Coaches

Jennifer Medgull

Baseball teams have a manager, several coaches, some therapists, dozens of players, and a handful of other staff members. Schools have a principal, assistant principals, supportive educators like media specialists and counselors, clerical staff, teachers, and a handful of other staff members. We're going to explore an extended comparison of these two kinds of organizations with particular focus on the coaches. So, look again at the lists. Coaches are an assumed part of a baseball team, and coaches are found in so few schools that we might not notice that they were missing from the above list.

Baseball coaches help players get better. They might be in a hitting slump, or they might be recovering from an injury that requires new ways of doing what used to come easy. One player might be hitting in the cleanup spot because they've got a hot bat these days. Pitching always has enough nuance that coaches are watching and talking to pitchers about their game.

If baseball teams are stacked with coaches who help their players get better, doesn't it stand to reason that schools ought to have coaches too?

Teachers might be in an assessment slump, or they might be returning from an extended leave that requires new ways of doing what used to come easy. One teacher might be asked to share strategies on classroom management because their classroom looks like a well-oiled machine. Special education always has enough nuances that coaches could be watching and talking to these educators about their work.

Coaches in schools are not for brand new teachers only. They're for middle-career teachers, those close to retirement, teachers who have new courses to teach, and teachers who have new curriculum from the state. Coaches also benefit teachers who are struggling to balance work and life or are navigating communication breakdowns with colleagues.

Why aren't coaches in every school in our country? Coaches cost money. They are paid at least as much as a teacher, but there are no students on a roster with the coach's name at the top. Funding for coaching is not allocated sufficiently, if at all. Coaches are hard to evaluate. How do we know if the money we do spend on coaches is paying off? Coaches can work best when they can work with teachers confidentially. A teacher who wants to improve their management of cooperative groups doesn't want that advertised to the evaluating administrator. A teaching team that is struggling to reach consensus on their common course doesn't want the district coordinator of their subject getting wind of the struggles and moving them to brand new courses right away to get rid of the problem. How is a principal supposed to evaluate the work coaches do in those situations? It's hard to rate that work on the "beginning, developing, proficient, distinguished" scale.

Many coaches aren't coaching even if they applied for a job with that title. They are proficient educators with no classes to prepare, so they seem to be available to address more pressing needs. Organizing testing logistics, evaluating teachers, substitute teaching when there are no more subs coming, and helping work through the backlog of parent phone calls needed for absent students all feel more critical than helping teachers improve their work. But, coaches are not test coordinators, administrators, substitute teachers, or clerical staff. Our education system does not yet value the work of coaching educators.

Coaches are best viewed in the support team of a school. Media specialists, counselors, and instructional coaches prepare special lessons, and they collaborate with teachers and administrators for the benefit of students. Coaches are certified teachers, and they often have additional credentials in coaching.

What DO coaches do? Coaches are conversation partners with teachers. They ask good questions to draw out of teachers their best ideas for teaching. If something isn't working anymore, coaches ask about what has changed. If something has never worked for a teacher, coaches point them to some colleagues who are excellent in that area and arrange for those teachers to share ideas.

Coaches lead professional learning for staff. They put together their own best adult teaching strategies to provide group learning experiences and then follow up with staff as they learn to incorporate the new skills into their teaching practices.

Coaches need not be experienced teachers in the exact same discipline as the teachers they coach. A science teacher can ask authentic questions when coaching an ELA teacher, and the result of that conversation can be richer than what might have come of a coach and teacher with matching expertise.

Coaches can mentor new teachers. But they should not be kept from working with veteran teachers as well. New teachers need different conversations than veteran teachers, and good coaches have the skills to participate fruitfully in both of those conversations. When functioning as a mentor to a new teacher, a coach serves the teacher best by helping them identify their own strengths and their own voice.

Coaches can support the research efforts of teachers pursuing advanced degrees. With meaningful topics, robust data, and multiple minds analyzing the data, the research findings can benefit an entire department or school, instead of going away after the paper is turned in for graduate course credit.

Coaches are the glue of the network of teachers in a school or district because they see the large picture and have opportunities to share implementation practices. When teachers from one school cannot visit another school to observe extended learning time, coaches can visit and bring back ideas that are worth trying in their own school. When teachers are struggling to navigate a new instructional platform, coaches can share great ideas and shortcuts from one team to another.

Coaches are confidants. If a coach reports to administration that they walked by a classroom out of control, they are not staying in their support role. Instead, they can check in with the struggling teacher outside of class to offer support. That might mean they get permission to come in the next time the class is out of control to demonstrate some strategies. They might instead help the teacher think through what precipitated the end of learning and ideas for ending those behaviors earlier in the process the next time. If a coach breaks the trust of a colleague, the cost is high to both the teacher and their students.

Coaches are supporters, not evaluators. If they are coaching well, then they may find themselves biased in their evaluations. Coaches are also not evaluators simply because they do not have the training in evaluation that administrators have. It is not appropriate for coaches to be sent in place of trained administrators to evaluate teachers in a school.

Coaches can join the administration in conversations about schoolwide data. Coaches have a unique perspective in such a group. They have been involved in conversations with teaching teams about the strengths of each team member and which classes are learning concepts faster. Coaches know what teachers have asked for help on. They also know which teams are working well together. Coaches also know about the learning preferences of teachers, and they can advise administrators on training strategies that will work well with teachers in the school.

For Administrators

Would you be the manager of a baseball team without coaches on your staff? Your teachers are professionals, but they do not have complete proficiency all the time in every skill needed for teaching. Highlight the work that your instructional coaches can do in your school, and speak with a growth mindset language about teaching, assessment, and teacher collaboration in your school. Set your coaches up for success by asking them to start the year with what they see that is right, and share those observations with the teachers.

Encourage teachers to work with coaches when they get low scores on evaluations; then let the teacher and the coach do their work confidentially. You will see the fruit of that work when you visit next, so there is no need to ask about it along the way. Seek the insight of instructional coaches when it comes to delivering training to the staff. Follow their advice when it is helpful for a faculty meeting, and share with the coach and the staff that you got help in delivering the information.

Ask a coach if they are available for substitute teaching; do not assume there is nothing on their schedule. And, only ask them to sub if you have other support staff also subbing in your school. Learn about research findings on the benefits of coaching, and insist from yourself and district leaders that coaching be prioritized highly in the budget. What benefits are lost in your school when you do not have coaches? What can coaches do that you wish you could do for your students and teachers?

For New Teachers

The title "instructional coach" means different things in different schools. Find out what it means in your school. The best scenario is that coaches do not evaluate you, and that they work with you confidentially. If you have that opportunity, pick something you want to improve by working with a coach. When you feel stronger in that area, share your successes with your colleagues. That helps show the worth of the coach so that you can continue to work with them over the years of your career. Be honest with your coach about your strengths and personality type as it influences your classroom. If you know your learning style, share that. Coaches can see things while they are in your classroom that you simply cannot see, so invite them in.

For Veteran Teachers

It is tempting to think you do not need to work with an instructional coach. You're expected to do everything right from your first day in the classroom, and you're told that student lives depend on you getting it right. So, it is no wonder you might bristle at working with an instructional coach. If your school values confidential coaching, it's worth the risk to try out some coaching. Maybe you know you need some ideas on closing a lesson so that it sticks better in students' minds. You can ask your coach for examples of teachers doing that well in your school. Maybe you just refuse to give group assignments anymore because it has never gone well for you.

You can ask your coach to come to your class and be another adult keeping groups on the right track until the groups can do that independently. Maybe the new technology is so overwhelming that you get frustrated when you're at home trying to make it do what everyone else says is easy. You can make an appointment with your coach to get some help. (Tell them ahead of time what you want to work on so they can learn it or bring in someone who can help you.) Maybe you've had a life event that caused you to lose your confidence managing the daily tasks of teaching. You can ask your coach to be a sounding board as you fumble your way through to getting your new rhythm. Wouldn't it be nice to have someone who shares your goals of keeping work in your classroom and offers ideas for doing that?

Professional baseball players have coaches because they can observe their swings from different perspectives and let them know that their eyes are not following the ball. Professional teachers have coaches because they can observe their instruction from different perspectives; coaches can let them know how their instructional emphases are not aligned to their assessments. Baseball coaches played once upon a time, but the stars of the team are the players now. Instructional coaches taught once upon a time, but those in front of students and parents are the teachers now. If coaches are hired to help professional athletes improve their play, then we must hire instructional coaches in schools to improve instruction. And, we must give them the freedom to do their work.

CHAPTER 16

All In and Burned Out:
Why Principals Are Leaving

ADAM DOVICO

THE BELL RINGS. IT'S 3:45 p.m. and I think to myself, "Time for the day to get started." Now the truth of the matter is, I have been at school since 7:00 a.m. But like most days, the things I had planned to accomplish changed by the unpredictable happenings of a school day, so I am left to do many of them after school. As the saying goes in the life of a principal, "The school day makes your schedule." And that's not a bad thing in my opinion because it makes the job exciting and it keeps each day unique. Of course, today flew by, and as always, and I think back to what the day was supposed to have looked like:

7:10 - Meet with Jacquez's mom
7:45 - Meet with School Improvement Team
8:15 - Morning news show and school rally
9:00 - Teacher observations
9:45 - Meet with human resources to discuss hiring for a position
10:00 - Meeting with legal department to discuss a teacher conduct situation
10:30 - Fire drill
11:00 - Lunch duty
12:00 - Classroom observations
12:45 - Meet with teacher about safety patrol
1:00 - Finalize Title 1 budget
1:30 - Classroom observations

2:00 - Debrief with teacher about morning observation
2:30 - 3rd grade PLC
3:00 - Meet with Shania's mom about PTA event
3:20 - Dismissal

To what it actually looked like:
6:30 - Text from my assistant principal that she is sick and won't be in today.
7:10 - Met with Jacquez's mom, but she had a parent advocate with her and the meeting took a much longer time.
8:00 - Showed up late for the School Improvement Team and caught the tail end of it where teacher concerns were raised. Teacher bathrooms are dirty again.
8:15 - We had a great school rally. It's my favorite part of the day.
8:45 - Cops arrive at school. There's been an alert that a volunteer who signed into our system at school was on a police suspect list. Spend the next hour investigating this, only to find out it was a misidentification because of the same name.
9:45 - Met with human resources and they denied the teacher I recommended for hire because of an ineligible teaching license.
10:00 - Met with the legal department and I have to put the teacher in question on unpaid leave while an investigation opens, active immediately. I had to go down to the room to explain this to her and find a teacher assistant to cover the room. I also had to craft a letter to the families explaining that the teacher would be taking time off due to a personal situation. Fire drill will have to be another day and lunch duty just didn't happen.
12:00 - A true joy to my day–getting to visit classrooms. I even jumped into a third grade lesson on multiplication.
12:45 - Got safety patrol sorted out.
1:00 - Emergency call on my cell phone from a kindergarten teacher. During recess a student fell off the monkey bars and their arm is clearly broken.
1:05 - Two fifth grade students were sent to the office because they were fighting on the playground. Since my assistant principal isn't here, I took care of this and sent my secretary outside to handle the broken

arm. The fighting situation took over an hour, after investigating what happened and calling the parents.

2:30 - Made it to PLCs and we had a great conversation about reading standards.

3:00 - Met with our PTA president and I had to explain to her that we were not allowed to have inflatables for an event. She was not happy, so I gave her legal's phone number.

3:20 - Found out that one of our new students did not have a bus route yet, so I moved from car rider dismissal to buses to beg the bus driver to take him to the bus stop, where his mom was waiting.

3:40 - Front office gets a phone call from a parent that their child did not get off the bus. We spent the next 30 minutes working with transportation to figure out what happened. He fell asleep on the bus.

Shoot, forgot to eat lunch again. A regular occurrence. But now that the students are gone, I get to start on the work that I didn't get to do during the day. There is paperwork with deadlines to finish, people who want to meet with me, and plenty of assigned tasks to check in on. Finally, at 6:00 p.m. I call it a day and head home, once again heading to the only car left in the parking lot.

Principal Burnout

Studies of principal burnout and turnover are not new. Almost a century ago, Williams (1932) wrote about the issue in the state of Illinois, finding that principal turnover was between 23%-35% over a 10-year period. "Professional factors" and "economic factors" were identified as leading reasons for turnover (p. 424). Forty-five years later, Blood and Miller (1978) studied the issue in New Mexico and found variables like power struggles, curriculum complexity, and role definition led to principals fleeing. Now almost another 50 years later, add on federal policies like No Child Left Behind (2002), Race to the Top (2009), Every Student Succeeds Act (2015), high stakes testing, social media, book bans, and a global pandemic, just to name a few, and you may be able to see why principal burnout is still an issue.

Interestingly, current principal turnover statistics remain largely consistent with historical data, hovering between 14%-36% over the past decade, and vary depending on state, data source, and method of calculation

(Béteille et al., 2012; Grissom & Bartanen, 2019; Levin & Bradley, 2019; National Center for Education Statistics, 2019). Since the pandemic, schools nationwide have faced high rates of principal turnover due to increased pressures of dealing with political unrest, learning loss, and making schools safe from disease and gun violence (DeMatthews et al., 2022). Scholars like David DeMatthews, Paul Carrola, Pedro Reyes, and Marcus Horwood have studied these most recent trends in principal turnover and have examined burnout from not only the working conditions present in today's schools, but the mental and psychological abuse that is associated with being in this type of leadership position. Many have found that the growing research and awareness of mental health contributes to the realization that principals are leaving because of mental health issues.

Principals in today's schools face unprecedented pressure to appease divisive community members, district administrators, and government officials. Studies show that principals are generally passionate about their job, more so than the average worker (Horwood et al., 2021). But what exists is a double-edged sword over trying to maintain your passion and battling never-ending strife from external factors. Over the past several decades, passion has been on the losing side, as principals have opted to retire early or simply just leave the profession (Whitaker, 1996; Horwood et al., 2021). This leaves the elephant in the room in districts across the United States as to when this issue of principal burnout will truly be confronted and addressed.

Why Do We Need to Keep Good Principals?

Teachers have been shown to stay or leave schools because of working conditions. Perceived value, protection of instructional time, support, and coaching are just a few ways that teachers have reported their satisfaction or displeasure. Likewise, principals are best situated to have an influence on those working conditions (Burkhauser, 2017). If we are to keep our best teachers in the profession, then we need to keep our best principals as well, since one exists because of the other (Boyce & Bowers, 2016). While there is no consensus for defining what qualifies one as an "effective principal," examining measures such as teacher responses regarding leadership practices, value-added scores, student achievement outcomes, and evaluation ratings can offer a high-level analysis of the term (Grissom & Bartanen, 2019). The reality is, though, that sometimes an effective school principal can't be measured by numbers or scales. Good principals demonstrate love, patience, understanding, equity, ingenuity, and so much more that accountability tests and surveys will never show.

Having a strong leader provides comfort, stability, and trust at a school. They communicate a vision that others can follow, provide the resources and support for teachers and students to be successful, and create a happy and safe environment where stakeholders can thrive (Burkhauser, 2017; Levin & Bradley, 2019). Unsurprisingly, when strong principals remain tenured at a school, these elements yield higher student achievement, teacher retention, and a stronger school community (Brockmeier et al., 2013; Huff et al., 2011; Soehner & Ryan, 2011). Then how has it remained the norm for one in five principals to turnover every year, negatively impacting school culture and achievement (Béteille et al., 2012)? What has not been addressed by school districts and state leaders that could ameliorate this crisis? And more importantly, how do we get them to stay?

My Story

In summer 2017, I received the phone call I was anxiously waiting for: "We would like to offer you a principal position." I had interviewed several weeks before, and I was beginning to accept that it may not work out. I had never been an assistant principal. I was not working in the district at the time, and it was generally understood that to become a principal there were certain rites of passage that you should experience. Luckily, the superintendent believed in me and the ambitious dreams I shared in my interview, and gave me the chance I needed. And I did not want to disappoint her.

I jumped into the position head first. In my first two weeks, I strategically prioritized people. I had learned this from a previous leadership position where I prioritized compliance, and that proved to be detrimental to relationships. This time, I met with every single staff member one-on-one, visited over fifty local businesses to introduce myself, and held a "meet the principal night" at a local restaurant for families. In between those events, I managed to squeeze in the administrative tasks that had to be done like budgets, student and staff handbooks, hiring, and finalizing schedules. It was tiring work, but exciting. Most of the time, I was flying the plane as I was building it, but I had excellent mentors whom I could call for help.

The time finally came when I had my staff together for the first time. I'll never forget that day. I jumped up on a table in the media center dressed in a neon yellow shirt, parachute pants, and fanny pack to go along with our 90s-themed back to school party. While I may not have known every principal competency and policy yet, I knew how to inspire people. And that's what I aimed to do. I took a staff that was drained and just going through routines and injected them with as much excitement and hope that I could. Of course, it's not hard to inspire people for one day. I was successful at that for many years leading up to this as I traveled around the country conducting keynote speeches for school districts. The true challenge was to maintain that through 180 school days. And now as the principal, I was tasked to do just that.

And I accepted the challenge with open arms. I gave my teachers permission to be creative, outside-the-box, innovative, and to break the script for what had always been done in school. And did they ever! My art teacher created beautiful murals around the school. My teachers got rid of their teacher desks and transformed their classrooms into works of art by adding stages, decorative lights, and portraits on the walls. We got rid of traditional morning work when students arrived and created morning choice, where kids could play board games, create art, work with Legos or Play-doh, and work on puzzles. We used a system I created called S.P.E.C.I.A.L., which taught students interpersonal and social skills, and after a local news station created a story on it, the school went viral and we had dozens of schools from around the United States visiting us. We were creating something that others wanted to be a part of.

There was optimism, excitement, and welcomeness as parents, community members, and district administrators walked into the building. But behind closed doors, there was a dark cloud that hovered over my head that threatened my presence. The mother who called the Board of Education to complain about me each week, the school's "D" grade on the state report card, the teachers who could not manage a classroom of kids, my supervisor chastening me because I spoke up again when she thought I should have kept my mouth shut. But as the principal, you have to keep that cloud in your office. Bringing it out into the building would destroy everything great that is going on. And so, you bear it. You let it weigh on you. And yes, sometimes it's just too much.

I had moments where I shut down; moments where I cried in my office. In talking to other principals, this is not uncommon. For some, it gets better over time. For others, the weight never lifts. There's no one right way to be a principal, but for me, I was going to put my all into it each and every day. It's just who I am. That meant I put my students and staff first, and I was going to do whatever it took to make that school the best it could be. Yes, that meant affronting others at times and spending nights and weekends at the school. Of course, it came at a price. My wife and I barely saw each other, and even though my son was a student at my school, I wasn't able to give him the full attention that I should have.

My family ended up moving to another city after my second year of being the principal at this school, as a result of my wife's new job. I had a tearful goodbye to the students, families, and staff. I never would have imagined how hard it would be to leave a place, but when you put your blood, sweat, and tears into something, moving on from it can be difficult. I had to make a decision at that point. Do I apply for another principal position in this new city? Do I start over again, knowing all that has to be done to get a school to the next level? Are the stress and pain that I felt in the chair of my office what I want to continue to feel each day?

I opted to take a year off. I decided that I needed to mentally, physically, and emotionally recover from the experience before I made my next move. It just so happened that during that year the pandemic hit, and it made me realize that my health and my family were the most important things to me. With that peace of mind, making the decision was much easier for me. And so I did go back to a school the following year, but as a curriculum facilitator. It allowed me to still have a great impact on school instruction and culture, but without the stress of being the principal. It also allowed me to begin doing things for pleasure like coaching my son's sports teams and picking up hobbies that I had not previously prioritized. I found that I was spending more time with my wife and we were doing more things as a family.

I share my story not to deter anyone from going into school administration. I cannot overstate enough how much I loved being the principal of my school. The position is a magnificent opportunity to share your passion, vision, and leadership with a broad audience and make a far-reaching impact.

But at the end of the day, I understand that I am a turnover statistic, in part due to burnout. And I feel that it is important to shed light on the challenges that the principal job carries with it. Without these stories and lived experiences, we may not get to address root issues that are causing thousands of principals to leave the profession each year. If we are to improve working conditions and outcomes for principals, then we need to make systemic changes.

How Do We Go All In Without Burning Out?

Statistics on principal turnover consistently demonstrate a higher rate at low-income schools and schools with a majority-minority student population, where less experienced principals disproportionately serve. These schools have also been equated with lower test scores, less experienced teachers, and higher accountability demands, causing additional stress on the school leader (Béteille et al., 2012; Boyce & Bowers, 2016; Gates et al., 2006; Levin & Bradley, 2019). As a counternarrative, in my experience, the hardest working, most creative, dedicated principals serve at these schools. But in the same breath, I acknowledge that these same principals remain at their schools for the shortest times. Many of them I have known over the years burn out quickly, while others start at low-income or struggling schools as a stepping stone to a higher-achieving or higher-income schools (Béteille et al., 2012).

How then can district officials support and help reduce the burnout and turnover rate, particularly at the highest needs schools? I share three ways that I believe we can help address this pressing issue.

1) Create a Collaborative Culture

By tradition, the principalship typically operates in silos. There is historically one principal at a school, and that person is responsible for the decision-making of their building. For obvious reasons, this can be problematic for new principals, who are learning policies, procedures, and practices. Building a culture of collaboration for principals has been shown to help retention by providing opportunities for dialogue and problem-solving between individuals in similar positions (Cieminski, 2018). Personally, my most impactful conversations as a principal were with fellow principals, particularly those who were at similar schools as mine. Essentially, we created our own professional learning community and tackled problems of practice with each other. This can be accomplished intentionally in school districts by designing designated time at meetings for leaders to collaborate.

2) Autonomy for Solutions

One size doesn't fit all in education. We have seen this true in curriculum adoptions, assessment measures, school calendars, and behavior policies, just to name a few. There is no one more equipped to make a decision about a school than its principal. They are privy to the day-to-day operations, personnel, community, finances, and school needs, which are invaluable nuggets of information when making decisions. Unfortunately, identifying and implementing solutions are often dictated from outside personnel, leading to compliance demands and accountability for decisions that were not made by the principal (Sparks, 2019). Misaligned decision-making between a principal and their supervisors yields frustration and resentment, which can lead to burnout. I was generally fortunate in my principalship to have the autonomy to make decisions about my school. Admittedly, sometimes I would forgo asking permission for certain decisions, but I always prepared myself with evidence and rationale for why I made that decision. Autonomy for solutions, coupled with support and constructive feedback from supervisors, is important for principals to feel empowered and trusted as professionals (Cieminski, 2018; Whitaker, 1996).

3) Compensation

My first year of teaching in North Carolina in 2004 I made $27,250 a year. By the time I became a principal, I added 13 years, two master's degrees, and National Board Certification; it came to $82,000 a year. On paper, I should have felt accomplished and satisfied, and I certainly felt that at times, but I also had moments of frustration knowing how much work I was putting in for the compensation I was receiving. I share this because I recognize that compensation in education is a complicated and important topic. Beside the fact that this is public record information, I feel it is important for transparency with this discussion. Not calculated in that time between those numbers is that I got married, had two children, bought a house, and had many more financial obligations than I did at age 22. The principal job is also 12 months versus 10 for a teacher. All of that to say there were days where I asked myself, "Is this all worth it?" Offering competitive compensation, signing bonuses, and benefits have been shown to attract principals; offering merit bonuses or incentives can retain veteran or accomplished principals, particularly at hard-to-staff schools such as rural or Title 1 (Burkhauser, 2017; Cieminski, 2018; Grissom & Bartanen, 2019; Kearney, 2010; Sparks, 2019). Getting there is not easy. It has been an age-old battle in education, and it requires elected officials to recognize the value and worth of educators at all levels. The principal crisis is real, and compensation is a tangible step in helping improve the issue.

Conclusion

The role and view of the principal has evolved over generations. A position that was once seen as managerial in nature has morphed into multidimensional leadership on many levels, including shaping school vision, leading instruction, cultivating teacher leadership, managing people and processes, and ensuring a hospitable environment for students and staff (Burkhauser, 2017). The dynamic expectations of the role have consequently led to detrimental outcomes for principal retention. While statistics remain largely unchanged, the lack of educators, the lack of educators looking to fill these voids have led to principal shortages across the nation, particularly in high-needs areas (Gates et al., 2006; Grissom & Bartanen, 2019; Whitaker, 1996). The result? Inexperienced principals enter schools where teacher turnover is high and student needs are intensified. This leads to high rates of principal turnover and perpetual change for these schools that desire stability. To address this crisis, several solutions were discussed above, including intentional collaborative opportunities for principals, autonomy in decision making, and better compensation formulas and incentives. Principals are passionate about their school and their work. This shows in their dedication to long hours, difficult conversations, unrelenting critical decision-making moments, and accountability for anything that occurs in their building. It's this same *all in* mentality, though, that is driving many principals to be *burned out*.

References

Béteille, T., Kalogrides, D., & Loeb, S. (2012). Stepping stones: Principal career paths and school outcomes. *Social Science Research, 41*(4), 904-919.

Blood, R. E., & Miller Jr., J. P. (1978). *The New Mexico principalship study. Part I. Factors affecting the principalship yesterday and today* (ED175143). ERIC. https://eric.ed.gov/?id=ED175143

Boyce, J., & Bowers, A. J. (2016). Principal turnover: Are there different types of principals who move from or leave their schools? A latent class analysis of the 2007-2008 schools and staffing survey and the 2008-2009 principal follow-up survey. *Leadership and Policy in Schools, 15*(3), 237-272.

Brockmeier, L. L., Starr, G., Green, R., Pate, J. L., & Leech, D. W. (2013). Principal and school-level effects on elementary school student achievement. *International Journal of Educational Leadership Preparation, 8*(1), 49-61.

Burkhauser, S. (2017). How much do school principals matter when it comes to teacher working conditions? *Educational Evaluation and Policy Analysis, 39*(1), 126-145.

Cieminski, A. B. (2018). Practices that support leadership succession and principal retention. *Education Leadership Review, 19*(1), 21-41.

DeMatthews, D. E., Childs, J., Knight, D., Cruz, P., & Clarida, K. (2022). More than meets the eye: Rural principal turnover and job-embeddedness before and during the COVID-19 pandemic. *Leadership and Policy in Schools, 22*(4), 905-928. www.tandfonline.com/doi/abs/10.1080/15700763.2022.2033273

Gates, S. M., Ringel, J. S., Santibanez, L., Guarino, C., Ghosh-Dastidar, B., & Brown, A. (2006). Mobility and turnover among school principals. *Economics of Education Review, 25*(3), 289-302.

Grissom, J. A., & Bartanen, B. (2019). Principal effectiveness and principal turnover. *Education Finance and Policy, 14*(3), 355-382.

Horwood, M., Marsh, H. W., Parker, P. D., Riley, P., Guo, J., & Dicke, T. (2021). Burning passion, burning out: The passionate school principal, burnout, job satisfaction, and extending the dualistic model of passion. *Journal of Educational Psychology, 113*(8), 1668-1688.

Huff, T. S., Brockmeier, L. L., Leech, D. W., Martin, E. P., Pate, J. L., & Siegrist, G. (2011). Principal and school-level effects on student achievement. *National Teacher Education Journal, 4*(2).

Kearney, K. (2010). *Effective principals for California schools: Building a coherent leadership development system.* WestEd. https://www2.wested.org/www-static/online_pubs/EffectivePrincipals.pdf

Levin, S., & Bradley, K. (2019). *Understanding and addressing principal turnover: A review of the research.* National Association of Secondary School Principals (NASSP). https://learningpolicyinstitute.org/product/nassp-understanding-addressing-principal-turnover-review-research-report

National Center for Education Statistics (NCES). (2019). *Principal turnover: Stayers, movers, and leavers.* Annual Reports and Information Staff. https://nces.ed.gov/programs/coe/indicator/slb

Soehner, D., & Ryan, T. (2011). The interdependence of principal school leadership and student achievement. *Scholar-Practitioner Quarterly, 5*(3), 274-288.

Sparks, S. D. (2019, March 12). Why teacher-student relationships matter. *Education Week, 38*(28), 44-55. www.edweek.org/teaching-learning/why-teacher-student-relationships-matter/2019/03

Whitaker, K. S. (1996). Exploring causes of principal burnout. *Journal of Educational Administration, 34*(1), 60-71. https://doi.org/10.1108/09578239610107165

Williams, L. W. (1932). Turnover among high-school teachers in Illinois. *The School Review, 40*(6), 416–428. http://www.jstor.org/stable/1080910

CHAPTER 17

Instruction, Identity, and Inclusivity:
What Can Teacher Preparation Programs Learn from Gay Male Teachers in the South?

JOSEPH R. JONES

Introduction

PRESENTLY, THERE IS A political attack on LGBTQ+ individuals, especially in southern states. In 2022, six southern states (Alabama, Florida, Louisiana, Mississippi, Oklahoma, Texas) enacted laws that prohibit discussing LGBTQ+ students or issues within P-12 schools. In Arkansas and Tennessee (also Montana and Arizona), teachers are required to notify parents of LGBTQ+ curricula and allow parents to opt out of the lesson. These laws create school climates that perpetuate heteronormativity, which can be detrimental for a number of LGBTQ+ individuals within schools. Further, these laws force teachers to allow intolerance to prevail in schools and in their classrooms because of fear of legal ramifications and job dismissal.

In the latest data from GLSEN (2019), a national surveyor of school climates, 59.1% of LGBTQ+ students felt unsafe in their schools, 32.7% missed at least one day from school because they were scared to attend, 68.7% were verbally assaulted because of their identity, and 25.7% were physically assaulted. Other data (Jones, 2017) posits that LGBTQ+ students who are harassed in schools believe college will be the same and choose not to attend. Further, the suicide rates for LGBTQ+ students are astronomical when compared to their non-LGBTQ+ student counterparts. I posit these numbers will increase in southern states because of these laws.

In 2017, I left higher education and returned to the secondary classroom in a southern state as a special education teacher in a co-taught English classroom. As a returning "new" teacher, I discovered the intolerance towards LGBTQ+ individuals had not decreased significantly over my 15-year absence. Specifically, I heard the homophobic slurs hailed at students, faculty, and staff on a regular basis (Jones, 2019). I witnessed students physically accosting LGBTQ+ students in the restrooms and in the hallways. Indeed, the intolerance for these students was as prominent as the intolerance towards non-heterosexual students during my first year of teaching.

Additionally, to better frame this discussion, it is necessary to explore teacher involvement in combating heteronormative actions that take place in schools. GLSEN (2016) reveals data from another national survey that depicts LGBTQ+ teachers and their attempts to create safe learning spaces, "LGBTQ teachers are more likely to engage in affirming and supportive teaching practices" (page 2). In fact, 74.5% of LGBTQ teachers implemented at least one affirming practice. That being said, only 43.9% of LGBTQ teachers displayed a visual sign of support, only 21.7% of LGBTQ teachers advocated for inclusive school and district policies, and 31.5% included LGBTQ+ topics in the curriculum. It should be noted that the GLSEN (2016) data is significant because it reveals that non-LGBTQ+ teachers are not as invested as LGBTQ+ teachers in creating safe environments. The survey reveals, only 10.3% of non-LGBTQ+ teachers displayed a visual sign of support, 7.8% advocated for inclusive school and district polices, and only 14% of non-LGBTQ+ teachers included LGBTQ+ topics in the curriculum. For all of the categories, non-LGBTQ+ educators were below their counterparts' percentages for attempting to create safe and affirming classroom spaces, which supports Taylor et al.'s, (2015) postulations that LGBTQ+ preservice teachers are the main proponents of addressing intolerance within their classrooms because they are more aware of the hatred that their students are facing.

The above data suggests teacher preparation programs must continue addressing this challenge. As such, there are numerous recent research studies that examine how teacher preparation programs are attempting to address this challenge; however, most of the literature focuses on how heterosexual identities can create tolerant spaces for LGBTQ+ individuals. Additionally, there are several recent studies examining LGBTQ+ new teachers' experiences within schools, but according to Sapp (2017) there are "very few studies that research the experience of queer people who are in the process of becoming teachers" (p. 13). This is especially true for articles published within the previous five years. A few of these recently published studies are worth mentioning. Tompkins et al., (2019) examined the experiences of new Canadian LGBTQ+ teachers and how those teachers became LGBTQ+ trainers in their respective schools. That being said, the study also revealed that school climate impacted the new teachers' ability to be their authentic selves.

Another study of music education majors revealed interesting findings concerning pre-service LGBTQ+ individuals. Taylor et al., (2020) examined the experiences of 95 music education pre-service majors, and one surprising finding revealed that most of the pre-service students felt comfortable supporting broad topics of social justice and inclusion; however, less than half felt they were able to support students with questions concerning gender identity and sexual orientation. Taylor et al., (2020) also revealed, "most music education majors who identify as LGBTQ+ were unsure how to negotiate personal identity in the classroom or handle issues that might arise one day with their own P–12 students who identify as LGBTQ+ (e.g., coming out to other students in class, transitioning gender identity, bullying)" (p. 20). This finding is significant because, as teacher educators, it is necessary to examine how our pre-service teachers' beliefs impact how these LGBTQ+ teachers' experiences will influence their pedagogical practices.

Similarly, Shannon-Baker and Wagner (2019) discovered that most LGBTQ+ pre-service teachers do not feel prepared to address hetronormativity within schools. In fact, a number of their participants felt overwhelmed when discussing possible intolerant acts and methods to address those acts, which appears to be a common theme in the most recent literature.

Though the findings of all of these studies are important to the overall academic discourse exploring teacher preparation in regard to preparing new teachers to address heteronormativity, there is a deficit in the recent literature because a majority of the research examines new teachers or preservice teachers' experiences, mainly from a heterosexual identity attempting to improve inclusivity.

I postulate it is important to conceptualize how gay male teachers with varying years of experience may utilize their past experiences to impact their pedagogical decisions. Moreover, it is also advantageous to examine gay male teachers' beliefs about the intersectionality of sexuality and pedagogy in secondary classrooms, and how that intersectionality impacts the creation of safe and affirming educational environments for their students. This data could influence how teacher preparation programs infuse LGBTQ+ topics into curriculum and clinical experiences. We must remember that teachers (regardless of sexuality), "bring with them a portmanteau of gender-based understandings that, in many cases, are invisible to them" (Lipka & Brinthaupt, 1999, p. 58). The individuals who are teaching are one of the most important critical aspects of instruction because teachers are constantly negotiating with their surroundings. Teaching is not simply content and strategies. Therefore, I argue it is beneficial to examine how gay male teachers' beliefs about gender and sexuality influence their classroom environment and their instructional choices. Moreover, an examination of this population may provide implications for teacher preparation programs as they attempt to prepare pre-service teachers to address heteronormativity within schools.

Additionally, I posit it may be advantageous to examine southern gay male teachers' experiences creating safe and affirming classrooms because such an examination may provide valuable information to combat the recent political attacks against LGBTQ+ individuals in southern states. As more states pass laws, teacher education programs will need to combat these attacks.

Therefore, the purpose of this study was to examine how gay male secondary teachers' personal lived experiences as gay males may or may not influence their current classroom practices. This was important because there is a lack of literature that explores the possible influence of gay male teachers' identities and beliefs about sexuality on their professional decisions and instructional strategies. This study could add to the literature discussing how teacher preparation programs prepare all teacher candidates to create safe and affirming secondary environments.

Specifically, I chose ten teachers through a convenient sampling process, with a majority of the participants having two degrees of separation from the researcher. Once chosen, each participant engaged in an unstructured Zoom interview with the researcher. I chose to use an unstructured interview because of its connections to the theoretical framework for the study, queer theory. I also utilized unstructured focus group interviews, classroom observations with field notes, and a research journal.

I chose to use these methods because of their connections to the theoretical framework for the study, queer theory. There is a power dynamic that is inherent in the research process. Thus, to help dismantle the power dynamic, an unstructured interview and unstructured focus group interview releases more power to the participant because the participant has more control in the direction of the interview process.

Queer Theory

Before discussing the findings of the study, it is beneficial to discuss briefly the theoretical framework for the study. Queer theory began gaining prominence in the early 1990s when a feminist scholar (De Laureitis, 1991) coined the term and postulated that there were three major aspects to queer theory: disrupting heteronormativity, dismantling the unification of lesbian and gay studies, and re-examining the development of sexual biases.

Queer theory explores how society defines non-heterosexual and heterosexual identities according to the hegemonic structures that exist within society. It examines how the construction of knowledge about sexual identity and heterosexism is socially situated. As such, the theory seeks to dismantle the hegemonic constructions surrounding gender and sexual identity that exist in society (Jones, 2010). Thus, queer theory offers a way to define what it means to have a fluid definition of gender and sexuality. In other words, queer theory seeks to show that there is no innate gender or sexual identity, which disrupts the binary opposition that controls society's constructions surrounding gender and sexuality (Jones, 2010).

I should note, queer theory informed this study ontologically, epistemologically, and methodologically (Browne & Nash, 2016), which is a recent concept in qualitative research, one that has not proliferated social science research.

The Teachers

Next, it is beneficial to discuss the demographics of the study. The participants live and work in a southern state in the United States. Traditionally, the state is a red state in national elections. Recently, the state passed a non-divisive law that bans teachers from teaching divisive concepts about racism. In essence, it was a law against critical race theory. 62% of the population identify as only white and 13% percent identify as only black (www.census.gov).

The participants in the study teach in school districts across the state, which I discuss more in depth below.

In order to allow participants to maintain power and agency in the collection of data, I emailed each participant a "demographic form," and I asked each participant to complete the form, which contained only questions. I did not offer identifiers from which the participant could choose. For example, each participant listed their own identifier for their race and gender. I chose this method because of its connection to the theoretical framework, which gives the participant the power to control parts of the data collection. It is important to allow the participants to retain as much power as possible. In addition to the form, I have also listed demographic information that emerged from interviews.

Jack teaches band at a middle school in a predominantly failing district, as determined by the state department of education, which is in one of the smaller metropolitan areas in the state. He graduated from a medium-sized state university. Jack is married, and he teaches in a school primarily populated by students of color.

Rob is the youngest teacher with whom I spoke. He is 23 years old, and is in his second year of teaching math. He identifies as a gay cis white male. He revealed in our interview that he is out to his students, but he is not out to his administration or colleagues. He graduated with an undergraduate degree in middle grades education from a small private institution in the state. He teaches in the suburbs of a metropolitan city in the state. His school population is primarily composed of White/Caucasian students.

Eric is a 27-year-old White gay cis male. He has taught science for four years at a socio-economically advantaged school, though his school exists within an overall failing district, as defined by state department of education. The district is in the top third largest districts in the state. He earned his undergraduate degree from a medium-sized state university. At this point, he has no plan to continue his education. His school population is divided equally between students of color and White/Caucasian students, though he believes that demographic is shifting to students of color.

Seth is a 35-year-old gay White male who has taught English for 13 years. He has been at the same high school for his entire career. He earned an undergraduate degree from a private school, a master's degree from a large state university, and he is currently working on a doctoral degree from the same large state university. Seth is married, and he teaches in a smaller metropolitan city in the state. His school population is primarily students of color.

Mark is a 36-year-old Black gay cis male. He has taught high school science for seven years. He entered the teaching profession after a career in pharmaceutical sales. He earned his undergraduate degree from a large state university, and he completed a master's with teaching certification from the same institution. He teaches in a district within a metropolitan area of the state. His school population is primarily students of color.

Steve is a 38-year-old gay White male who has taught high school English for 16 years. He teaches in a rural district, which contains one elementary school, one middle school, and one high school. He earned his undergraduate degree, his master's degree, and his educational specialist from a medium-sized state university close to his current school district. His school is a Title I school, and it is primarily populated by White/Caucasian students.

Michael is a 39-year-old Black male, and he has taught high school math for 16 years. He currently teaches in a large metropolitan area. He has taught in the district his entire career at three different high schools. He earned his undergraduate, his master's, and his educational specialist degrees from a large state university. His current school is primarily populated by White/Caucasian students.

Matt is a 40-year-old White male who has taught English for 18 years. He also teaches in a socio-economically advantaged school, within a more affluent district. The district is one of the largest districts in the state. He has taught in three districts over his career, all of which have been in the state, and all of which have been socio-economically advantaged. His school is primarily populated by White/Caucasian students.

Jeff has taught high school biology for 25 years. In his interview, he revealed a strong desire to retire in five years. He is a 47-years-old White male. He teaches in a school district in a rural community in the eastern part of the state. He has spent his entire career in the same district and the same high school. He earned his undergraduate, his master's, his educational specialist, and his doctorate from a large state university. His school is primarily populated by White/Caucasian students.

John is a 52-year-old African American male who teaches history in a medium-sized school district. He has taught in the district his entire career, though he has been at several schools including two middle schools. His undergraduate and his master's is from a medium-sized state university. His school population is equally divided between students of color and white/Caucasian students.

From the analysis of the findings in the study, several themes emerged; however, for the purpose of this discussion, I will focus on three themes: instruction, identity, and inclusivity.

Instruction

In examining how the participant's personal experiences impact their pedagogy, the theme of instruction emerged. By "instruction," I am concerned with the participants' epistemological construction of instructional practices and if those constructions were influenced by their own beliefs surrounding sexuality and gender.

When asked if his beliefs about sexuality informed his instructional decisions, Jack stated, "this wave of legislation that came out against talking about transgender bathrooms, legalizing gay marriage, and then the kids all talk about it because their parents talk about it. But the kids are uneducated. So they're just copying what their parents are saying. And a lot of it is just backwards and just not respectful or conducive to a learning environment, because if we're all supposed to work towards an end goal of learning and building a positive educational experience, then yes, it needs to inform my classroom decisions. Otherwise, we are letting the ignorance win."

Similarly, Seth believes his classroom practices should be informed by his philosophical beliefs about education. He states, "I do not do it because

I am gay. I do it because it is the right thing to do. I address hate language towards students of color and students with special needs because I believe it is the right thing to do. I believe schools are responsible for creating a more tolerant society."

Jack and Seth recognize the impact of hegemony on their students' construction of knowledge and believe they must address their students' beliefs about LGBTQ+ individuals. However, both teachers view the challenge through a professional ethical dilemma that is not related to their sexuality. In this manner, they have separated their sexual identity from their professional responsibilities, which is similar to Steve's beliefs.

In the focus group interview, Steve shared his beliefs about his classroom practices, "Although I have never allowed my sexuality to inform my classroom choices, I definitely would not do it in the political climate schools are in right now. I don't stop reading a text with students to discuss a gay reference, unless it is necessary for the broader understanding of the novel. Part of that is probably because when I started teaching I could be fired for being gay. It was the culture of the south in those days."

Later in the focus group interview, Matt made the following comment, "I do not want students nor administration to know that I am gay because I am not sure how they would respond. Can I be fired? Who knows with what's going on in society. But, I have always felt that way. I grew up in a society where gay people were abused and killed. Maybe I have brought that into my professional life. But, that doesn't mean that I can't use curriculum to change the society. It will just take time. I just don't think I should make it personal."

For Steve and Matt, the current political regime dictates how they address issues surrounding sexuality in their classrooms. Both are afraid of retaliation from the district, even being dismissed from their teaching position. In essence, the regime has accomplished its intentions, to control these teachers' treatment of gender and sexuality within schools.

Rob followed up with Matt during the focus group interview, "I can see where the political climate can impact your pedagogy, but we can't let them win. I have a rainbow flag in my room. I talk about LGBTQ+ contributors to mathematics whenever it is feasible. I believe it's important because students need to know that some of the important discoveries came from LGBTQ+ individuals. It helps them create a different identity."

After Rob's comment, I offered a follow-up question, "So, do you think that it is teachers' jobs to do that?" Rob fervently stated, "yes." Matt responded, "as long as it is connected to the curriculum." Similarly, Steve said, "no, we can't privilege one difference over another. That's why they claim we have a gay agenda. We can't give them evidence for their beliefs."

During my classroom observations, I visited Rob's classroom. I noted in my field notes an incident that happened while I was there. "A student was sitting at his desk completing the assignment. His nails were painted blue, which his neighbor noticed. The neighbor fake whispered, 'stupid fag' to the student. I use the term fake whispered because he said it loud enough for the students close by could hear it, and he didn't think Rob would hear it. Rob publicly reprimanded the student and had a class discussion about kindness and language. Afterward, he removed the student from the room." When speaking to Rob after the observation I learned that it was important to Rob that the student be present in the room for the discussion about kindness, and it was also important that the class witnessed the student's discipline. He was not able to have a conversation without the consequences of his actions.

For Rob, who is the youngest teacher in the study, it is imperative to advocate for LGBTQ+ individuals within his classroom. His statement, "we can't let them win" establishes an us versus them binary, through which he is constructing meaning about gender and sexuality within schools. Conversely, the older teachers continue to construct a meaning that allows the power regime to remain in control.

It should be noted, I asked the following question in each individual interview, "Did your teacher preparation program prepare you to address challenges within the LGBTQ+ community in schools?" None of the participants received formalized training to create safe and affirming classrooms for this population. The state requires a diversity introductory course in education, but the course does not provide specific methods to address challenges surrounding LGBTQ+ youth.

The lack of preparation may have an influence in how these participants view their role as an LGBTQ+ advocate in their classrooms and schools.

For these participants, sexuality influenced their instructional decisions in various ways. Some participants advocated for complete dedication to LGBTQ+ issues, while others believe the instructional decisions concerning

LGBTQ+ issues should be grounded in the curriculum. It is important to note, the differences of approaches tended to be generational.

Identity

Next, the theme of identity emerged from the data analysis. "Identity" references the ways the participants constructed meaning about identity and how that construction impacted their classroom practices. Moreover, it is important to note that the participants' own definitional parameters of "identity" are also important to examine.

Identity plays a tremendous role in these participants' beliefs surrounding their classroom environments. Jack stated, "In the past five years, I've had kids come to me and say, I'd rather go by John rather than Lucy. I'd rather be called Lucy rather than John, like, they've decided that they're transitioning, or they don't feel comfortable in their own skin. And they'd like to be called something different. And my response is always okay. Just have to make sure I'm on point with what you want to be called, because I want to respect your choice… we had a couple kids in class who were identified as transgender. And they said their friends said openly defending their friend, 'no, they go by whatever they go by.' You're calling them by the wrong name now."

Indeed, names play a vital role in Jack's class. Later in the interview, he states, "we're not going to call somebody outside of their name because it normally results in somebody using the N word or using faggot or gay, or their new favorite thing is to call somebody fruity. And every time they use one of these words, that is not the kid's name. I asked them the question I said, So could you replace that word with something else? What would you replace that word with? A student called somebody gay a couple times and I said, so if you need to replace the word, and he said fruity. And I said, what does that mean? Fruity? Can you define that for me? Can you change it again? What would you get? What would you say? The student said, 'weird'. Okay. So they're just weird. And that's appropriate to call somebody just weird randomly? You just get to know them or just ignore them all together. You don't have to be friends with them, but you also don't have to call them outside of their name." For Jack, identity was more than a sexualized understanding of someone. Identity includes the basic core of someone's name.

For Matt, identity also included one's name. He stated, "I remember having a student, and I did not pronounce her name right the first time. She said, 'call me M.' I replied, "but that's not your name. It is important for me to call you by your name." Eventually, I did pronounce it correctly because it was important for me to allow her whole self to be welcomed in my classroom." Similarly, Rob refuses to use one's dead name in his classroom.

For Steve, identity was a pivotal point in his philosophical beliefs about education. In the focus group interview, he commented, "all students come into our classes with an identity, whether that is Christian white football player or MTF trans. Identity matters. We all know that. I struggle with how supportive I should be. I don't want administration to believe that I am favoring one identity over another, so I attempt to value all identities. I don't think I do it well."

Matt supported Steve's belief in failure, "yes, I am the same way. I don't do it well. When I was in high school, I was a closeted gay male. There were not so many identities. You were gay or straight, lesbian or gay. No one in my education classes taught me anything about gay issues. I had to learn on the job. So, yes, I struggle with the identity thing. I am sure I am an epic failure. But, it was not my childhood experience."

To which Rob replied, "it's not that difficult. Teachers need to educate themselves on these topics. It's too important." Mark agreed with Rob, "it is too important. As a black male though, it is also important for teachers to educate themselves on the challenges of being a black gay male, or a black trans student. When black identity mixes with sexuality and gender identity, it is very different in my community versus the white community."

Throughout the data, it is apparent that identity plays a tremendous role in these participants' pedagogical practices. The data also illuminate the generational differences of these participants and their beliefs about sexuality and gender identity within their classrooms. Specifically, the veteran teachers are more traditional in their approach to addressing LGBTQ+ issues within their classrooms. Additionally, it is important to note that teacher preparation programs did not prepare these teachers, regardless of generation, to address challenges with identity.

It is also important to consider these teachers' treatment of sexuality and gender as it relates to instruction and to identity. Rob was the only philosophically consistent teacher in regards to these topics. Jack, Matt, and Steve were in favor of supporting students and their identity, but they held nearly antithetical beliefs concerning instructional practices. In this manner, the individuality of the student is more important than a broad curricular or instructional decision that may impact other belief systems within the room. Therefore, the justification of action is premised on individualism not the collective.

Inclusivity

In addition to instructional practices and identity, inclusivity also emerged as a theme from the data analysis. By inclusivity, I mean a purposeful attempt to increase or decrease inclusive practices within the participants' classrooms and their school buildings. In this capacity, a majority of the teachers believed that their classroom spaces were more inclusive than many of their counterparts throughout the building. For example, Eric stated, "I have found that many of the students that are part of the LGBTQ+ community have really felt comfortable in my class, like not using their dead name in class. For instance, in any other class, they might go by their dead name just to keep the teacher from feeling dissonance on what the roster says." Similarly, Matt suggested that a majority of his students were more expressive of their positive support for LGBTQ+ students. When asked if he believed LGBTQ+ students felt safer in his room, he responded, "I do believe they feel safer in my room as compared to other teachers. I have a couple of trans kids who are very open about their identity in my room. During a department meeting, someone mentioned the student's name and a colleague indicated he had no clue the student was trans." The other teacher's statement attests to Matt's beliefs about how his student felt in his room compared to the other teacher's room. Matt also credits his desire to create an inclusive classroom as the conduit for this atmosphere.

For Eric, he makes some specific pedagogical decisions to address inclusivity in his classroom, but his choices attempt to address a broad definition of inclusivity, not simply the LGBTQ+ inclusion. Specifically, he states, "I've tried to structure my classroom and some of the expectations and some of the activities we do throughout the year towards inclusivity and understanding and checking your perspective. I try to stay away from privilege because it's a triggering word for a lot of people, but I call it checking your perspective, which is essentially the same thing, just a triggering word because I like to think of privilege as perspective driven by opportunity, and the opportunity part is where it starts to get triggering for a lot of people."

Likewise, Rob is an advocate for inclusive practices, "I think it is important that LGBTQ+ students who walk into my room feel welcomed and affirmed. They see the rainbow flag. I discuss my own sexuality with them, which I did receive a few phone calls from parents last year, but I teach in a super liberal suburb, so I knew my principal would support me. Students walk into straight teachers' rooms and see pictures of their spouses. Straight couples talk about trying to have a child. I have several straight colleagues who talk about date nights with their husbands. LGBTQ+ students need the same opportunities to have role models."

Conversely, three of the participants (who are the older participants) in the study did not purposefully change their instructional practices to create a safer classroom environment for LGBTQ+ students. John stated, "I am not going to change what I do specifically for one group of students. Everything I do in my classroom has to benefit the entire class. No one is allowed to hit another student, or to scream at another student. If someone calls another student a gay slur, I am going to address it the same way. I am not going to stop what I am doing to have a mini-lesson on the word. I have heard some faculty do that in their classrooms. I am going to treat it the same way as if I heard a sexist slur or a racial slur." Similarly, Jeff made the following comment, "I am not going to let my sexuality cause me to treat hate language differently. My sexuality can't define my classroom and how I teach my students. They have to be separate."

In addition to the participants' individual classrooms, the data analysis revealed findings concerning the inclusivity of the participants' school buildings. When asked if his administrators know about his sexuality, Eric responded, "It gives me a weird level of anxiety in the same way that not knowing whether the kids know or what the kids think. I don't care what the kids think, because that's not my job. What the administration thinks of me is definitely an important thing... I wonder whether their preexisting biases of me and who I am will impact my job."

Moreover, when I observed Eric's classroom, there were no classroom paraphernalia that indicated anything about his sexuality.

Matt stated, "I don't know who knows? I think the administration knows based on conversations I've had with some of the assistant principals, particularly one who is very, I'd say he is very inquisitive. But I have never told anyone because I do not want them to know. We are in an important political climate. So, many things could potentially happen, and I want to hide behind my male Christian whiteness."

As with Eric, I did not document any classroom décor that would lead one to believe Matt was gay or an ally. That being said, there were numerous posters of people of color discussing their contributions to literature. There were also numerous posters discussing women and their contributions to literature. When I visited his class he was lecturing on feminism. He stated, "So, we mostly make you read white female authors who committed suicide. Right. Virginia Woolf. Sylvia Plath. Charlotte Perkins Gilman. We are going to read a powerful author who is an icon in literature. Toni Morrison." He continued with an autobiographical discussion of Morrison's life. During the focus group interview, I asked Matt about the lesson. He commented, "students need to see themselves in the literature. They need to see that someone like them can do great things. For years, English classrooms have avoided the powerful woman writers who made an amazing impact on society. We don't teach those women in schools unless you are in AP."

For Matt, inclusivity is an important ideal in his pedagogy. From this statement and others, it is obvious that Matt values inclusivity in this classroom as long as it can be connected to the curriculum, as he stated, "But, that doesn't mean that I can't use curriculum to change the society. It will just take time. I just don't think I should make it personal."

Jack remarked in his interview, "So, I'm married and my husband's great. Love him. We married five years ago. We were engaged six years ago. Instead of going to my graduation for my master's degree, we went to Disneyland and got engaged or went to Disney World to get engaged. When I came back, all the kids noticed the ring on my finger. They're like, so you got married. And I'm like, I'm getting married. That's what the ring means. But I've tried really hard to not talk about that personal stuff with the kids. They don't need to know that I'm married to a man. I have yet to say in front of my students, I'm gay, I have a husband. That sentence has never come out of my mouth. It's not something that I still, I guess, don't feel comfortable doing for the students because what business is it of theirs?"

For a majority of the teachers, inclusivity should not be connected to personal feelings about sexuality and gender. As such, a majority of the teachers did not discuss their own sexuality with their students, even though such actions improve levels of tolerance in educational settings (Jones, 2014). For these teachers, the hegemonic structures that marginalize LGBTQ+ individuals are also controlling these teachers' classroom practices as they relate to inclusivity. Specifically, Matt must connect any practice that improves inclusivity to the curriculum, which in the south is derived by heteronormative power regimes. It is also interesting that Matt feels safer hiding behind his white Christian maleness; in doing so, the action attests to the power of heteronormativity within his beliefs and classroom practices. Similarly, Jack believes his students should not be privy to his personal life, specifically his marriage to his husband. His belief, as with the others, emerges from the heteronormativity that pervades society, especially southern culture and society.

For a majority of these teachers, inclusivity is important, but it must be premised within the power regime and structure of their community. As such, these teachers are perpetuating the heteronormativity that exists in society; thereby, their own marginalized status does not influence their classroom practices.

Discussion

This study examined southern gay male teachers' beliefs about the intersectionality of sexuality, gender identity, and pedagogy in secondary classrooms. For this discussion, three important themes emerged from the data analysis: instruction, identity, and inclusivity. Thus, it is important for teacher preparation programs to consider the findings from this study; so that, we can ensure our graduates are prepared to address the challenges that arise concerning LGBTQ+ students.

First, these participants did not receive training in their educational programs to address the challenges surrounding LGBTQ+ students within schools. I posit it is imperative for teacher preparation programs to examine how they discuss LGBTQ+ issues in their curriculum. This is an important aspect to consider given the current political climate towards all forms of difference. As Jones (2019) and GLSEN (2019) postulate, the challenges surrounding LGBTQ+ students are rampant in secondary schools, and teachers are not adequately addressing the challenges.

Moreover, it is important for teacher preparation programs to focus on LGBTQ+ challenges because of the lack of support for LGBTQ+ students. The hatred against LGBTQ+ students is more damaging. If someone calls a student of color a slur, they can go home and most likely have familial support, which is less likely the case in situations of sexuality and gender discrimination, especially in southern states. Thus, in a majority of cases the harassed student must carry the pain of the hatred without an outlet of familial support to reassure the student that they are understood. Teachers should be trained to specifically address challenges that create hostile school environments for LGBTQ+ students.

It is also important to note the generational divide in these participants' beliefs about their involvement in supporting LGBTQ+ students and how that finding informs teacher preparation. In this study, the younger generation was more adamant about advocating specifically for students who identified as LGBTQ+. Conversely, the older generation of participants believed in the importance of advocacy, but they preferred to frame it within a broader understanding of all marginalized identities. This is important for teacher preparation programs to consider because preparation programs may need to prepare their younger candidates to navigate the belief systems of the older teachers and administrators in the building. The navigation should provide new teachers with the theoretical underpinnings to support a belief in advocacy for LGBTQ+ students.

Finally, though the purpose of this study was not to examine the influence of divisive curriculum laws and the political power regimes in southern states, the finding emerged from the study, which merits a discussion. In relation to creating an inclusive and affirming classroom, the political climate is a stronger influence than the personal lived experiences of a majority of the men in this study. Specifically, there are numerous mentions of the role of the current political regime and its influence on a majority of these teachers' pedagogical decisions. Many refused to mention LGBTQ+ topics because of the fear the current political regime has imposed on education in the state. One teacher indicated that he wants to hide behind his white Christian male identity because of the current political climate in his state.

For further context, in one southern state, higher education leaders were asked "to gather information about courses, curriculum, jobs and research that focus on topics such as anti-racism and social justice" (Stirgus, 2022). According to the article, the state legislation wants to reduce funding if state institutions use allocations for social justice issues.

In this capacity, I argue it is necessary to explore how educators are prepared to think critically about the methods to address all areas of difference (especially LGBTQ+ students) as it relates to the scope of the current political climate. Specifically, teacher preparation programs should prepare teachers to examine the laws about divisive curriculum and engage in critical conversations with candidates about the laws' influence on the process of schooling and their employment. For a majority of the participants, the current political climate in the state caused trepidation and influenced their instructional decisions, which perpetuates heteronormativity and intolerance.

The current political regime of power in a number of states is influencing higher education, as well as K-12 education. As such, teacher education programs must examine how the political actions will influence the methods through which we prepare future teachers. As the data (GLSEN, 2016) suggest, LGBTQ+ teachers provide more advocacy for LGBTQ+ students, and the findings of this study reveal that the political influence is greater than their own beliefs about advocacy, which harms the lives of LGBTQ+ students in our schools.

In addition to an examination, teacher education faculty must enter the conversations surrounding the current political climate. It is imperative that the academy support all marginalized identities within P-12 schools and higher education.

Conclusion

According to GLSEN (2019), 59.1% of LGBTQ+ students felt unsafe in their schools, and 25.7% were physically assaulted in schools across the United States. This data, among other discussed earlier, is alarming. As an academic who prepares pre-service teachers, it is apparent that changes should occur in teacher preparation programs. We must engage in methods to prepare all candidates to become advocates and to create safe and affirming educational environments for all students, but especially for LGBTQ+ students. We must begin conceptualizing how to better prepare teacher candidates to enter the profession with the skills to combat these challenges while functioning within the divisive curriculum laws that a number of states are passing. Students are depending on teachers to provide safe learning environments, and it is imperative that teacher preparation programs are producing teachers who are dedicated to these principles.

This article first appeared in *Taboo: The Journal of Culture and Education*
Jones, J. R. (2023). Instruction, Identity, and Inclusivity: What can Teacher Preparation Programs Learn from Gay Male Teachers in the South. *Taboo: The Journal of Culture and Education, 22*(1). https://digitalscholarship.unlv.edu/taboo/vol22/iss1/4

References

Browne, K., & Nash, C. (2016). Queer methods and methodologies: An introduction. In K. Browne & C. Nash (Eds.), *Queer methods and methodologies: Intersectingqueer theories and social science research*, 1-23. Routledge.

De Lauretis, T. (1991). Queer Theory: Lesbian and gay sexualities. *Differences: A Journal of Feminist Cultural Studies, 3*(2), iv-xviii.

GLSEN. (2016). *LGBTQ-Inclusive and supportive teaching practices: The experiences of LGBTQ and non-LGBTQ educators.* https://www.glsen.org/research/lgbtq-supportive-teaching

GLSEN. (2019). *2019 national school climate survey.* https://www.glsen.org/research/2019-national-school-climate-survey

Jones, J. R. (2010). *Homophobia in secondary schools: An investigation of teachers' perceptions of homophobia through a collaborative professional development program.* (Publication No. 3442769) [Doctoral dissertation, University of Rochester]. ProQuest.

Jones, J. R. (2014). Purple boas, lesbian affection, and John Deere hats: Teacher educators' role in addressing homophobia in secondary schools. *Teacher Education and Practice, 27*(1), 154-59.

Jones, J. R. (Ed.). (2017). *Feather boas, black hoodies, and John Deere hats: Reflections of diversity in K-12 schools and higher education.* Sense Publishing.

Jones, J. (2019). *My second first year: Leaving the academia for a high school classroom.* IAP.

Lipka, R. P., & Brinthaupt, T. M. (1999). *The role of self in teacher development.*

SUNY Press.
Sapp, J. (2017). *Introduction*. In W. DeJean & J. Sapp (Eds.), *Dear Gay, Lesbian, Bisexual, And Transgender Teacher: Letters Of Advice To Help You Find Your Way*, 147-160. IAP
Shannon-Baker, P., & Wagner, I. (2019). Battling heteronormativity in teacher education: Reflections on human development course from teacher and student. In D. Martin (Ed.), *Exploring gender and LGBTQ+ issues in K-12 education: A rainbow assemblage*, 147-163. IAP.
Stirgus, E. (2022, February 10). Georgia lawmaker targets work focused on anti-racism, social justice. *Atlanta Journal Constitution*. https://www.ajc.com/education/georgia-lawmaker-targets-work-focused-on-anti-racism-social-justice/A7ZDE6Q7GNE3HGUU5MPY3KJFZU/
Taylor, D., Talbot, B., Holmes, E., & Petrie, T. (2020). Experiences of LGBTQ+ students in music education programs across Texas. *Journal of Music Education, 30*(1) 11-23.
Taylor, C., Peter, T., Campbell, C., Meyer, E., Ristock, J., & Short, D. (2015). *The every teacher project on LGBTQ-inclusive education in Canada's K–12 schools: Final report*. The Manitoba Teachers' Society. https://winnspace.uwinnipeg.ca/bitstream/handle/10680/1264/Every%20Teacher%20Project%20Final%20Report%20WEBc.pdf?sequence=1&isAllowed=y
Thompkins, J., Kearns, L., & Mitton-Kükner, J. (2019). Queer educators in schools: The experiences of four beginning teachers. *Canadian Journal of Education 42*(2), 384-414.

CHAPTER 18

Superhumans:
Student Teachers in a Time of Crisis

Erinn Bentley

We're all familiar with the phrase: *I teach. What's your superpower?* Whether it's on a t-shirt or a coffee mug, it is a rallying cry for us educators. It confirms that the work we do often requires a superhero level of patience, energy, enthusiasm, and stamina. It's validation that the work we do really *is* making a difference, even when our students' blank stares and slumped shoulders say otherwise. As a life-long educator, I have embraced being a superhero. But, the superhero-self I knew taught in a brick-and-mortar classroom. I was there *with* my students, giving them a high-five for a thought-provoking answer or a raised eyebrow for mumbling, "I dunno". I had colleagues down the hall I could turn to for help. Then came the announcement on March 14, 2020. The COVID-19 pandemic had reached our education community. All K-12 and university campuses were closed, face-to-face instruction was suspended, and instruction was moved online. None of us teachers had the superpowers needed to avert this world-wide crisis. I was not even sure if I had the superpowers needed to support my own students.

Still, superheroes don't give up.

For the past 12 years, I have mentored future and current secondary English teachers at a regional public university in the south. My roles as a professor range from teaching methods courses, to supervising pre-service teachers in local schools, to providing students at all levels with academic advising. When our university and the local K-12 schools shifted to online instruction due to the COVID-19 pandemic, I was supervising five student teachers. For the six remaining weeks of the semester, they were instructed to assist their classroom teachers in providing online instruction. My student teachers quickly launched into panic-mode, texting me: *How will this work? How can I put an entire Shakespeare unit online? I don't know what I'm doing!* I did not have the power to see into the future and answer all of their questions. I only had the power to listen, to encourage, and to support. This is our story –from the start of the crisis to our current situation.

Prior to the pandemic, my student teachers and I met weekly on campus for seven months, and I had shared countless hours with them in their high school classrooms. We weathered active shooter drills and laughed when our lesson plans went off the rails. We hosted a baby shower for Rachel (pseudonyms used throughout), whose little one arrived just before Thanksgiving break. We were a tight group. These folks were creative, vibrant, and determined to change the world. Seeing them with their students, I believed they would.

When both our university and their high schools closed their doors in March of 2020, we shifted to virtual meetings. As each of them popped on to my computer screen, I saw familiar faces with unfamiliar expressions: tired eyes, tight-lipped smiles. Gone were my superheroes. Hailey started the conversation: "I feel like I'm starting student teaching all over again." Eva agreed, saying, "I was just about to take over teaching all of the classes. I had my unit all planned, and now I either don't get to teach it or have to revise the whole thing." From their perspective, the pivot to online instruction could not have come at a worse time. In our program's model, student teachers spend the first half of the semester co-teaching and assisting their mentors before assuming the planning and instructional responsibility for all classes. Their "solo" teaching time was supposed to begin the day the schools closed.

Jonathan was also frustrated with the new online model. He said, "This is not how I wanted to be trained. I wanted to learn how to actually be a teacher. Anyone can just post stuff online. I feel like I'm taking steps backward." Rachel felt similarly. She explained, "I miss being with my seniors. Since they are about to graduate and their grades are basically set, almost none of them log into my Zoom meetings. I'm still planning lessons, but for whom? I'm basically teaching no one." When the local district shifted to online learning, K-12 students had just completed their third 9-week grading period. Only one more period remained in the academic year. Students' final grades were an average of the first three periods. If students wanted to improve their grades, they could complete the optional online work. "I guess a lot of my students are fine with their As, Bs, and Cs," Rachel sighed, "because they've stopped doing anything." Eva countered, "My A students keep logging in; it's the students with Ds and Fs I'm worried about. They are the ones who need this opportunity, but I haven't heard from many of them yet."

Teaching, they all agreed, was connected to talking–having discussions with students, whether it's part of a lesson or a quick chat in the hallway between classes. By talking, we figure out what our students are thinking, feeling, and wondering. We don't teach algebra, American literature, or physical education. We teach humans. And now we were teaching in a new world, one where my student teachers and their classroom teachers seemed to be talking into a void.

As a mentor, part of my job is to model best practices that pre-service teachers can adopt as they plan their lessons. Sometimes these pedagogical practices come from experts in the field, such as podcasts, textbooks, exemplary lesson plans, scholarly articles, and videos. Other times, I draw from my own experiences. There was no how-to guide on shifting teaching, learning, and mentoring online during a worldwide pandemic. And I certainly did not have any experience in this area. We could accept this moment as a crisis by simply posting content online and giving up teaching. But, as we know, superheroes don't give up. My student teachers were no exception.

By the end of our first virtual meeting, I could see we felt overwhelmed and anxious. It was hard for any of us to envision our next six weeks. I wondered, if we could not look forward, what if we looked back? In our first meeting, seven months ago, we started with the question: Who is your teaching hero? We each then wrote a narrative describing the teacher, coach, counselor, or mentor who most impacted us as a student, and we shared our stories. I now told my student teachers–go back and read your narratives. When we meet next week, tell me again about your heroes. Tell me the biggest lesson you've learned from them. I will do the same.

Back in August, I wrote the following: *I still remember walking into my 7th grade advanced English classroom. The desks and chairs were not lined* up in tidy rows. Instead, they sat side-by-side around the room, forming a wide circle. In its center stood a tall metal stool. It had been painted an electric blue at one time; however, the paint was now chipped and pealing. He called it the Venerable Blue Stool.

Mr. M., perched on the edge of the Venerable Blue Stool, read aloud the lilting lines of Poe and Frost. Every so often he paused, swiveled, and asked, "What do YOU think?" When he spoke, he looked you straight in the eye. He leaned in. The Stool was his stage; he was the director. We were his actors, his audience. One day, the circle of desks was gone. All of our chairs were lined up facing the classroom's wall of windows. Mr. M. told us: "Behold! Observe! Write about the outdoors." My window overlooked the parking lot. Half-melted snow mixed with mud and slush. A single plastic trash bag turned in the breeze. We whined, "But, there's nothing there. What do we write about?" From the Venerable Blue Stool–"There is always a story, you just need to find it." And we did.

On Thursdays, the Stool towered before us, empty. It was there for those who chose it. We could recite something we had read: a song, a story, or a poem. We could recite our own words. It was our open mic, our spotlight. Who could have guessed that sitting on this surface–hard, cold, and rusted–would make a 12-year-old feel like her world was okay, if only for the 60 seconds it took to read, "'Hope' is the Thing with Feathers."

Let's face it. Seventh grade is a time most adults would rather forget. The middle school years are just that–a time when we are stuck in the middle of outgrowing childhood, but not quite growing into our new bodies, roles, and responsibilities. Honestly, I don't remember much from that time. I do remember the Venerable Blue Stool. Years later, I became a middle school English teacher too. Standing in front of my students and their wary eyes, I quickly discovered that Mr. M. made it all look easy. I began to worry. I didn't have his charisma and charm. I didn't have a Stool. But, being a good teacher isn't really about having a certain kind personality or having an electric blue prop. Good teachers make sure that each student knows they belong. They are accepted. They are heard.

As I looked back over the words I wrote months ago, one thing was clear. Whether our classroom is online, in a building, or some combination of the two—teaching isn't about the teacher; it's about the student too. Each student belongs. In our meeting, I was eager to hear my student teachers' reflections on their narratives. Instead, Hailey talked about one of her 11th grade students, who also was a member of the track team she had been coaching. This student was not checking in, not turning in any work. "There's no way my star sprinter would just drop out of school," Hailey insisted. "She's hoping to get a track scholarship for college." She finally got a hold of her student on the phone and discovered this 16-year-old was babysitting three younger siblings. All children had online learning to complete and their home's internet could only sustain one learner at a time. This student had to wait until her parents got home and the computer was free, so her classes started after dinner. She had been trying to follow along, but managing seven classes alone every night wasn't working. Hailey could have just told her to do her best and send questions via email. Instead, she met with her via videoconference for one-on-one tutoring.

Eva then jumped into the conversation. She had designed a four-week unit and was frustrated that only her straight-A students were logging in to do the work. Several students were on the cusp of failing the class, and this was their last chance to raise their grade. What did she do? She calculated what those students needed to do to pass. She contacted them with this information. In our meeting, she laughed. "I am terrible at math, as you know," she said. "And maybe my kids are too." She thought about her students. Did they know that a passing grade was within their reach? Smiling, she talked about the kids who were now logging in, chatting in Zoom meetings, and doing the work. Her hours spent calculating grades and reaching out was worth it. Sometimes a nudge from a teacher, who clarifies the grading system and encourages that student to keep on going, is all that is needed. That student knows they belong.

I could go on and on about my student teachers. They were superheroes for their students. I was proud to see how our conversations had shifted in one short week. Before, they were worried about their lesson plans and university requirements; now, they were focused on their learners. The mentor in me wondered: *Was there something guiding their teaching decisions and beliefs?* We never got a chance to talk about their thoughts on their hero-narratives, so I decided to re-read them. In those stories, I saw a 5th grade student who found her hero in a teacher who–finally–spelled her name just as it was written on her birth certificate. She admitted, "For years I got used to teachers telling me I didn't know how to spell my own name. It's my name. To have a teacher correct you for years.... It hurt."

Another wrote about feeling like she wasn't "smart enough" and assumed her teachers did not see potential in her because they never recommended her for an advanced or honors class. As her peers moved on to advanced classes together, she felt stuck—until 9th grade. For the first time, a teacher gave her a "yellow paper"–a recommendation form to take Advanced Placement chemistry. She reflected, "At the time I believed you weren't smart if you weren't in advanced classes. Now I know that is not true. All students have potential. They just need encouragement." A third described what it felt like to never have a teacher who looked like her. "Even when we were reading stories or novels, the only time I saw a character who was like me was during Black History Month." She became a teacher, determined to change the curriculum and serve as a role model.

Re-reading my student teachers' narratives, I was reminded of my own education journey. I did not become an English teacher because I love to read Shakespeare or write poems. Instead, I remember what it felt like to be that vulnerable, awkward, and shy 7th grade student who preferred to sit in the back of the room, unnoticed. And I remember what it felt like to finally be comfortable enough to sit in the center and let my teacher and peers notice me. Thinking of my student teachers, did this narrative assignment really impact their practices? Probably not. Did the experiences described in those narratives impact them? Most definitely.

In fact, scholars acknowledge that by the time student teachers arrive to their classrooms, they have spent thousands of hours as learners themselves. Observing various teachers, they witness strategies, behaviors, and lessons which mold their beliefs regarding the profession. In *Schoolteacher: A Sociological Study* (1975), Dan Lortie named this phenomenon *the apprenticeship of observation*. As a result, pre-service teachers often teach the way they were taught, mimicking former learning experiences. One potential danger is that simply mimicking another's actions does not take into account context. Every group of students is unique. Every classroom situation is different. For instance, while the Venerable Blue Stool worked for Mr. M. back in the 1980s, his strategy may not be appropriate for students today. As my student teachers adjusted to their new online teaching context, they could have relied on strategies they observed their mentor teachers or former K-12 teachers use previously. Instead of focusing on the *how* and *what* of teaching, they focused on the *who*–their students.

As I write these words, it is now Fall of 2023. My student teachers never got to see their graduating seniors again or even attend their own commencement ceremony. I did not have the power to prevent those heartaches. They worried whether this abbreviated teaching experience had *really* prepared them to be full-time teachers. Three years later, I can attest that all five are still teaching; two were even nominated by their districts for the First-Year Teacher of the Year Award. Their success makes them my heroes, yet I still worry as a mentor: *How do I help my current and future student teachers work in spaces and circumstances none of us have experienced? What if all of this uncertainty is so discouraging, they choose to leave the profession?*

I cannot, of course, speak for all mentors; however, here is what I have noticed among my student teachers these past three years. They are resilient. When told to pivot, they don't complain. They just figure out how to do it (whatever "it" may be). They are empathetic. When their students complain because they missed out on Homecoming dances or birthday parties during the pandemic, they listen. They can relate. Their university Homecomings, social events, and sports were cancelled, postponed, or moved online as well. Student teachers are patient. They see their students' learning gaps and understand what it is like to lose years of instruction. They are willing to put in the work to get their students back on track.

To say those pandemic years were challenging is an understatement. Many of us are still exhausted and anxious. Alongside our students, we feel the emotional, psychological, physical, and academic impacts from those experiences. Talking with veteran teachers, I see some (myself included) taking solace reminiscing about the "good ol' teaching days" or skipping ahead to imagine a fresh start next fall. Perhaps, though, we all could learn from our student teachers, who seem to live in the present moment. They understand, better than I do, just how much is out of our control. Rather than resist the uncertain, they walk into their classrooms each day and are resilient, empathetic, and positive. They focus on what *is* in their control: Their students.

A while back, I joined a faculty learning community at my university focused on *Small Teaching Online* (Darby & Lang, 2019). I was drawn to this book study not necessarily to discover new strategies and assignments. It was the title of the second section that got me–"Teaching Humans." Here, Darby and Lang (2019) encourage teachers to "nudge" students who are struggling or need extra attention (p. 149). They explain, "Students might not be doing the work in your course for a variety of reasons. Some of them might have overextended themselves ... many of them will not do the work because they doubt their own abilities, or because they don't understand the amount of work and self-discipline required to succeed" (Darby & Lang, 2019, p. 151). These descriptions reminded me of my student teachers' narratives, both the stories written at the start of the pandemic and those composed just a few weeks ago. My folks know how it feels to not be chosen for an advanced class. They know how it feels to be invisible in a classroom. They know how important it is for teachers to call students by their names, to care about them as humans.

Like all good superheroes, we teachers have alter-egos. We are coaches, parents, spouses, band directors, and senior class sponsors–just to name a few. In other words, we are human. Darby and Lang (2019) remind us to view our students similarly:

> [Our students] are not just names on a screen, although it can sometimes feel that way. Our students are living, breathing people. They come to us with hopes and dreams, pressures and concerns, competing demands on their time. It's important to remember that students have lives outside the LMS. Their whole world does not revolve around our class. From time to time, they may need additional support or flexibility. (p. 95)

Whether our students are learning online or in a physical classroom, they have outside lives–extra-curricular activities, jobs, family members, and so on. Not every student has the same amount of resources at home to support their learning, such as purchasing a graphing calculator, paying field trip fees, having access to technology, having a quiet and safe space to study, having meals and housing, or having reliable transportation. The pivot to online learning during the pandemic did not cause these issues, they already existed. As my student teachers discovered, many of their students did not choose to drop out or vanish when their school doors closed. Other parts of their lives made it challenging for them to tune into a Zoom meeting or complete work independently.

Since that time, we have also discovered how challenging it is when students are in hybrid learning spaces–with some peers online and some in-person. Who receives attention? Who is ignored or allowed to disconnect? How do we help those students who have years' worth of learning gaps? How do we balance meeting students at their levels and preparing them for high-stakes, rigorous tests? Our current teaching and learning situations are far from perfect. Again, many of these issues predated the pandemic, and no single teacher can fix them. Still, I am proud of my folks for finding flexible ways for supporting their students. Most importantly, they honed their greatest teacher trait–the power of caring.

Each semester, my student teachers ask if they are *truly* ready to be full-time teachers. Whether their classrooms are in virtual or physical spaces, these future teachers have shown me just how powerful it is to listen, hope, and empathize. None of these are superpowers. They are human powers. Moving forward, I am not sure I want to embrace being a superhero or encourage my pre-service teachers to do the same. While I know we can–and will–change the world, we do not need this infallible, larger-than-life persona to do it. We just need to be human.

References

Darby. F., & Lang, J. (2019). *Small teaching online: Applying learning science in online classes.* Jossey-Bass.

Lortie, D. (1975). *Schoolteacher: A sociological study.* University of Chicago Press.

CHAPTER 19

Promoting Student Engagement and Enhancing Outcomes Through Community Involvement

Noah Lawton Harrell

Student engagement and outcomes are the bread and butter of teaching: educators want to see students super engaged in their learning and producing products that showcase what they have learned. Community involvement can play a huge role in helping both engagement and outcomes. Our students are a part of a community. In fact, a school is a microcosm of the community it serves. The diversity in that population plays a role in the educational experience of every student, whether we recognize that truth or not. According to a report from Wells et al., "research demonstrates the important educational benefits—cognitive, social, and emotional—for all students who interact with classmates from different backgrounds, cultures, and orientations to the world" (Para. 2). We need instructional strategies that take advantage of the great opportunity community involvement offers.

Despite data showing shifting demographics of American schools, many districts remain fairly monoethnic. Students who do not live in culturally diverse areas often manifest implicit bias. This is created because the student has not experienced anything else and has internalized that their lived experiences are the lived experiences of others. Breaking that implicit bias is crucial to being able to give students the benefit of cultural diversity in a school.

Research shows that "the mere inclusion of different perspectives, and especially divergent ones, in any course of discussion leads to the kind of learning outcomes (for example, critical thinking, perspective-taking) that educators, regardless of field, are interested in" (Drexel University, 2021, para. 2). The push for more cultural diversity can lead to other benefits in a school as well: students become more empathetic, students gain a better understanding of lessons and people, students become more open-minded, students feel more confident and safer, and students are better prepared for a diverse workplace (Drexel University, 2021). In my opinion, understanding other points of views strengthens our students' thought processes. When there is a lack of diversity, close-mindedness about other cultures is prevalent.

One area of focus for me as a vice principal is the effect of community engagement and ways in which the diversities of that population and our school can lead to better student outcomes. Any such effort could certainly have different looks. This could mean more parent involvement in schools, and leadership opportunities or training about ways they can help their students succeed. Another look could involve local businesses and other stakeholders coming into schools to help promote the importance of education. The next generation of the workforce will come out of our schools after all, so businesses should want to tap into that. They want to have well developed and thoughtful individuals ready and prepared to join their companies. For their part, students seeing real world implications that relate to their learning leads to more engagement. More, seeing the immediate benefits of something they are learning or working on can push the engagement and outcomes that students produce.

In thinking about how societal diversity and community involvement can lead to better student engagement and outcomes, I took a long look at my own school to see what we could do. There have been two opportunities that I have been able to assist with and promote in my school building. The first was a community night in which students of different classes were able to share and show off work they had been completing in the building. The idea was that at the end of first term we would invite stakeholders from the community to a showcase of our student talent and products. Teachers worked with students on coming up with outcomes that they could show off. When we first started the process, we sat down as an administrative team to discuss where and when we wanted to complete the showcase night.

Ideally, we wanted to host the event in the downtown area of the community. I was able to work with our local government to acquire a permit to present the showcase. Teachers were given a timeline to submit progress of student work to make sure that their students were doing their part. A major piece of this plan was to have students look at their outcomes and link them to a standard, whether it was for that class or another. Students had to discuss outcomes with their teachers and administration, and how they would look at the showcase.

We were also able to get other stakeholders from the community to link up with these groups to help enrich the experience. For example, we had a dog grooming business created by one of our agriculture classes. They were able to partner with a local vet and the local humane society. They were given tools and resources by the vet, and they helped the local humane society with dog adoptions. Unfortunately, due to weather conditions, we had to move the event from the community venue to our school; nevertheless, the showcase took place and was a huge success. Students of diverse backgrounds were able to work together to produce successful outcomes.

The second plan focused on societal diversity and community involvement; how they impacted student engagement and outcomes involving our Career, Technical, and Agricultural Education Department (CTAE). Our school demographics are: approximately 55% identifying as White, 40% identifying as African American, and 5% indicating "other" on school documents. Fortunately, these demographics allow us to promote more cultural diversity in our school building than some other schools are able to.

At the beginning of the school year, I sat down with one of the other assistant principals and discussed the opportunity of exploring community within the CTAE department. The administrator had the idea that all students complete an employability unit at the beginning of their CTAE course. This would push students to create a resume, look at what kind of jobs they would like to have, and also work on interviewing skills. The timeline would be for CTAE teachers to go through the unit within the first three weeks of term. Since one of the objectives of the plan was to have students work with others on their interviewing skills, we asked members from community businesses to work on those skills with classes. Students at the end of the unit had an active resume that they could use, along with enhanced interviewing skills.

The idea of a diverse community working alongside teachers and students to promote student engagement and outcomes is extremely important to the overall success of a school impacting its community. Such partnerships are mutually beneficial. All educators should advocate for the implementation of programs like the ones described in this chapter because they enrich student lives in numerous ways. The current P-12 schooling process will greatly benefit from diversity education.

References

Drexel University. (2021, January 20). *The importance of diversity and multicultural awareness in education.* Drexel University School of Education. https://drexel.edu/soe/resources/student-teaching/advice/importance-of-cultural-diversity-in-classroom/

Wells, A. S., Fox, L., & Cordova-Cobo, D. (2016, February 9). *How racially diverse schools and classrooms can benefit all students.* The Century Foundation. https://tcf.org/content/report/how-racially-diverse-schools-and-classrooms-can-benefit-all-students/?session=1

Wood, L., & Bauman, E. (2017, June 23). *How family, school, and community engagement canimprove student achievement and influence school reform.* Nellie Mae Education Foundation. https://nmefoundation.org/how-family-school-and-community-engagement-can-improve-student-achievement-and-influence-school-reform/

CHAPTER 20

Pressing Issues and Contemporary Concerns

FRAN DUNDORE

>A jury of eleven white and
>one black citizen
>of the deep south
>found
>three white males
>Guilty
>of the Murder of
>Ahmaud Arbery
>A man
>A Black man
>A young Black man
>A Beautiful Young Black man
>who went for a jog
>and wandered through
>the new construction
>was caught on camera admiring the home,
>maybe dreaming about
>a home
>a plot where
>a man
>any man
>could claim the land
>and put down roots and be

permanent.
He left with nothing.
He walked away
empty handed
He fought
empty handed
He died empty handed.
He died empty handed.

The fact that a jury comprised of eleven white people and one Black person seated in a courtroom in the deep south convicted three white males (one with ties to law enforcement) is worthy of celebration and praise. It is a feat to see justice served in a courtroom in Southern Georgia, in a country where the things that divide us seem to cast a shadow on the things that unite us. We are bearing witness to a time where the breakdown in communication, on a local and a global level, is stark and terrifying–where we are quick to fire off words and weapons triggered by pundits, propaganda, and pure hate.

Coming off the heels of the election of a divisive president, oppressors in all forms have come out of their thinly veiled hiding places to bask in the shadows they have cast across human decency. We have a lot to talk about as a nation and as a people who share the same resources on this planet, and we have to find a common language that will allow us to engage in divergent thinking without permanently silencing the thinker. Jay Parini (2008) offers that we are living in an "age of identity politics, in which marginalized groups–women, gays, immigrant communities, or racial minorities of one kind or another–struggle to 'find a voice'" (p. 47). The issues we are facing are not just pressing, they are persistent, and they are pervasive. The voices of the *other* continue to be pulled under, like a landmass drawn deep beneath the surface of the Earth.

Their voices
    submerged,
   subjugated
      substandard,
     sinking,

> silent,
>
> > subsumed when they collide with power.

We need to hear the voices of the poets. Eliot (1943) writes that the poet has a duty to language because poetry is local. It belongs to the people, and it lives inside a language unique to a culture. Poetry thereby plays a social function in a culture by curating the language of experience and emotion, and crafting it together in such a way that it represents the shared experiences of the collective group.

On January 20th, 2021, only 14 days after an assault on our nation's Capital by a mob of American citizens, a poet offered her voice to heal our nation. Amanda Gorman (2021) challenged us to "find light in this never-ending shade." Through a poem, she used her voice to make sense of the madness we had witnessed, and she offered her words as social commentary on our shared human experience and the state of our nation. The poet gives us language to express something we have experienced, but for which we have no words. They enlarge our consciousness and refine our sensibility (Eliot, 1943). We are educating the citizenry to maintain our democratic ideals as well as to develop social relationships that promote human dignity. We are responsible for providing experiences in the classroom that allow students a safe space to explore–and to question–the values of our society. We have chosen a vocation that affords us the opportunity to use our voices to empower our students as thinkers who are ready to engage in dialogue about content that matters: freedom, equity, opportunity, justice. We certainly won't prepare them for this task by continuing to perpetuate a pedagogy that is packaged and programmatic–one which avoids the difficult conversations that students deserve the opportunity to take part in– one that asks very little of the student as an intellectual, and even less of the teacher.

A Pedagogy of Poetry–An Overview of Poetic Inquiry

> I was a poem before I was anything else
> My first division–
> syllables into cells into sound
> the poem
> and me.

And you were my first verse.
Your metered feet traipsing out and away from me in a rhythm
only you could hear, but one I tried with desperation to follow.
Another divide–
> making your pattern and path in this world with that free, un-
> hindered music you work so hard to keep in line.

Chasing your dreams down slanted streets and atop buildings 45
stanzas high–each one a story.
And I, who have been working to make sound into sense,
am silenced by the thought that we who are so different
are made of the same stuff–I am particle,
You are light.
I am your story and you are mine.
We are tangled up in verse
Iambic feet that sound like beating hearts.

I wrote these words without having any idea how I might explain them if someone ever asked about them, but knowing fully the weight of the truth they held for me. I was a poem before I was anything else. About this, I am certain. I did not choose to be a poet; the muse was born in me. There are no degrees to which I am a poet—a good one, a bad one. A poem can launch an entire metacognitive state for me. I want to hold it out in front of me, examine every word, ask how it could possibly know exactly the right thing to say. T.S. Eliot (1943) describes the poet as one who is able to "[make] people more aware of what they feel, and therefore [teach] them something about themselves" (p. 9). Poetry is the lens through which I have come to know this world and know my place in it. It is the way I best communicate who I am. It is as much an instinct for me to write as it is to hold my breath under water. I have lived an entire lifetime hearing words strung together in my head voice—my muse catching me off guard, startling me, waking me up to find myself on the edge of awareness, or to see myself in the words of someone else–their truths laid bare so that I may get a glimpse of my own humanity. The urgings are sometimes subtle, a word or phrase I can't let go of, a line from a poem I read yesterday or thirty years ago. I can be digging in the garden or driving to work and I *hear* the lines.

Mary Oliver (2017) delivers my mantra:

you do not have to be good; you do not have to crawl on your knees for a hundred miles repenting.

And Wordsworth (2007/1807) is there, as I am ringing up my purchases at the TJ Maxx with his reproving commentary on the dangers of capitalism...
The world is too much with us late or soon
getting and spending we lay waste our powers

And Berry (1999/1973) helps keep me in check so as not to let the politicos get into my head.
Every day do something that won't compute
　Love the lord, Love the world,
　Take all that you have and be poor.

Poems come as reminders,
as warnings,
as harbingers of peace.
They are faithful, steadfast,
persistent.

Playing with words in this way–stringing them into verse and then untangling them again—it is that series of breaking and mending that is also how I learned to speak for myself about topics I hadn't otherwise been able to share, and it is also how I connected with my students. What I didn't know as a young writer and teacher is that what I was doing–using a poem as a lens for viewing the world and my place in it—had a name.

Galvin and Prendergast (2016) describe this form of inquiry—*poetic inquiry*–and the expression that results as a "young branch on the older tree of qualitative research" (p. xi). Poems allow for a unique way to use language that predates codification. It is distilled; it is precise, and is the language of feeling and emotion. Reading and writing poetry enable us to edge closer and closer to knowing ourselves and knowing others. This method of both utilizing poetry as a means of understanding a research topic, as well as generating poetry from the research, opens the researcher up for a more nuanced understanding.

Poetic inquiry can be expressed as found or generated poems from field notes or other research material. Poems can be embedded to provide a depth of understanding various phenomenon and expressed in memoirs, autobiography, or fiction. For my research and dissertation, I plan to use poetic inquiry to explore the teachers' lived experiences with poetry. I want to use poetic inquiry to study and analyze secondary teachers' lived experiences with poetry and how those experiences influence their use of poetry in instruction, as well as studying the extent that secondary teachers use poetry as a means of giving students access to language and the power it conveys.

To what extent do teachers utilize poetry as a method for students to recognize and exercise their own identity and power? Using critical pedagogy as a theoretical framework, and engaging hermeneutic inquiry on some level (although I am still processing how that will look) I want to reflect on my own experiences as a public school student, a teacher, and an administrator and the ways in which the poem has continued to provide a means to claiming voice and power. I share Freire's (1997/1970) call to action that teachers must use their voices to give students the opportunity to grapple with the fact that poverty, prejudice, and injustice have become normalized in the wealthiest countries on earth. They must be revolutionaries who are willing to help to pull others out from under the weight of oppression, and who help their students become critically aware of their social situations and empower them to take action. Educators are intellectuals who must dare to fight to circulate their power–channel it into their students–to free their body, mind, and soul. If the teacher is to be the revolutionary, I add to that premise that the poem is a beacon for social justice.

Exploring Theoretical Traditions

In the decades between the 1960s and 1980, educational researchers such as John Mann, Dwayne Heubner, Eliot Eisner, and Maxine Greene sought to include the aspects of an educational setting that could not be quantified and reproduced in the ways that prevailing educational researchers were attempting (Vallance, 1991). These theorists argued that the happenings in any classroom—the decisions that we make, the texts that we choose, the ways in which we direct a discussion—are influenced by the experiences that have shaped the individuals, both teacher and student. Putting all of our human experiences into the mix, the variables become too great for the learning environment to be predictable or reproducible.

Schwab's (1973) Curriculum Commonplaces comes to mind in thinking about all that intersects when we make curriculum: the learner, the teacher, the subject matter, and the milieu. Vallance (1991) describes how as early as the 1920s, Dewey was grappling with how to lay scientific boundaries around the process of making meaning, a struggle which eventually yielded to the birth of education as a *social science* that embodied the learner's individual experiences and value judgments. Ultimately, there were experiences of great value to an individual's education that could not be quantified, but that undoubtedly contributed to the process of teaching and learning, and an aesthetic approach to exploring and describing the classroom experience bridged some gaps in understanding the phenomenon.

The use of arts-based research in general, and *poetic inquiry* specifically, only began to garner widespread acceptance in the late 1980s and early 1990s with the use of poetry in the fields of nursing and science (Prendergast et al., 2009) as a means to get closer to the human experience. More than just producing poetry as a byproduct of the inquiry, Butler-Kisber (2010) contends that poetic inquiry is an artful way of being a researcher that provides a more complete picture of the subject and situation.

Poetry uncovers what our biases assume cannot exist–it shows us that *other* is not something to be ostracized/cast out, but simply a part of the phenomenon of being. The phenomenon that is normalized (white, heterosexual, male,) exists in society in such a way that anything that exists outside of the norms they represent must exist in negative space–in a vacuum created by the construct of normal, but that notion is illusory. It is when we take responsibility for the other and enter into dialogue with them, that we address the limit situations that Freire (1997/1970) describes in order that we may recognize those limitations as the "frontier between being and being more human" (p. 102).

Epistemological Compatibilities and Challenges

Maxine Greene (2001) describes taking "imaginative adventures into meaning" (p. 67), where meaning encompasses the connections we make in our lived experiences. My first awakening to this kind of meaning came from a teacher who introduced me to metaphor. It was not my first encounter with the poetic device, but it was certainly my first experience. This experience showed me the give and take of loving the poetic: the gift of words that ring of a truth so clear I could feel them, believe them, and the rush of reading my own writing aloud, of being called an author, of having the power to share my voice. Her assignment was that we write a poem without naming our subject—one that was a metaphor in its entirety, and I wrote this:

> Mysterious I know I seem, complex and unexplained,
> But I am just the shell of life, and this I will remain.
>
> I hold beneath my roaring waves a strength you cannot see:
> The rivers and the flowing streams bow down to worship me.
>
> The ships–triumphant as they sailed with passengers on deck–
> I now hold here upon my floor disfigured, broken, wrecked.
>
> The traces of a time before are present here in me.
> I am the story of the past; I tell it brilliantly.
>
> Now listen to my laughter as I crash upon the shore,
> And you will know all that I am, and you will love me more.

Ms. Hallford asked if I would share my work with the class, and she introduced me by saying, *Students, we are so fortunate to have the author with us today to read and discuss her words.* And their response was not the stereotypical shame-filled scenes you see in films that so often miss the mark in the ways in which they represent teenagers and underestimate the compassion they are capable of. They were supportive; they asked me questions; they asked me to read it again. This experience was transformative for me both as a learner and as the teacher I was becoming. I particularly appreciate Frost's (1931) representation of the sensations I felt:

> Enthusiasm…is taken through the prism of the intellect and spread

on the screen in a color, all the way from hyperbole at one end–or overstatement, at one end–to understatement at the other end. It is a long strip of dark lines and many colors. Such enthusiasm is one object of all teaching in poetry. (p. 37)

The dialogue between my teacher and my classmates about my own writing etched a new trajectory for me. It awakened in me a feeling I had never had—an awareness to what it could feel like to be a participant in the thinking and discussion in the classroom. My classmates and I created an understanding of metaphor through reading and discussing each other's poetry. On some level, we defined the parameters as the ways in which metaphor works in constructing meaning. Ms. Hallford brought into being what Frost (1931) describes as education by poetry or an education through metaphor. As she must have known, and Frost (1931) argues, poetry begins in trivial metaphors, pretty metaphors, "grace" metaphors, and goes on to become the profoundest thinking that we have.

My classmates responded the way they did because Mrs. Hallford had created an environment where we trusted each other, and where we shared our voices openly. In this instance, poetry was the vessel my teacher used to give us a voice, and my experiences in her classroom as a reader and a writer would form an outline for my identity and divide school for me into before and after. Eliot (1943) argues that poetry allows us to share the phenomenon of the human condition–the experiences unique to each of us–across time and space. It is the poem, and the criticism that comes from inquiring through or into the poem, that sets us face to face with a thing, a situation, or a person we have never seen before, free from eyes clouded by prejudice– and leaves us alone with it.

While poetry can bridge gaps in communication and offer existential insight, there are epistemological challenges inherent within this mode of inquiry. Among those challenges is addressing the ambiguity often inherent in poetry, and in defining all that poetic inquiry encompasses. Still, poetic inquiry also offers insight into our shared experiences and the emotions they produce in ways that cannot be managed with prose. That very ambiguity, the natural ability for a poem to live in the gray–in a space outside of either-or-is what makes poetry such a haven for divergent thoughts. It is a place where we can project our imaginations in such a way that we edge closer to empathy. We move towards understanding the lived experience of something or someone other than ourselves.

> We exit egocentricism
> to experience
> to empathize –
> explain
> engage
> (co) exist.

It seems appropriate here to reiterate Eliot's point:

Poetry
brings us
face to face
with
other –
and
leaves us
alone
to figure it out.

Poetic Inquiry Continues to Challenge, Advance, and Contradict Traditional Forms of Inquiry

Prendergast (2009) argues that an aesthetic approach to research does not have to stand in opposition to more traditional forms of analysis. The work of the poet is to reflect back a clearer image of who we are. It clarifies and magnifies being (Butler-Kisber, 2010). So, using poetry to explore lived experiences of ourselves and others is not a replacement for more traditional forms of curriculum inquiry. It is an extension, allowing us to push deeper into parts of a subject or phenomenon and to understand more about ourselves through that study. As educators, our first priority must be bringing the student into the learning space and honoring them with the ability to recognize their unique voices and the power structures that exist around them. We must take heed of the questions Kincheloe (2012) proposed as essential to Curriculum Studies: "What is the relationship between classroom practice and issues of justice? How do schools reflect or subvert democratic practices and the larger culture of democracy? How do schools operate to validate or challenge the power dynamics of race, class, gender, sexuality, religion, indigenous/aboriginal issues, physical ability-related concerns, etc.?" (p. 151).

I posit that we add to those essential questions other questions such as, *how can art in general–and poetry in particular–help students embrace the democratic ideals for which we stand, while recognizing the places where those ideals fall short and where liberty and justice are not afforded to all Americans?* A pedagogy that not only included poetry, but demanded that students have the freedom to explore the lived experiences of others through the poem and express their awareness of self through the poem is essential to actualizing fundamental values of democracy, the criteria of dignity, and the worth of the human being (Rosenblatt, 1995).

References

Berry, W. (1999). *The country of marriage.* Counterpoint. (Original work published in 1973).

Butler-Kisber, L. (2010). *Qualitative inquiry: Thematic, narrative, and arts-based perspectives.* SAGE.

Eliot, T.S. (1943). *On poetry and poets.* Farrar, Straus, and Giroux.

Freire, P. (1997). *Pedagogy of hope: Reliving pedagogy of the oppressed.* (R. Barr, Trans.). Bloomsbury. (Original work published 1970).

Frost, R. (1931). Education by poetry. In H. Cox & E.C. Lathem (Eds.), *Selected prose of Robert Frost* (pp. 33-46). Holt, Rinehart, and Winston.

Galvin, K., & Prendergast, M. (2016). *Poetic inquiry II–seeing, caring, and understanding: Using poetry as and for inquiry.* Sense.

Gorman, A. (2021). *The Hill We Climb.* Viking.

Greene, M. (2001). *Variations on a blue guitar: The Lincoln Center Institute lecture on aesthetic education.* Teachers College Press. https://archive.org/details/variationsonblue0000gree

Kincheloe, J. (2012). Critical pedagogy in the new dark ages: Challenges and possibilities. *Counterpoints, 422,* 147-183.

Oliver, M. (2017). *Devotions: The selected poems of Mary Oliver.* Penguin.
Parini, J. (2008). *Why poetry matters.* Yale University Press.
Prendergast, M. (2009). Poem is what? Poetic inquiry in qualitative social science research. *International Review of Qualitative Research, 1*(4), 541-568. https://journals.sagepub.com/doi/10.1525/irqr.2009.1.4.541
Prendergast, M., Leggo, C., & Sameshima, P. (Eds.). (2009). *Poetic inquiry: Vibrant voices in the social sciences.* Sense.
Rosenblatt, L. M. (1995). *Literature as exploration.* Modern Language Association of America. https://archive.org/details/literatureasexpl00rose
Schwab, J. J. (1973). The practical 3: Translation into curriculum. *The School Review, 81*(4), 501-522.
Vallance, E. (1991). Aesthetic inquiry. In E. C. Short (Ed.), *Forms of curriculum inquiry* (pp. 155-186). SUNY.
Wordsworth, W. (2007). The world is too much with us. (Antonia Till, Ed.) *The collected poems of William Wordsworth.* Wordsworth Editions. (Original work published in 1807).

CHAPTER 21

Violence In Schools

FORREST R. PARKER III

IN RECENT YEARS, THE United States has faced a growing concern over the perceived escalation of violence within its educational institutions. Acts of aggression, ranging from physical assaults to bullying and even shootings have had devastating consequences on students, families, and communities. However, there has been a steady decline in school violence within our schools in nearly all areas over the past two decades. This is not to say that school violence is no longer a major issue; however, the type of school violence that is increasing has changed. Also, with the advent of smartphones, viral videos have played a large part in the perception of a larger problem than the current data demonstrates. Violence in schools still calls for a deeper understanding of its root causes, examination of its consequences, and exploration of potential solutions.

One significant factor contributing to violence in schools is rooted in socioeconomic issues (Brown et al., 2009; Turanovic & Siennick, 2022; Warner et al., 1999). Poverty, inequality, and the lack of resources in certain communities create an environment where students may feel marginalized, frustrated, and hopeless. This vulnerability can lead to aggressive behavior and a cycle of violence within schools. Additionally, psychological factors such as untreated mental health issues and emotional distress can significantly impact a student's behavior, making them more susceptible to violent acts or becoming victims themselves (Brown et al., 2009; Turanovic & Siennick, 2022; Warner et al., 1999).

Social dynamics also play a crucial role in school violence (Brown et al., 2009; Turanovic & Siennick, 2022; Warner et al., 1999), with bullying, peer pressure, and social exclusion leading to resentment and anger among students. The rise of technology and social media has further compounded these issues; cyberbullying has become prevalent, causing emotional harm to victims (Giumetti & Kowalski, 2022). Moreover, the influence of violent media content can desensitize students to aggression and normalize violent behavior as a means of problem-solving (Giumetti & Kowalski, 2022; Kowalski et al., 2019).

The consequences of school violence are far-reaching and multifaceted. Not only do victims suffer physical and psychological harm, but the overall educational environment is disrupted. Students who experience violence often struggle academically, leading to decreased educational outcomes (Irwin et al., 2022; Steffgen et al., 2013). Witnesses and bystanders also bear emotional scars, affecting their mental well-being and ability to focus on their studies. Furthermore, the long-term effects of school violence can extend beyond the immediate school years with studies indicating an increased likelihood of involvement in criminal behavior and the imposition of significant societal costs (Irwin et al., 2022; Klomek et al., 2011; Steffgen et al., 2013).

Understanding current trends and patterns of violence in schools is crucial for effective intervention and prevention strategies. Analyzing statistical data allows us to identify high-risk groups and tailor interventions accordingly. By studying the various types of violence prevalent in schools, such as threats to harm, physical assault, bullying, and weapons possession, we can develop targeted approaches to address these specific issues.

Addressing the problem of violence in schools requires a collaborative effort involving schools, educators, government agencies, law enforcement, families, and communities. Schools must strive to create safe and inclusive environments that prioritize the well-being of students. Implementing comprehensive anti-bullying programs, conflict resolution initiatives, and mental health support services can foster positive relationships and equip students with the necessary skills to navigate conflicts peacefully.

Government initiatives and policy interventions also play a critical role in curbing school violence. This includes enacting laws and regulations related to gun control, adopting zero-tolerance policies for violent behavior, and reforming disciplinary practices to emphasize rehabilitation and restorative justice. Additionally, community involvement and grassroots movements can generate awareness, promote dialogue, and create a culture that rejects violence in schools.

While the problem of increased violence in U.S. schools is a pressing concern, there is hope for a safer future. Promising practices and innovative approaches, such as restorative justice models, social-emotional learning, early intervention programs, and involving students in creating safer school environments, have shown positive results in preventing and reducing violence (Cornell, 2020; Steffgen et al., 2013). The issue of school violence in the United States carries significant importance, as its impact extends beyond the walls of educational institutions. The prevalence of violence in schools deeply affects the well-being and safety of students, including the emotional toll on families and the overall health of communities. Addressing this issue becomes essential to ensure the healthy development and the academic success of students, as well as the overall social fabric of society.

The purpose of this chapter is to explore the root causes of violence in U.S. public schools, examine the consequences this violence has on stakeholders, and discuss potential solutions to this problem.

Definition of Terms

School Violence. The multifaceted construct of "school violence" includes a wide variety of acts, such as physical assault and battery, physical aggression, noncontact aggression (e.g., throwing things), broadly defined externalizing behavior, bullying, fighting, robbery, unwanted sexual contact, weapon possession, and verbal threats.

Bullying. Unwanted, aggressive behavior among school-aged children that involves a real or perceived power imbalance.

Cyberbullying. The act of using digital technologies, such as the internet, social media platforms, or mobile devices to harass, intimidate, or harm individuals or groups. It involves repeated and deliberate aggressive behavior intended to cause emotional distress, humiliation, or fear in the targeted person. Cyberbullying can take various forms, including sending threatening or derogatory messages, spreading rumors, sharing private or embarrassing information, creating fake profiles or accounts to impersonate or humiliate someone, or sharing manipulated or explicit content without consent.

Understanding Root Causes of School Violence

The literature on school violence generally groups causes of school violence into the following categories: socioeconomic factors, psychological factors, social factors, and the influence of media and technology. The following vignettes attempt to demonstrate how these factors are relevant in a typical U.S. school setting.

Socioeconomic Factors

The issue of violence in U.S. schools cannot be dissociated from the socioeconomic factors that shape the lives of students. Poverty, inequality, and the lack of resources in certain communities contribute to an environment where violence can thrive. Understanding these socioeconomic factors is crucial for developing effective strategies to address and prevent school violence.

Vignette One

The school bell rang, signaling the end of another grueling day. Joss, a 16-year-old student, gathered her belongings and headed out of the classroom. Her footsteps echoed through the hallways as she made her way toward the exit. She couldn't help but notice the stark contrast between her school and the well-to-do schools she had seen in movies. The walls were faded, lockers were dented, and the ceilings leaked when it rained. This environment, along with a myriad of other socioeconomic factors, had silently contributed to a growing undercurrent of violence within the school.

Joss hailed from a low-income neighborhood plagued by poverty and crime. The school she attended reflected the community it served where many students faced daily struggles just to meet their basic needs. As she stepped outside, she was met with a crumbling infrastructure surrounded by dilapidated buildings and vacant lots. The lack of investment in the area was a constant reminder of the systemic neglect that had taken hold in her community.

Inside the classroom, the weight of these socioeconomic burdens marred Joss's day. Overcrowded classrooms made it difficult for teachers to provide individual attention, leaving many students feeling marginalized and overlooked. Limited resources meant outdated textbooks, inadequate technology, and a shortage of extracurricular activities that could have provided a healthy outlet for the students' energy and creativity.

As Joss walked home, she navigated through a neighborhood rife with gang activity. Violence was an everyday occurrence, leaving both physical and emotional scars on the community. She had seen friends succumb to the allure of joining a gang, seeking protection and a sense of belonging that they couldn't find elsewhere.

Feeling isolated and trapped, Joss yearned for an escape. But without access to quality education and limited job prospects, the cycle of poverty seemed inescapable. Her dreams of a better future dwindled with each passing day; in its place was a simmering frustration that threatened to boil over.

The next morning, tension hung heavy in the air as Joss returned to school. It was just another day in the struggle to survive where trivial disputes could quickly escalate into something much more sinister. Shared experiences of poverty, violence, and hopelessness fueled the students' emotions, and they responded like tinder waiting for a spark.

Amid this volatile mix, a minor altercation erupted between two students. The insults and threats escalated, and their pent-up frustrations poured out in a frenzy of rage. The neglected school environment, lack of resources, and constant exposure to violence created a pressure cooker, pushing some students to their breaking point.

As Joss watched the situation unfold, she couldn't help but feel a mixture of anger, frustration, and sadness. She realized that addressing school violence required more than disciplinary measures or reactive responses. It demanded a comprehensive approach that addressed the underlying socioeconomic factors, invested in education, and provided support systems to break the cycle of violence.

But for now, Joss and her fellow classmates were left to navigate the treacherous waters of their troubled school and were caught in a storm of violence that had its roots in a society that had failed them.

As described in Vignette One, students who live and attend school in an impoverished area can be more susceptible to violence in schools. The consequences of socioeconomic factors are unmistakable in this vignette. The absence of a nurturing environment, limited access to opportunities, and the omnipresence of violence created an atmosphere where school violence became a grim reality. In the absence of meaningful interventions addressing the root causes of these issues, the cycle threatened to perpetuate itself, trapping future generations in the same web of violence and despair.

Psychological Factors

In understanding the complex issue of school violence, it is essential to consider the psychological factors that contribute to aggressive behavior and victimization among students. Mental health issues and emotional distress play a significant role in shaping individual responses to conflicts, interactions, and stressors within the school environment. Exploring these psychological factors is crucial for implementing effective prevention and intervention strategies.

Vignette Two

Sitting alone in the school cafeteria, Kweisi stared at his lunch tray as his mind was lost in a whirlwind of emotions. He felt isolated, rejected, and invisible. For weeks, he had been struggling with mounting pressure both academically and socially. The weight of it all seemed unbearable, and it was taking a toll on his mental well-being.

Kweisi's once bright and jovial demeanor had slowly faded away; it was replaced by a simmering anger and frustration. Each day, he found himself dwelling on the numerous incidents of bullying he had endured over the past year. Taunts, insults, and even physical assaults had become a routine part of his daily life. He had tried seeking help from teachers and counselors, but it seemed like nobody truly understood the depths of his pain.

As the lunch period progressed, Kweisi watched his classmates from a distance. They laughed, chatted, and formed tight-knit groups. Their joyful interactions only served to further amplify his feelings of alienation. He wondered why he couldn't fit in, why he couldn't be accepted for who he was. These thoughts gnawed at his mind, fueling an inner turmoil that he struggled to contain.

The bell rang, signaling the end of lunchtime. As Kweisi walked through the crowded hallways, he couldn't help but notice the glaring disparities between his reality and that of his peers. Some students received accolades for their achievements, while others basked in the glory of popularity. Meanwhile, he felt invisible, unnoticed, and overshadowed by his own insecurities.

Over time, these psychological factors began to shape Kweisi's perception of the world. He started feeling resentment toward his classmates, the school, and even himself. The weight of his emotions became unbearable, and a dark, sinister idea began to take root in his mind—a desperate attempt to regain control and to make others notice the pain he had been silently enduring.

One fateful day, Kweisi's anger reached its boiling point. The culmination of social isolation, academic pressure, and untreated psychological distress led him to bring a weapon to school. In his mind, it was the only way to express his anguish and force the world to acknowledge his existence.

This harrowing vignette serves as a somber reminder of the profound impact that psychological factors can have on individuals and the potential consequences when they are left unattended. It underscores the importance of fostering inclusive environments, promoting mental health awareness, and providing appropriate support systems for students facing psychological distress. Only through such proactive measures can we hope to prevent the tragedy of school violence and create safer, more nurturing educational spaces for all.

Social Factors

Social factors within the school environment play a significant role in the occurrence of violence among students. Bullying, peer pressure, and social exclusion are social dynamics that contribute to a hostile and unsafe atmosphere, leading to increased risks of violence. Understanding these social factors is crucial for implementing effective prevention and intervention strategies.

Vignette Three

The bell rang, signaling the end of another long and tiresome school day. Students poured out of the classrooms while their laughter and chatter filled the air. Among them was Drew, a quiet and introverted teenager who often walked the halls unnoticed. Today, however, something was different. A veil of anger seemed to shroud him, and a simmering rage replaced his usually calm demeanor.

Drew had always been an outcast, a misfit in the intricate social web of high school. Bullied for his nerdy interests and awkward appearance, he had endured years of relentless taunts and isolation. The daily onslaught of ridicule and humiliation had taken its toll on his fragile psyche, nurturing a seed of bitterness deep within him.

As Drew made his way through the crowded hallway, he couldn't help but notice the obliviousness of his peers. They laughed and joked, oblivious to the silent battles being fought within their midst. Each laugh and each snicker served as a reminder of his own torment. Anguish and resentment intertwined within him, fueling a dangerous fire that threatened to consume everything in its path.

A group of popular kids passed by and their laughter pierced through Drew's ears like shards of glass. In their midst was Zach, the unofficial king of the school. With his athletic build and confident demeanor, he effortlessly commanded the attention and admiration of his peers. Zach's charisma and status made him untouchable, a shield against the harsh realities that others faced.

Drew's eyes narrowed as he watched Zach, his fists clenching involuntarily. The sight of the very person who symbolized the unattainable acceptance and happiness he yearned for ignited a storm of emotions within him. Jealousy, anger, and a profound sense of injustice swirled together, obscuring his vision of reason.

As the students dispersed, Drew found himself alone in the empty hallway, consumed by a dangerous concoction of emotions. The world seemed to shrink, leaving only him and the torment that had plagued him for years. In that moment, he reached a tipping point—a thin line between surrendering to the darkness within or lashing out to regain control.

The following days passed in a haze of turmoil and contemplation. Drew's mind oscillated between the allure of vengeance and the weight of consequence. Years of neglect, humiliation, and a society that seemed to turn a blind eye to the struggles of its youth nurtured the seed of violence.

The school violence that would unfold was not a sudden explosion, but rather the culmination of a toxic mix of pain, isolation, and a deep-seated desire for retribution.

In the end, it was the silent cries for help that went unheard, and the lack of empathy and understanding that allowed this dangerous seed to flourish. As society grapples with the aftermath, it is essential to recognize that school violence is not born out of a single moment of madness, but rather the culmination of a myriad of underlying issues left unaddressed and festering in the shadows.

As demonstrated by Vignette Three, school violence is not necessarily caused by a single event that can be clearly traced such as in a cause-and-effect exercise. School violence is far more nuanced, making it a difficult topic to study quantitatively. Social factors play a key role in school violence.

Influence of Media and Technology

The rapid advancement of media and technology has had a profound impact on the lives of young people, including their experiences within the school environment. The influence of media, particularly exposure to violence and the prevalence of cyberbullying, contribute to the occurrence and perpetuation of school violence. Understanding these influences is crucial for addressing and mitigating the impact of media and technology on student well-being.

Vignette Four

As the sun set behind the school building, casting long shadows across the empty playground, Emma sat alone in her room staring at her laptop screen. She had just finished another exhausting day at school filled with whispers, stares, and unkind remarks. The once bubbly and confident teenager had become a victim of cyberbullying, a dark cloud that had slowly consumed her life.

Emma's torment began innocently enough with a few hurtful comments posted on a social media platform. At first, she brushed them off thinking they were just the cruel words of a few misguided individuals seeking attention. But soon, the comments multiplied, spreading like wildfire through the digital realm. Friends turned into foes, and even strangers joined in, hiding behind the anonymity of their screens.

Each day, Emma logged into her social media accounts with a sense of dread, knowing that she would be bombarded with a barrage of hurtful messages and derogatory memes. The power of technology had turned her schoolyard into a 24/7 battlefield where the torment never ceased. The once vibrant hallways had become dark, twisted versions of themselves, infested with virtual monsters eager to tear her apart.

As the cyberbullying intensified, so did Emma's isolation. The world outside her bedroom window felt like an alien place, a distant reality with which she could no longer connect. The constant bombardment of negativity eroded her self-esteem, replacing her joyful spirit with a nagging voice of self-doubt. She wondered why she had become a target, and what she had done to deserve such hatred.

Unable to find solace in the digital realm, Emma retreated into the silence of her thoughts. She wore a mask of strength during the day, concealing her pain from her parents and teachers. But behind closed doors, tears stained her pillow, and the weight of the world pressed down upon her fragile shoulders.

One gloomy evening, Emma's parents sat her down with deep concern etched on their faces. They had noticed the change in their daughter in the way her laughter had grown scarce and her once gleaming eyes had dimmed. Their hearts ached as they watched their child crumble under the weight of virtual cruelty.

This vignette has become all too common in U.S. schools. This type of cyber bullying is in and of itself violent. Furthermore, it can lead to acts of physical violence that include self-harm.

Consequences of School Violence

The consequences of students being exposed to school violence cannot be overstated. One obvious consequence of school violence are the physical injuries that may occur as a direct result of school violence. There may also be psychological harm to the victims of school violence. Besides the offending students, the victims of violence have an increased likelihood of offending themselves. Even witnessing violence has been shown to have a lasting and traumatic effect on students (CDC, 2016). According to the Centers for Disease Control and Prevention (2016), students who have experienced violence may be at a higher risk of drug and alcohol abuse. The American Psychological Association (APA) also reported that students who experience school violence may have lower self-esteem, higher levels of anxiety, and are at greater risk for suffering from depression and loneliness (Hawker & Boulton, 2000; Rigby, 2003). These same students are also at a higher risk for attempting suicide throughout their lives (Dempsey et al., 2011; Klomek et al., 2011; Meltzer et al., 2011).

Another consequence can be felt in the academic performance of entire groups of students who experience school violence. Victims of school violence may have lower academic performance over time due to witnessing and experiencing violence in their schools (Glew et al., 2005). When students experience forms of school violence, they may avoid school and are more likely to drop out of school (Fried & Fried, 1996). When the school environment is chaotic, it makes learning difficult for students.

Exploring Current Trends and Patterns

Unfortunately, the most current data on school performance and school violence since 2021 have not been released as I write this in 2023. It is a severe limitation because schools were shut down in 2020 because of the pandemic; some limited survey data suggested a surge in school violence since schools reopened in 2021. One interesting indication of the perceived higher levels of violence can be found in the number of school shootings that have taken place since schools reopened in 2021.

According to the most recent NCES report, there were 93 fatal school shootings in the 2020-2021 school year. This is the highest number of fatal school shootings since data collection on this topic began. According to an article from the *Washington Post*, over 357,000 students have experienced gun violence at school since 1999's Columbine High School shooting through to school year 2023 (Cox et al., 2023).

A national survey from the Centers for Disease Control and Prevention (2016) found 6.6% of students reported being threatened or injured with a weapon within a year of taking the survey. That same survey reported 8.7% of students skipped school due to feeling unsafe during the month prior to taking the survey. Although it is still too early to predict a trend, percentages increased from prior years. According to this CDC survey (2016), reasons included high school students carrying a weapon on school property, cyberbullying, high school students who felt sad or hopeless, and all suicide-related questions. The NCES 2021 report (2022) also documented a two-fold increase in cyberbullying and widespread disorder in the classroom from 10 years ago. There was also an increase in disrespect for teachers as well as increases in verbal abuse toward teachers in 2019-2020, up from 10 years prior.

Recent studies reported 16% of all threats made by students were directed at teachers (Curran et al., 2019; Maeng et al., 2020; Moon & McCluskey, 2020). Of these threats toward teachers, 6% were carried out by the student making the threat. Most of these teachers being threatened and assaulted were newer teachers and teachers of students with special needs. These same studies predicted that 4%-8% of teachers will be assaulted each year. Violence against teachers is an under investigated issue that may have profound effects on schools, teacher retention, and student performance (Espelage et al., 2013). This is an interesting development as trends shift from overt physical fights between students in school to more covert and misplaced methods of violence to teachers appearing to be on the rise.

Public Perceptions

It is important to note public opinion regarding school violence shows a growing concern. A Gallup poll found 44% of adults nationwide were fearful for their child's physical safety at school. This alarming number seems to be largely influenced by media coverage of mass shootings in schools. National perceptions could also be influenced by cell phone footage of violent incidents in schools. With the advent of cell phone cameras and videos, the public has access to many horrifying and consistently occurring events that had lacked widespread awareness in earlier decades. Currently, many cell phone videos showing police mistreatment of people of color are common. The American public has also been exposed to video footage of school violence on TV news and online. The rapid dissemination of these videos has certainly had an impact on public perceptions, but the level of this impact remains unclear. These videos have the added effect of amplifying isolated incidents and making them seem more widespread than they really are.

School Violence Predictors

The U.S. Department of Justice (DOJ) defines school violence as: "the multifaceted construct of 'school violence' includes a wide variety of acts, such as physical assault and battery, physical aggression, noncontact aggression (e.g., throwing things), broadly defined externalizing behavior, bullying, fighting, robbery, unwanted sexual contact, weapon possession, and verbal threats" (Turanovic & Siennick, 2022, p. i). This meta-analysis also outlined the leading predictors of students who engaged in school violence.

The strongest predictor of a student committing a defined act of violence at school was "delinquent/antisocial behavior" (Turanovic & Siennick, 2022, p. ii). Other strong predictors of violent perpetration were if a student had attention deficit hyperactivity disorder (ADHD), if they had experienced maltreatment while growing up, if they had been rejected by peers, and if the students were morally disengaged.

Turanovic and Siennick's (2022) meta-analysis for the DOJ showed a weak relationship between school attachment, immigrant status, race and ethnicity, school size, student socioeconomic status, involvement in extracurricular activities, presence of an officer or guard, and the use of visible school security devices. Some of these results may be surprising; however, these results do not suggest there are no overtly interdependent relationships, but rather, that there is only a weak relationship.

Turanovic and Siennick's (2022) meta-analysis reported the top predictor of a student being the victim of school violence was "peer acceptance/social preference" (p. ii). The more likable a student is to their peers, the less likely they were to be victimized. The data showed students who have been victimized outside of school are more likely to be victimized at school. Students who are being victimized are usually victimized in many ways. Once a student has been victimized, they are at a greater risk of being victimized again and again.

The Role of Schools and Educators in Preventing Violence

This section outlines what schools can do to help prevent school violence. Readers should take note of these ideas and determine the strategies their schools are already employing, plus other ideas that can be adopted to help prevent school violence.

- Schools should implement measures to ensure the physical safety of students, such as appropriate security protocols, monitoring systems, and safety drills. They should increase supervision in high-risk areas such as hallways, cafeterias, and playgrounds. Schools should implement security measures like surveillance cameras, controlled access points, and visitor management systems. Schools should continuously evaluate and update safety policies and procedures based on the evolving needs and emerging best practices in school safety. They should stay informed about relevant research, training, and resources.

- Schools should establish clear anti-bullying and anti-discrimination policies. These policies should explicitly address bullying, harassment, and discrimination based on set factors such as race, gender, sexual orientation, disability, and religion.

- Schools should educate students and staff about diversity, inclusivity, and respectful behavior. This can be done through workshops, assemblies, guest speakers, or integrating relevant topics into the curriculum.

- Schools can create opportunities to celebrate and showcase the diverse backgrounds and talents of students. Schools can organize cultural events, heritage months, or other activities that promote understanding and appreciation of different cultures.

- Schools can provide counseling and support services to address the diverse needs of students. This includes mental health support, therapy, interventions for students who exhibit concerning behaviors, access to special education resources, and resources for students from marginalized backgrounds.

- Schools can use conflict resolution strategies schoolwide. Schools could incorporate conflict resolution programs that seek to educate students, staff, and parents on methods and strategies for deescalating situations and finding solutions to problems between individuals. One example of this is the restorative justice practice that focuses on repairing harm and fostering empathy rather than punitive measures.

- School personnel can foster strong relationships with students. They should encourage meaningful connections between students and trusted adults, such as teachers, counselors, and administrators. Building positive relationships can help identify and address potential issues before they escalate.

- School leaders, teachers, and staff should model respectful behavior and create an environment where students feel valued and supported. Encourage empathy, kindness, and open dialogue among students.

- Schools should involve students in decision-making processes and provide platforms for them to voice their opinions and concerns. This can be done through student councils, clubs, an anonymous tip system to report threats or concerns, or other channels for student participation.

- Schools can train staff on inclusivity by providing professional development and training for teachers and staff on topics like cultural competency, LGBTQ+ inclusion, and understanding diverse learning needs. This equips them with the knowledge and skills to create an inclusive classroom environment.

- Schools can establish partnerships with the community by collaborating with community organizations, local leaders, and families to support and reinforce the values of inclusivity and safety. Schools can engage parents and guardians in discussions and workshops related to creating a safe and inclusive school environment. They can establish partnerships with local law enforcement agencies and mental health providers to enhance safety measures, share information, and coordinate emergency response plans.

- Schools should regularly evaluate and improve their systems to ensure school safety and inclusivity. Schools should regularly assess their policies, programs, and initiatives to identify areas for improvement. They should seek feedback from students, staff, and parents to ensure continuous growth and adaptation to changing needs.

By implementing these strategies, schools can foster a safe and inclusive environment that supports the well-being and success of all students. These strategies can help reduce school violence.

Collaborative Efforts and Policy Interventions

Government initiatives and policy interventions play a crucial role curbing school violence by providing a structured framework and resources to address this complex issue. These efforts aim to create safer learning environments for students and promote the well-being of entire school communities.

One key aspect of government initiatives is the establishment of interagency collaborations. By bringing together educational institutions, law enforcement agencies, mental health services, and community organizations, these collaborations facilitate information sharing, coordination, and joint efforts in preventing and responding to school violence. Through coordinated action, these stakeholders can pool their expertise, resources, and strategies to effectively address the various factors contributing to violence in schools.

Government initiatives also prioritize the implementation of evidence-based prevention programs and policies that foster positive school climates. This includes initiatives such as anti-bullying campaigns, character education, social-emotional learning programs, and conflict resolution training. By promoting respectful and inclusive environments, these efforts help reduce incidents of violence, promote empathy and understanding, and equip students with the skills to peacefully resolve conflicts.

Enhanced security measures are another important aspect of government interventions. These measures may include controlled access to school premises, surveillance systems, metal detectors, and trained security personnel. While physical security measures alone may not eliminate the risk of violence, they serve as deterrents and provide a sense of safety for students and staff. Effective security measures work hand in hand with prevention and intervention strategies to create a comprehensive approach to school safety.

Government initiatives also focus on mental health support within schools. By increasing access to counseling, therapy, and early intervention programs, students can receive the necessary support to address their emotional and mental well-being. By identifying and addressing mental health challenges early on, government interventions aim to prevent potential violent behavior by providing appropriate support and interventions.

Furthermore, legislative measures play a crucial role curbing school violence. Governments enact comprehensive legislation and policies that allocate funding for prevention efforts, staff training, emergency preparedness, and collaboration between educational and law enforcement agencies. These measures may also include gun control regulations, such as background checks and safe firearm storage practices, which can help prevent unauthorized access to firearms by individuals at risk of violence.

Overall, government initiatives and policy interventions provide the necessary structure, coordination, and resources to effectively address school violence. By prioritizing prevention, fostering positive school climates, enhancing security measures, promoting mental health support, and enacting legislation, governments play a vital role in curbing school violence and ensuring the safety and well-being of students and the entire school community.

Promising Practices and Innovative Approaches

Promising practices and innovative approaches are continually being developed to prevent and reduce violence in schools. These strategies often emphasize proactive measures, community engagement, and comprehensive support systems. Here are a few examples.

- **Restorative Justice Practices.** Restorative justice approaches focus on repairing harm and fostering accountability rather than punitive measures alone. These practices involve bringing together individuals involved in a conflict to discuss its impact, find solutions, and rebuild relationships. Restorative justice encourages empathy, understanding, and personal growth, ultimately reducing the likelihood of recurring violence.

- **Peer Mediation and Conflict Resolution.** Empowering students to take an active role in resolving conflicts can be effective. Programs that train students as peer mediators enable them to mediate conflicts between their peers, teaching valuable communication and problem-solving skills. By promoting dialogue and peaceful resolutions, peer mediation programs contribute to a positive and nonviolent school environment.

- **Threat Assessment and Early Intervention.** Implementing threat assessment protocols within schools help identify individuals who may pose risks of violence. These multidisciplinary teams assess threats, gather information, and intervene appropriately. Early intervention can involve counseling, support services, or referrals to mental health professionals, with the aim to address underlying issues and prevent potential violence.

- **Anonymous Reporting Systems and Tip Lines.** Creating avenues for students, staff, and parents to report concerns or suspicious activities anonymously is critical. Anonymous reporting systems and tip lines encourage individuals to come forward with information about potential threats or acts of violence. This facilitates early intervention and provides a mechanism for individuals to share their concerns without fear of retaliation.

- **Digital Citizenship and Online Safety Education.** With the rise of technology and social media, promoting digital citizenship and online safety is essential. Innovative approaches include educating students on responsible online behavior, cyberbullying prevention, and recognizing the consequences of sharing harmful content. By fostering a culture of respect and responsible digital engagement, schools can mitigate the risk of online violence and harassment.

- **Trauma-Informed Practices.** Recognizing the impact of trauma on student behavior and well-being is crucial. Trauma-informed approaches integrate trauma knowledge into school policies, practices, and staff training. By creating supportive and safe environments, schools can help students heal from traumatic experiences and reduce the likelihood of violence associated with unresolved trauma.

- **Positive Behavioral Interventions and Supports (PBIS).** PBIS is a proactive approach that promotes positive behavior by establishing clear expectations, providing incentives, and teaching social skills. It emphasizes prevention rather than solely focusing on disciplinary actions. PBIS frameworks create a positive school climate, fostering a sense of belonging and reducing instances of disruptive and aggressive behavior.

- **Community Partnerships and Wraparound Services.** Engaging community organizations, mental health agencies, and other service providers can enhance the support system for students. Collaborative efforts can offer comprehensive services such as mental health counseling, after-school programs, and mentorship opportunities. By addressing the various needs of students holistically, these partnerships contribute to healthier and safer school environments and their communities.

- **Social-Emotional Learning (SEL).** Social-emotional learning programs integrate the development of essential social and emotional skills into the school curriculum. These programs promote self-awareness, self-regulation, empathy, and positive relationship-building. By teaching students these skills, SEL programs foster a supportive and respectful school climate, reduce conflict, and enhance overall well-being.

In summary, promising practices and innovative approaches that help prevent and reduce violence in schools often prioritize proactive measures, restorative justice practices, early intervention, community involvement, and holistic support systems. By implementing these strategies, schools can create safer and more inclusive environments that support the well-being and success of all students.

Conclusion

School violence is a complex and multifaceted issue that requires a comprehensive approach to effectively address its causes and consequences. This chapter has explored various aspects of school violence, including its impact on students, families, and communities, as well as the socio-economic, psychological, and social-emotional factors that contribute to increasing violence occurring in schools.

It is evident that school violence has far-reaching consequences, negatively affecting the academic achievement, emotional well-being, and overall development of students. Families and communities also bear the burden of violence, experiencing heightened fear, stress, and the erosion of trust in educational institutions. The socio-economic factors of poverty, inequality, and limited resources exacerbate the risk of violence, creating environments where students face significant challenges.

Psychological factors, such as mental health issues and emotional distress, further contribute to the occurrence of violence within schools. Untreated mental health conditions, emotional dysregulation, and the experience of trauma can undermine student abilities to navigate conflicts and cope with stressors; these conditions can also increase their susceptibilities to engage in, or become victims of, violence. Additionally, social factors, including bullying, peer pressure, and social exclusion, play critical roles in shaping the dynamics of violence within the school environment. The normalization of violence in media and the prevalence of cyberbullying amplify these social factors, leading to increased aggression and victimization among students.

Addressing school violence requires a collective effort from all stakeholders involved. Schools must create safe, inclusive, and supportive environments that prioritize the mental health and well-being of students. This involves implementing evidence-based prevention programs, promoting social-emotional learning, and providing accessible mental health services. Furthermore, collaboration between schools, families, and communities is crucial. Engaging parents and caregivers in violence prevention efforts, fostering partnerships with community organizations, and advocating for policies that address the underlying socio-economic factors of violence are essential for creating sustainable change.

Tackling school violence necessitates a holistic and proactive approach that addresses its root causes and supports the well-being of students. By promoting empathy, fostering positive relationships, providing the necessary resources for prevention mitigation, and support systems, we can create a school environment where violence is minimized and students can thrive academically, emotionally, and socially.

References

Bennett-Johnson, E. (2004). The root of school violence: Causes and recommendations for a plan of action. *College Student Journal, 38*(2). https://link.gale.com/apps/doc/A119741926/AONE?u=anon~42ba340a&sid=googleScholar&xid=6a54e7e5

Brown, R. P., Osterman, L. L., & Barnes, C. D. (2009). School violence and the culture of honor. *Psychological Science, 20*(11), 1400-1405.

Centers for Disease Control and Prevention. 2016. *Explore youth risk behavior survey questions—United States, 2021.* https://yrbs-explorer.services.cdc.gov/#/

Cornell, D. G. (2020). Threat assessment as a school violence prevention strategy. *Criminology & Public Policy, 19*, 235–252. https://doi.org/10.1111/1745-9133.12471

Cox, J. W., Rich, S., Chong, L., Trevor, L., Muyskens, J., & Ulmanu, M. (2023, April 3). More than 357,000 students have experienced gun violence at school since Columbine: There have been 389 school shootings since Columbine. *The Washington Post.* https://www.washingtonpost.com/education/interactive/school-shootings-database/

Curran, F. C., Viano, S. L., & Fisher, B. W. (2017). Teacher victimization, turnover, and contextual factors promoting resilience. *Journal of School Violence, 18*(1), 21–38. https://nam02.safelinks.protection.outlook.com/?url=https%3A%2F%2Fdoi.org%2F10.1080%2F15388220.2017.1368394&data=05%7C02%7Cjjones1%40gordonstate.edu%7C49aed1db1d734f4d524608dc31aeaeb7%7C9450bf80253743819ecba433616fae0c%7C0%7C0%7C638439873543387509%7CUnknown%7CTWFpbGZsb3d8eyJWIjoiMC4wLjAwMDAiLCJQIjoiV2luMzIiLCJBTiI6Ik1haWwiLCJXVCI6Mn0%3D%7C0%7C%7C%7C&sdata=05WmenXr2DFvYaaJE38WlDJOavUcJbGoQ1wszNEKL%2F0%3D&reserved=0"https://doi.org/10.1080/15388220.2017.1368394

Dempsey, A. G., Haden, S. C., Goldman, J., Sivinski, J., & Wiens, B. A. (2011). Relational and overt victimization in middle and high schools: Associations with suicidality. *Journal of School Violence, 10*, 374-392. doi:10.1080/15388220.2011.602612

Espelage, D., Anderman, E. M., Brown, V. E., Jones, A., Lane, K. L., McMahon, S. D., Reddy, L. A., & Reynolds, C. R. (2013). Understanding and preventing violence directed against teachers: Recommendations for a national research, practice, and policy agenda. *American Psychologist, 68*(2), 75–87. https://doi.org/10.1037/a0031307

Flannery, D. J., Wester, K. L., & Singer, M. I. (2004). Impact of exposure to violence in school on child and adolescent mental health and behavior. *Journal of Community Psychology, 32*(5), 559-573.

Fried, S., & Fried, P. (1996). *Bullies and victims: Helping your child survive the schoolyard battlefield*. M. Evans.

Giumetti, G. W., & Kowalski, R. M. (2022). Cyberbullying via social media and well-being. *Current Opinion in Psychology, 45*, 101314. https://doi.org/10.1016/j.copsyc.2022.101314

Glew, G. M., Fan, M., Katon, W., Rivara, F. P., & Kernic, M. A. (2005). Bullying, psychosocial adjustment, and academic performance in elementary school. *Archives of Pediatric Adolescent Medicine, 159*, 1026-1031.

Green, E. (2020, November 23). *Exploring school violence and safety concerns*. Illinois Criminal Justice Information Authority. https://icjia.illinois.gov/researchhub/articles/exploring-school-violence-and-safety-concerns

Hawker, D. S. J., & Boulton, M. J. (2000). Twenty years' research on peer victimization and psychosocial maladjustment: A meta-analytic review of cross-sectional studies. *Journal of Child Psychology and Psychiatry and Allied Disciplines*, 41, 441- 455. doi:10.1111/1469-7610.00629

Henry, S. (2009). School violence beyond Columbine: A complex problem in need of an interdisciplinary analysis. *American Behavioral Scientist*, 52(9), 1246-1265. https://doi.org/10.1177/0002764209332544

Irwin, V., Wang, K., Cui, J., & Thompson, A. (2022). *Report on indicators of school crime and safety: 2021*. National Center for Education Statistics, U.S. Department of Education, Office of Justice Programs, U.S. Department of Justice. nces.ed.gov/pubs2022/2022092.pdf

Klomek, A. B., Kleinman, M., Altschuler, E., Marrocco, F., Amakawa, L., & Gould, M. S. (2011). High school bullying as a risk for later depression and suicidality. *Suicide and Life-Threatening Behavior*, 41(5), 501-516. doi:10.1111/j.1943-278X.2011.00046.x

Kowalski, R. M., Limber, S. P., & McCord, A. (2019). A developmental approach to cyberbullying: Prevalence and protective factors. *Aggression and Violent Behavior*, 45, 20–32. https://doi.org/10.1016/j.avb.2018.02.009

Meltzer, H., Vostanis, P., Ford, T., Bebbington, P., & Dennis, M. S. (2011). Victims of bullying in childhood and suicide attempts in adulthood. *European Psychiatry*, 26, 498-503. doi:10.1016/j.eurpsy.2010.11.006

Maeng, J. L., Malone, M., & Cornell, D. (2020). Student threats of violence against teachers: Prevalence and outcomes using a threat assessment approach. *Teaching and Teacher Education*, 87, 102934. https://nam02.safelinks.protection.outlook.com/?url=https%3A%2F%2Fdoi.org%2F10.1016%2Fj.tate.2019.102934&data=05%7C02%7Cjjones1%40gordonstate.edu%7C49aed1db1d734f4d524608dc31aeaeb7%7C9450bf80253743819ecba433616fae0c%7C0%7C0%7C638439873543368385%7CUnknown%7CTWFpbGZsb3d8eyJWIjoiMC4wLjAwMDAiLCJQIjoiV2luMzIiLCJBTiI6Ik1haWwiLCJXVCI6Mn0%3D%7C0%7C%7C%7C&sdata=eR2CcfWMT9rVSdIGUQBolQ7MRR%2BY6dIe3YUoST5Lngs%3D&reserved=0"https://doi.org/10.1016/j.tate.2019.102934

Moon, B., Saw, G., & McCluskey, J. (2020). Teacher victimization and turnover: Focusing on different types and multiple victimization. Journal of School Violence, 19(3), 406–420. https://nam02.safelinks.protection.outlook.com/?url=https%3A%2F%2Fpsycnet.apa.org%2Fdoi%2F10.1080%2F15388220.2020.1725529&data=05%7C02%7Cjjones1%40gordonstate.edu%7C49aed1db1d734f4d524608dc31aeaeb7%7C9450b

f80253743819ecba433616fae0c%7C0%7C0%7C638439873543391860%7CUnknown%7CTWFpbGZsb3d8eyJWIjoiMC4wLjAwMDAiLCJQIjoiV2luMzIiLCJBTiI6Ik1haWwiLCJXVCI6Mn0%3D%7C0%7C%7C%7C&sdata=AJSqC3bmy7rPuERWRuHgwuT4kSLcxCOXvM0PsW0S7L4%3D&reserved=0"https://doi.org/10.1080/15388220.2020.1725529

Myers, L. (2000). *Violence in schools*. U.S. Dept. of Health and Human Services, Substance Abuse and Mental Health Services Administration, Center for Substance Abuse Prevention.

National Center for Education Statistics (NCES), (2022). *Report on indicators of school crime and safety: 2021*. US Department of Education.

Rigby, K. (2003). Consequences of bullying in schools. *Canadian Journal of Psychiatry, 48*(9), 583-590.

Steffgen, G., Recchia, S., & Viechtbauer, W. (2013). The link between school climate and violence in school: A meta-analytic review. *Aggression and Violent Behavior, 18*(2), 300–309. https://doi.org/10.1016/j.avb.2012.12.001

Turanovic, J. J., & Siennick, S. E. (2022). *The causes and consequences of school violence: A review*. National Institute of Justice. https://www.ojp.gov/pdffiles1/nij/302346.pdf

Warner, B. S., Weist, M. D., & Krulak, A. (1999). Risk factors for school violence. *Urban Education, 34*(1), 52–68. https://doi.org/10.1177/0042085999341004

CHAPTER 22

Recruiting Teacher Candidates from Marginalized Groups

Stephen Raynie

In the last century, I attended a kindergarten class taught by a nice woman who claimed to be from Mars. We made butter by shaking jars of cream, built forts with large blocks, learned the alphabet song, counted to 100, played with sand tables, went to recess, and colored between the lines. Like another planet, the school was apart from the turmoil of Vietnam War protests and the righteous struggles of the Civil Rights Movement. But I think for my Martian teacher, the classroom was a place where she felt she could model creating a good life, one built on meaningful relationships with others.

Our own students at Gordon State College express that need to help make life meaningful for others. Julie, who is a junior in our traditional, face-to-face cohort, declares:

> My elementary and middle school teachers helped give me encouragement when I wanted to give up and help me understand a grade doesn't define who I am. Every single day won't be the same and will come with challenges, but that doesn't mean giving up on a student or situation. (personal communication, August 30, 2023).

Anna, a candidate in our online parapro-to-teacher program, explains her desire this way: "I want to be a teacher because I love seeing children learn and grow. I specifically want to be an elementary school teacher because I enjoy building lasting relationships from a young age" (personal communication, September 8, 2023). A recent survey of Gordon State parapro-to-teacher students about why they chose education confirms this sentiment. The comments focus on a love of children and a desire to create safety for them (Student Survey, September 16, 2023). Many also mention that one of their own teachers inspired them and that they want to make that difference in the lives of others. All see education as challenging and personally meaningful, and they reflect the Japanese idea of *ikigai*, popularized by Héctor García and Francesc Miralles (2017). The authors recommend that in order to make a good life, find work where these ideas intersect: something you love, something that the world needs, something that you are good at, and something that you can get paid for. Finding joy in daily life, in fact, does not depend on money, and one of the privileges of becoming college-educated is broad freedom to pursue work that one has defined as meaningful.

That impulse to serve and nurture is still in the hearts of teacher candidates and in the faculty; they desire to be the person who helps others lead their best lives. As I reflect on my own experience as a child, however, I cannot recall ever having a teacher from a marginalized group. While my kindergarten teacher helped me imagine the concept of "difference" by claiming to be from Mars, the perspective of my teachers was familiar to me because as a white male, I easily identified with the white women and men who kindled my imagination as a child. They looked like me, they were members of the same social class as me, and they of course had all graduated college just like my father had.

I was already a member of a privileged group without knowing that my path had been smoothed over by social forces I could not yet see, unaware even during my adolescence of riots occurring in North Carolina in the 1970s documented by Timothy Tyson in his memoir, *Blood Done Sign My Name* (2004); or of the 1986 school boycott in the town and county where I now live, Barnesville, Georgia. The Associated Press story published in *The New York Times* (1986) read: "Civil rights leaders... assert that the school district is running black teachers away, but school officials say they cannot find enough qualified black [sic] teachers to match the racial ratio of the schools" (p. 28). It is still a deeply rooted social problem: in order to have more teachers from marginalized groups, opportunities need to exist for marginalized students. In order for more opportunities to exist for marginalized students, social constructs—even if unintentional—that perpetuate racism and discrimination must be made visible and open to challenge. As the surveyed teacher candidates say, the foundation of the desire to teach is relational. That relational desire is certainly antithetical to continuing marginalization.

Racial division lingers in Barnesville, marked literally by the railroad tracks that run through town. Until 2007, Fred Crane, who played Brent Tarleton in *Gone with the Wind*, owned a large antebellum house on Greenwood Street that had been built for cotton magnate, Josiah Holmes in 1849. Crane was the last surviving adult male actor from the film (Crane, n.d.); he ran the place as a museum and bed and breakfast. He called it Tarleton Oaks; its size and prominence marked it as a time-bound landmark, perhaps a little like Emily Grierson's house in Faulkner's *A Rose for Emily*.

Gordon State College is named after John Brown Gordon, a Civil War general, senator, and governor whose statue still stands outside the state capitol in Atlanta and whose portrait was hanging in the library when I interviewed for a position at Gordon State in 2001. Russell Hall on the west side of campus is named for Richard B. Russell, Jr., who, according to his biography on the United States Senate webpage (n.d.), resisted desegregation and "used his parliamentary skills and knowledge of Senate rules and procedures, including the filibuster, to defeat bills banning lynching, abolishing the poll tax, and upholding civil rights for Black Americans" (para. 1). Off campus, the lived experience of Gordon State students is filled with other reminders of that scarred history.

Other visible signs of that legacy of racial conflict are still present in Georgia. For example, the state recently enacted a new law that governs classroom discussions of "divisive topics" like race and gender identity (Bernstein, 2022). The tension also recently surfaced in the University System of Georgia's renaming controversy, a movement to change the names of more than 70 buildings and campus locations that carried the echoes of slavery and segregation. Although the Board of Regents appointed a task force to study the issue, rather than accepting its counsel, it simply "thanked the group for its 'diligent work on this complex matter' but said that it 'will not pursue name changes on USG [University System of Georgia] buildings and colleges as recommended by the advisory group's report'" (Beals, 2021).

Moreover, in June 2023, the Georgia Professional Standards Commission, which oversees education program providers in the state, voted to remove "diversity," "equity," and "inclusion" from education program standards (McCray, 2023). Thus, systemic barriers not only still exist for access to education and for marginalized citizens generally, but there are also continuing state-sponsored and persistent reminders of separateness, oppression, and impediments to social mobility for marginalized groups.

We teach in our educator preparation programs (and rightly so) that an appreciation for diversity is essential to a healthy society, yet our culture continues to reproduce the inequities of past generations through practices and structures that restrict deconstruction and reform. For example, Darrius Stanley (2022) found that "White [sic] educators continue to lack cultural awareness, comprehension of White [sic] privilege, and deep understanding of the unique needs and assets of racially minoritized students" (p. 202). Citing a 2016 study from the U.S. Department of Education, Stanley further concluded that "the persistent underachievement of racially minoritized students across the country ... is related to the lack of diversity in the educator workforce" (p. 202).

Perhaps more alarming, in Georgia, African American high school students are more likely to be punished for misbehavior than white high school students. For example, in Cobb County, 33% of students are African American, but account for 52% of all disciplinary actions. In Dekalb County, 68% of students are African American, but account for 82% of disciplinary actions. Clayton County, Atlanta Public Schools, and Gwinnett County all have similar data (Givens, 2021). According to the 2021 Georgia K-12 Teacher & Leader Workforce Report, only 26.5% of teachers in Georgia's public schools are African American (Flamini & Steed, 2021, p. 2). Not surprisingly, 44.8% of teachers in high-poverty schools are African American, and 79.9% of teachers that work in low-poverty schools are white (Flamini & Steed, 2021, p. 13).

I bring up this context of continuing racial divisions in Georgia because the state is facing a shortage of teachers, and at the same time, our education program students were once overwhelmingly white. I wondered why this would be the case since every year almost half of Gordon State College's new students come from marginalized groups. At the same time, the retention rate for students from marginalized groups lags significantly (Gordon State College, 2021, p. 22). The number of faculty members from marginalized groups was low, and the number of students from marginalized groups graduating from our education program was also low. But the solution had to be outside of the existing program structure, and perhaps even outside of the traditional educational structure that reinscribed marginalized status. The education program was trying to address a structural problem while operating within the very structure that perpetuated it.

Some might want to attribute the teacher shortage to pay, but it is difficult to make that case in Georgia. Factors such as inter-district mobility certainly play a role since counties supplement the state minimum scale at different rates, but in the metropolitan area of Fulton County, Georgia, for example, newly minted bachelor's degree graduates start at $56,488, and if new hires are certified in special education, there is an additional $3,000 added (L. Burton, personal communication, August 1, 2023). This rate is significantly above the National Education Association's calculation of the average starting rate nationally of $42,844 (2023) and is well above the official state salary scale (Georgia Department of Education, 2023).

One might also attribute the teacher shortage to the fact that teacher salaries do not increase at the same rate as they do in other professions. According to the National Education Association (2023), the average teacher salary nationally is $3,644 less than it was 10 years ago after being adjusted for inflation. This finding is supported by similar data from the National Center for Educational Statistics (2023; Table 22.1)

Data from just a few years ago, moreover, show that even though Georgia's average teacher salary compared favorably to all neighboring states, it still lagged behind the national average and had not kept up with inflation as calculated by the national Consumer Price Index (NCES, 2023). In Georgia and in all surrounding states, inflation-adjusted teacher salaries had, in fact, been declining for a decade even though Georgia remained on top in comparison with neighboring states. Table 22.1 shows the decline in real wages for teachers in constant 2020-2021 dollars. Although it is the case that through 2021 Georgia teacher salaries in inflation-adjusted dollars did decline, it would not be accurate to say that Georgia teacher salaries have continued that slide. For the last two fiscal years, the State of Georgia has increased state employee salaries (including public school teachers) by $5,000 (Fiscal Year 2023) and $2,000 (Fiscal Year 2024). The $5,000 raise in FY 2023 was retroactive to FY 2022, and state employees received this extra money in spring 2023.

Table 22.1

Decline in 2020-2021 Constant Dollar Wages for Teachers in the Southeast, 2009-2010 to 2020-2021			
	Average Teacher Salary 2009-2010	Average Teacher Salary 2020-2021	Constant Dollar Change from 2009-2010
National Average	$67,228	$65,090	-3.2%
Georgia	$64,486	$60,553	-6.1%
Alabama	$57,759	$54,271	-6.0%
Florida	$56,711	$49,583	-12.6%
Louisiana	$59,376	$51,851	-12.7%
Mississippi	$55,419	$47,655	-14.0%
North Carolina	$56,883	$54,392	-4.4%
Tennessee	$56,203	$52,380	-6.8%
South Carolina	$57,682	$53,361	-7.5%

Source: National Center for Education Statistics (NCES).

Although a number of issues can contribute to an organization's staff recruitment and retention (Yontz & Wilson, 2021), Hough and Loeb (2013) note that salaries do increase teacher applicant pools, allowing districts to be more selective in their staffing. While teacher salaries should be higher, and while teacher salaries have generally not kept up with inflation, it seems dubious that students considering teaching as a profession would be deterred by entry-level salaries in Georgia. Georgia teachers find work at salaries higher than others in their general areas. For example, while it is certainly true that Georgia's college graduates in accounting, business, and engineering earn more than their peers in education, it is also true, according to the University System of Georgia's website Georgia Degrees Pay (2023), that educators earn more than their recently graduated peers in the same fields who are not certified to teach. (See Table 22.2.) It is also true that Georgia's teacher salaries flatten out relative to the market over time, and this trend might account for teacher turnover. Still, the starting salaries for teachers of biology, English, foreign language, and mathematics are significantly higher than those for graduates in the same field who do not work in public schools. For students interested in fields taught in the public school system, entry-level teacher salaries compare favorably to the market. Even so, students do not always choose majors based on anticipated salaries. They are not thinking in such utilitarian terms, or else more of them would take hard math courses and become engineers.

Table 22.2

Georgia College Graduate Median Salaries (Georgia Professional Degrees Pay)			
	One Year After Graduation	Five Years After Graduation	10 Years After Graduation
Accountancy	$45,553	$63,430	$78,411
Business	$43,378	$61,377	$75,721
Civil Engineering	$62,972	$79,735	$106,207
Communication	$32,846	$47,458	No Data
Criminal Justice	$33,418	No Data	No Data
Electrical Engineering	$72,427	$93,341	$124,241
Economics	$40,625	63,006	$81,235
Human Services	$33,157	$42,019	$54,252
Political Science	$32,813	$51,819	$67,023
Biology	$28,763	$47,704	$71,824
Biology Teacher	$47,370	$54,434	$64,405
English	$30,268	$44,045	$56,509
English Teacher	$43,974	$51,249	$58,698
Foreign Language	$37,115	$44,980	No Data
Foreign Language Teacher	$43,952	$52,197	$55,123
Mathematics	$41,600	$56,209	$69,055
Mathematics Teacher	$48,883	$54,223	$57,992
Elementary Education	$38,928	$48,110	$55,228

Source: Georgia State Department of Education

The larger issue with attributing the teacher shortage to a macroeconomic factor like salaries is that it ignores what actually happens in the classroom resulting from marginalizing social constructs that obstruct the certification of new teachers. The strain between education as professional citizenship and education as workforce development is heightened when groups are marginalized because the desire to enter the economic middle class occurs simultaneously with other reminders to subaltern groups that they are, perhaps, unqualified for full citizenship after all. If public education means making productive citizens and workers, the question arises: who wants to be a citizen or even a worker within a structure that perpetuates inequity? Education ought to come with the promise of autonomy and prosperity, but the lived experience of individuals from marginalized groups might not match these ideals. Conditions of implicit and explicit bias within the classroom mimic the social milieu as a whole (Blackson et al., 2022). The idea of the classroom as a utopic space distanced from socio-political conflict is an illusion.

If public education sets itself up as an engine of social mobility—just as Gordon State College has with its access mission—it also sets itself up to be judged on that basis. In Georgia there is a clear anti-progressive strain in education and in education program governance, which, frankly, seeks—even if unconsciously—to perpetuate the divisions it purports to oppose. It is easier to blame poor teaching, bad teachers and administrators, and even substandard education program providers for failures than it is to blame the larger social and systemic forces within which teachers and their students are operating.

It raises the question of whether the teacher shortage generally and the shortage of teachers from marginalized groups in particular, is simply the result of disrespect and deprofessionalization. Aronson et al., (2022) succinctly aver:

> Because schools were discursively constructed as a "problem" to be solved, then teachers must be contributors as well. This type of blame thus called into question their deserving of professional status. Relatedly, the racial, ethnic, and economic inequalities of the 21st century have been discursively constructed as the product of failing schools, as the result of which elite policy actors have

blunted progressive era moves toward professionalization and have justified a move toward the technocratic management of an underperforming labor force. (p. 25)

Public perception of teachers also suffers from frenzied media coverage; examples of unprofessional and even criminal behaviors abound and help solidify the rhetorical deprofessionalization and provide the political rationale for salaries that generally do not respond to market forces. In the face of deprofessionalization, the moral passion of just wanting to do some good in the world wanes.

Teacher deprofessionalization is sustained by two umbrella forces: added work (Ginsburg & Megahed, 2009) or intensification of work (Apple, 1987) and standardization of curriculum, pedagogy, and assessment (Frostenson, 2015; Milner, 2013; Newkirk, 2009). These forces lead to loss of autonomy (Darling-Hammond, 2007; Ginsburg & Megahed, 2009; Wronowski & Urick, 2019), however nuanced (Frostenson, 2015), and feelings of demoralization which occurs when teachers become unable to find moral rewards from their teaching (Santoro, 2011,pp. 25-26).

Certainly, employees of any organization desire autonomy, good leadership, and a positive interpersonal environment, all free from social constructs that perpetuate inequity. Turning teaching from an altruistic, relational, and liberatory enterprise into a high-efficiency, high-stakes cash nexus function that devalues and demoralizes teachers and students both is bound to discourage the passion that the best students and teacher candidates have.

The process described here accounts for declining interest in teaching: it has become increasingly difficult to find moral rewards, the sense of making a meaningful difference in the world. Remember the principles of *ikigai* to find meaningful work: something you love, something the world needs, something you are good at, and something you can get paid for. It is not the money alone that governs entry and exit from teaching as a profession, although certainly it is important to have enough that one's basic needs can be comfortably taken care of. It is the sense of passion and joy that comes from work that is beyond the self, work that is treated at least in part with political suspicion because it carries with it the possibility of reforming or even undermining the status quo. Yet that desire for autonomous, creative work increasingly scrapes against a technocratic impulse to reproduce what are essentially characteristics of factory work: standardized curriculum, testing and assessment, large and increasing workloads, strict pacing guides, legislatures and school boards with ideological demands that preserve inequity, and, perhaps, rationalizations for downward pressure on wages and benefits. The double consciousness of teaching as a profession—the promotion of democratic values and social mobility together with what looks like a systemic impulse to reproduce conditions of oppression using a Taylorist methodology—generates the stress of cognitive dissonance.

Our teacher candidates want to enter the profession for all the right reasons. When they encounter the reality of being less able to create an autonomous space to make a difference individually, deprofessionalization becomes depersonalization. Teaching is not respected or valued because it is seen as a function not worthy of status or independence. Indeed, as mentioned earlier, this contradiction is played out in the construction of teachers in public discourse as lacking moral and ethical judgment or as engaged in a heroic struggle against an oppressive regime denying them basic religious or other freedoms. Both narratives reinforce the public perception that education as a whole needs to be better regulated, better controlled, and under-compensated.

In spite of the socio-economic and political contradictions surrounding teaching, with the exception of the period from 2014-2018, the University System of Georgia Degrees Conferred Reports show that traditional elementary education graduates have remained relatively steady since 2010 (see Table 22.3). But these numbers do not account for turnover, and the 2015 report from the Georgia Department of Education rang alarms statewide, for it found that "47% of the state's public school teachers leave education within five years" (Owens, p. 3). While from 2016-2021, the Governor's Office of Student Achievement reports noted that the total number of teachers increased from 110,059 to 122,466, the shortage still exists (Flamini & Steed, 2021; Tio, 2016). According to the U.S. Census Bureau (n.d.), Georgia's population has increased from 9,687,653 in 2010 to 10,912,876 in 2022, a percentage gain of 12.6%.

Table 22.3

University System of Georgia Elementary Education Teacher Production (CIP Code 13.1202)												
2010	2011	2012	2013	2014	2015	2016	2017	2018	2019	2020	2021	2022
979	993	1260	898	799	844	656	602	629	933	902	908	1043

There is a solution, one that promises to undo over time the structural problems of Georgia's teacher shortage while producing more new teachers from marginalized groups. Non-traditional teacher preparation programs typically begin with the premise that the candidate has a bachelor's degree, but what if the question were instead, how can we help those already in the school and already passionate about their work complete certification to become teachers? Often paraprofessionals are adults whom we know already make more motivated and better-performing students. For paraprofessionals, the starting salary of a teacher is a huge leap from their current circumstances, and they already know the same frustrations of the teachers they work with.

Unfortunately, the Governor's Office of Student Achievement reports do not track paraprofessional teachers in public schools, and no one appears to track the retention of teachers who completed a bachelor's degree and received certification through parapro-to-teacher programs. But parapros are the unseen and grossly underpaid workers of the public school system for whom teaching as a profession is truly aspirational. They are already accustomed to the stresses of the profession, and for most, the starting teacher's salary is twice what they make as a parapro.

Why are more parapros not becoming certified teachers? The largest barrier to degree completion for working adults is the sheer number of credit hours, which translates into clock hours, and when someone is working during the day full time and taking care of children in the evening, getting to classes is problematic. Another issue is the structural incompatibility between many Associate of Applied Science degrees in early childhood education and Bachelor's degrees in Education. In addition, cost is often prohibitive. Tuition and fees at a regional university in Georgia can be as much as $298.27 per credit hour and in the state university sector, it is $169.33 (University System of Georgia Fiscal Affairs, 2023). Private college tuition is generally more. Bachelor's degree tuition at Brenau University, for example, is $754 per credit hour (Brenau University, 2023). The University of Phoenix is a little lower, at $398 per credit hour (University of Phoenix, 2023). The cost to complete a degree for what a parapro makes can seem especially discouraging.

In addition to the on-going issues relating to public perception of teachers, political leadership, and working conditions, solving the teacher shortage is really a function of access, and in this case, connecting those who want to be teachers to an accessible program is the key to resolving unmet demand. At Georgia's state colleges, tuition is much more modest. Gordon State College's tuition, for example, is $106.80 per credit hour. A parapro starting with an Associate of Science or Associate of Arts degree from a University System of Georgia school could complete a bachelor's degree for about $6,400.00, a cost that could easily be recouped in the first year of teaching. What is perhaps more essential to the access mission at Gordon State, however, is that through the parapro-to-teacher program, the college has been able to increase the percentage of teacher candidates from marginalized groups to over 24% in the fall 2023 cohort. While college and education program providers in Georgia generally have a lot more work to do in this area, this access pathway works because it leverages the motivation in working adults to become certified teachers with affordability and instructional access. It sets the conditions to accelerate the underlying social justice imperative of education to eliminate structural barriers to continuing inequity. While it does not entirely reconcile the structural issues resulting in the teacher shortage, it does offer a meaningful personal path that allows for the greater self-determination and social mobility that comes with prosperity.

Teacher preparation programs, therefore, should look beyond the traditional structure of higher education and find ways to include those already more firmly committed to working in schools. Reprofessionalizing public education by increasing both salaries and autonomy must be part of the solution, and at the same time, structural barriers that deter access by students from marginalized groups must be eliminated.

In addition, when our parapro-to-teacher students were asked what drew them to our program at Gordon State College, a consistent theme was the ability to continue to work at what they love while earning their degrees (Student Survey, September 16, 2023). While there is no shortage of people who love children and want to create safe learning spaces for them, many lack opportunity. The world of higher education as a separate space that is in the world but not a part of it, does not reflect the reality of the postmodern economy in which the path to a bachelor's degree and participation in the middle class is often fraught with financial struggles and frequent detours. The way forward to addressing the teacher shortage while improving degree completion for students from marginalized groups is complex and multi-faceted, but a large part of the solution must be driven by access.

References

Aronson, B., Anderson, A., Ellison, S., Barczak, K., & Bennett-Kinne, A. (2021). The last refuge of the incompetent: Urban teacher perceptions of their positions in public discourse. *Educational Studies 57*(1), 21-36.

Associated Press. (1986, August 24). Race disputes spur boycotts of school systems in two southern states. *The New York Times*, Section 1, p. 28. www.nytimes.com/1986/08/24/us/race-disputes-spur-boycotts-of-schools-in-2-southern-states.html

Beals, M. (2021, November 22). Georgia college system not changing names associated with slavery, White supremacy. *The Hill*. https://thehill.com/homenews/state-watch/582744-georgia-college-system-not-changing-names-associated-with-slavery-white/

Bernstein, S. (2022, April 28). Georgia becomes latest U.S. state to ban 'divisive' concepts in teaching about race. *Reuters.com*. https://www.reuters.com/world/us/georgia-becomes-latest-us-state-ban-divisive-concepts-teaching-about-race-2022-04-28/

Blackson, E., Gerdes, M., Segan, E., Anokam, C., & Johnson, T. (2022). Racial bias toward children in the early childhood education setting. *Journal of Early Childhood Research*, 20(3), 277–292. https://doi.org/10.1177/1476718X221087051

Brenau University. (2023). *Brenau University Tuition*. https://www.brenau.edu/tuition-financial-aid/tuition/

Crane, F. (n.d.). *Internet Movie Database*. https://imbd.com/name/nm0186347/bio/?ref_=nm_ov_bio_sm

Flamini, M., & Steed, H. (2021). *2020 Georgia K-12 teacher & leader workforce report*. Governor's Office of Student Achievement. https://gosa.georgia.gov/georgia-k-12-teacher-and-leader-workforce-report

García, H., & Miralles, F. (2017). *Ikigai. The Japanese Secret to a Long and Happy Life*. Penguin/Random House.

Georgia Degrees Conferred Reports. (n.d.). *University System of Georgia Degrees*. https://www.usg.edu/research/usgbythenumbers

Georgia Department of Education. (2023). *Georgia State Salary Schedule*. https://www.gadoe.org/Finance-and-Business-Operations/Budget-Services/Documents/FY2023SalarySch.pdf

Givens, L. (2021, February 17). *State data shows Black students punished more often, severely than other races*. 11 Alive. https://www.11alive.com/article/news/community/voices-for-equality/state-data-black-students-punished-more/85-49fbfbc2-8c0e-4b07-9c91-56b7bb7af8c2

Gordon State College. (2021). *Gordon State College Factbook*. https://www.gordonstate.edu/documents/departments/institutional-resesarch/gsc-fact-book-2020-2021.pdf

Hough, H., & Loeb, S. (2013). *Can a district-level teacher salary incentive policy improve teacher recruitment and retention?* Policy Analysis for California Education. https://cepa.stanford.edu/sites/default/files/PACE%20Policy%20Brief%2013-4_LowRes.pdf

McCray, V. (2023, June 8). Anger grows as Georgia panel further cuts diversity from teacher prep rules. *Atlanta Journal Constitution*. www.ajc.com/education/anger-grows-as-georgia-panel-further-cuts-diversity-from-teacher-prep-rules/LSWK5HDSAZC6JN74QVDFK6XEYA/

National Center for Education Statistics (NCES). (2023). *Constant dollar average teacher salaries*. https://nces.ed.gov/programs/digest/d21/tables/dt21_211.60.asp

National Education Association. (2023). https://www.nea.org/resource-library/educator-pay-and-student-spending-how-does-your-state-rank

Owens, S. (2015). *Georgia's teacher drop-out crisis: A look at why nearly half of Georgia public school teachers are leaving the profession*. Georgia Department of Education. https://www.gadoe.org/External-Affairs-and Policy/communications/Documents/Teacher%20Survey%20Results.pdf

United States Senate. (n.d.) *Richard B. Russell: A featured biography*. https://senate.gov/senators/FeaturedBios/Featured_Bio_Russell.htm

Stanley, D. (2022). Still in search of a home: A critical analysis of Black teacher turnover and exclusion. *The Journal of Negro Education* 91(2), 202-212.

Tio, R. (2016). *2016 Georgia K-12 Teacher and Leader Workforce Report*. Georgia

Department of Education. https://gosa.georgia.gov/georgia-k-12-teacher-and-leader-workforce-report

Tyson, T. (2004). *Blood Done Sign My Name*. Crown.

University of Phoenix. (September 28, 2023). *Tuition,*. https://www.phoenix.edu/tuition-financial-aid.html

University System of Georgia Fiscal Affairs. (2023). *Tuition and fees FY 2024*. https://www.usg.edu/fiscal_affairs/tuition_and_fees

University System of Georgia. (2023). *Georgia Degrees Pay*. https://usg.edu/your-future-earnings

University System of Georgia. (2023). *USG By the Numbers, Degrees Conferred Reports*. https://www.usg.edu/research/usgbythenumbers

U.S. Census Bureau. (n.d). *Population of Georgia*. https://www.census.gov/quickfacts/fact/table/GA/PST045222

Yontz, B., & Wilson, R. (2021). Teacher salary differentials and student performance: Are they connected? *Journal of Educational Issues*, 7(1), 168-83.

CHAPTER 23

From Great Challenge Comes Great Gain:
Promoting Collaborative Planning in K-12 Schools

NOAH LAWTON HARRELL

THE ADAGE "IRON SHARPENS iron" rings true in all walks of life. In the world of education, it's especially true; sadly, it's also true that teachers tend to stick to their own classes and their own ways. I did too, when I was a teacher. As an administrator now, I have witnessed the incredible growth that is possible when teachers meet and bounce ideas off each other, and because of that, I feel that is essential for the growth of an educator to participate in collaborative planning, which in turn ensures the growth of students in each educator's care. In my school, I explored the benefits of good collaborative planning and ways to get teachers on board; then I proposed a collaborative planning protocol to help teachers in their collaborative efforts.

Collaborative planning is the practice of having teachers who teach the same course work together in order to enhance their instructional planning. From a school district perspective, "Collaborative planning provides opportunities for teachers to work together during the school day to make those connections through examining their practice, consulting with colleagues, and developing their skills" (Caskey & Carpenter, 2014, para. 4). When teachers work together, they look beyond their own classrooms, which is beneficial for both the teacher and the student. In truth, teachers have a mentality of their classroom being theirs and theirs alone. I was a teacher for 14 years, so I include myself in that description. I stayed in my lane, and I wanted no one else in my lane. I now know that allowing others to look at what is happening in our classes, along with sharing ideas from our own experiences, enhances the instruction going on in all classes.

In fact, in looking at the benefits of collaborative planning, I understand why school districts are pushing more and more for this approach to teacher development. According to Gates (2018), for the National Education Association (NEA), there are three benefits: collaboration helps brainstorm creative ideas, professional collaboration teaches you about yourself, and learning collaboratively helps students.

The first NEA-identified benefit helps teachers by giving them a "safety net" in terms of bouncing ideas off other professionals. Hearing feedback from another colleague can lead to a new spark or idea when it comes to planning for instruction. The process is metacognitive; while you are sharing through collaborative planning, you learn about yourself as an educator. In sharing honestly about your approaches and strategies, you have to evaluate what you are doing in the classroom in order to make collaborative planning effective. From the perspective of a teacher-turned-administrator, the more self-reflection and self-evaluation a teacher can do, the more they can grow in the profession. The third and last NEA-identified benefit is that collaborative planning can lead to concerted practices for students. While working as a collective unit, teachers can plan collaborative activities for students, which in turn will encourage the benefits that teachers gain and pass them on to students.

Getting teachers on board with collaborative planning is certainly a barrier to successful outcomes for any school implementing collaborative planning. The hard truth is that some veteran teachers don't necessarily want to listen to younger or newer teachers in the profession; the converse is equally true. However, all of us can grow as educators. One difference I see in my school that affects participation is the idea of teachers "having to" versus "wanting to" engage in collaborative planning. Since districts are pushing teachers to basically get on board with collaborative planning, changing the mindset of some educators is crucial for teacher buy-in. According to Caskey & Carpenter (2014), for the Association of Middle Level

Education (AMLE), there are five ways to build buy-in:

- create a truly shared vision with specific goals,

- develop a sense of community,

- identify group norms,

- use discussion and dialogue, and

- work through any conflict that arises.

Each of those elements make sense to me. Having teachers be a part of both the construction of a collaborative vision and team goals can help lead to more ownership, which in turn leads to more buy-in. Creating a sense of community among the teachers involved is especially crucial because collaborative planning is at its core relational: building a sense of trust among group members is key. Collaborating teachers are making themselves vulnerable, pouring themselves out, and sharing their practices with each other.

One way that administrators can assist with the trust-building is to set group norms, which will encourage trust and transparency. Agreeing to group norms and sticking to them results in teachers feeling more comfortable in the collaborative setting. Additionally, when developing a collaborative planning program, administrators will want to make sure that group norms establish guidelines for maintaining the discussion format (versus one member venting or another oversharing personal details) and for keeping discussions on target. Teachers are too busy for collaborative planning sessions to turn into one teacher's personal soap box time.

The last element that administrators will want to guide teachers toward is conflict resolution. People do not always agree on everything; openly evaluating practices can lead to people challenging and questioning each other. Creating a conflict management plan can lead to more productive outcomes for teachers, in turn increasing comfort levels for participating teachers.

And, of course, administrators can encourage collaborative planning in practical ways. Such practicality begins with the simple (at least on the surface) step of scheduling common planning periods. Giving teachers the built-in time to be able to meet and discuss courses eliminates the barrier of teachers having to come early or stay later at work. I believe having administrators as part of this type of professional learning community (PLC) is another practical and crucial element to successful implementation—and it's a huge show of confidence in the process. Lastly, administrators need to have genuine conversations with participating teachers about the effectiveness of the process. In that way, they can change the mindset of "have" to "want to."

To establish a healthy collaborative planning system at my school, I first worked with our instructional lead in order to create a protocol that teachers could use in their meetings. We spent time talking to and then receiving feedback from teachers when it came to the process. I was able to help create the protocol and lead the charge in implementation. We have set the standard that at least once a week our teachers will meet collaboratively to discuss lesson plans, unit plans, student data, and assessments.

Already, there have been gains in expectations of participating teachers for collaborative planning, even if we still have work to do in the building overall. For a variety of reasons, some PLCs do not necessarily get to all the different topics that need to be discussed during any one session. Despite an imperfect implementation thus far, however, I have great hope. When I was still in the teaching ranks, I looked at collaborative planning as a means to check off a box. As an administrator, I now see the value of good collaborative planning. It makes me want to sit down and come up with a more effective plan moving forward, to help with more teacher buy-in. The barriers that lead to poor collaborative planning really stem from attitudes of teachers regarding the process. Being able to change that attitude will be crucial in starting off the next school year with a great plan. I look forward to the challenges that lie ahead because with those can come great gains for our students.

References

Caskey, M. M., & Carpenter, J. (2014, October). *Building teacher collaboration school-wide*. Association for Middle Level Education (AMLE). https://www.amle.org/building-teacher-collaboration-school-wide/

Gates, S. (2018, October 18). *Benefits of collaboration*. NEA. https://www.nea.org/professional-excellence/student-engagement/tools-tips/benefits-collaboration

CHAPTER 24

Schools in Crisis:

The Importance of Social-Emotional Learning in the Lives of Rural Middle School Students

KRAIG HOWELL

SOCIAL-EMOTIONAL LEARNING (SEL) REFERS to a set of skills and competencies that allow students to effectively establish, develop, and maintain interpersonal relationships with others; as well as, manage their intrapersonal feelings, emotions, and responses to social situations. Students who receive SEL instruction have been shown to demonstrate higher levels of academic achievement, in addition to improved behavioral and social competence. Furthermore, rural communities and schools face significant challenges in addressing the social-emotional needs of students due to limited resources and other factors. Middle school is the time when many students face social-emotional challenges for a variety of reasons.

Research indicates adolescence is when social-emotional needs are most prevalent (Yeager, 2017). Rural communities are often ill equipped to identify needs, provide responses, and demonstrate a lack of resources to meet adolescent SEL needs (Stokes et al., 2021). Indicators of perceived needs identified within the study came from teacher responses gathered in focus groups and interviews. Additionally, a 2017 survey indicated only 35% percent of middle schools are consistently implementing SEL interventions and programming (DePaoli et al., 2017).

In my state of Georgia, Student Health Survey data collected in spring

2022 indicated that, within the last 30 days, 16% of middle school students felt sad or hopeless for 10 or more days; 12% considered suicide on more than one occasion in the last 12 months; 10% used alcohol daily for 11 or more days in the last 30 days; and 10% used marijuana for 11 or more days in the last 30 days (Ga DOE, 2022).

Therefore, social-emotional learning (SEL) is a viable avenue to address the current crisis in rural middle schools. In conceptualizing the argument presented in this chapter, I discuss: i) the history of SEL, ii) its effectiveness and barriers, iii) middle school implementation, and iv) rural school implementation.

History of Social-Emotional Learning

The origins of social-emotional learning (SEL) can arguably be traced back to the initial promotion of engaged citizenship and the Mental Hygiene Movement led by John Dewey and Jane Addams. In Dewey's Laboratory School at the University of Chicago in 1896, he posited the idea that education

> forms a character which not only does the particular deed socially necessary but one which is interested in that continuous readjustment which is essential to growth. Interest in learning from all the contacts of life is the essential moral interest. (Dewey, 1916, p. 223)

While the tenets of Dewey's message remain the same today, the current context in which education occurs has certainly evolved into something entirely different. Over the course of the next century, what would eventually become known as SEL would undergo a myriad of changes from encompassing what skills to include, how to teach the skills, and what impact, if any, these skills had on academic achievement (Dewey, 1933; Elias et al., 2008; Islam, 2015).

The evolution of SEL involves many curricular experts, each contributing new knowledge and information to a body of research and practices towards our understanding today. In addition to Dewey, Edward Thorndike developed a theory of learning highlighting connections among participants as key components (Islam, 2015). Thorndike (1905) set forth laws of learning to explain how people, or learners, engage with stimuli and with one another. Additionally, Islam (2015) wrote that Thorndike clarified how through repetition, reward, and skill development, these skills were transferred from familiar situations and environments to unfamiliar or unknown situations and environments. Thus, cultivating connection and interaction with others, as well as the generalization of skill application, show strong correlations to the goals of SEL.

In his book *Social Intelligence*, Daniel Goleman (2006) wrote about lifting the "curtain on an emerging science... one that reveals that we are wired to connect" (p. 4). Goleman informed the world about connections to each other, oneself, organizations, and religions. Goleman's expansion of Salovey and Mayer's (1990) theory of emotional intelligence, Comer's (1968) whole child work, and Gardner's (1983) interpersonal intelligences brought to light the science behind social connections (Goleman, 2001). Goleman, in collaboration with Tim Shriver, founded the Collaborative for Academic, Social, and Emotional Learning (CASEL) in 1994, with the goal to establish "high-quality, evidence-based SEL as an essential part of preschool through high school education" (CASEL, 2021a, p. 1). CASEL named these skills "social-emotional learning," to communicate learning that "links academic achievement with the skills necessary for succeeding in school, in the family, in the community, in the workplace, and in life in general" (Elias et al., 2008, p. 252).

CASEL (2013) identified direct instruction, integration with academic content, and infusion with teaching practices as three strategies to develop students' social and emotional skills in the classroom. However, while many teachers have expressed an interest in the integration of SEL into their classroom practices, they also highlight the need for support and resources to effectively do so (Bridgeland et al., 2013; Buchanan et al., 2009). Research found that teacher attitudes about and in support for SEL affected the implementation, impact, and sustainability of SEL programming (Bowen & Graham,; Gingiss et al., 1994). Specifically, teacher attitudes and perceptions directly relate to outcomes; therefore, positive attitudes and perceptions lead to positive outcomes and negative attitudes and perceptions lead to no change in outcomes or negative outcomes (Bowen et al., 2013; Gingiss et al., 1994). Assessing the beliefs, attitudes, and perceptions of teachers is critical to understanding how to improve and sustain SEL programming in classrooms.

Effective SEL Programming

In 2021, CASEL published a guide for schoolwide implementation of SEL programming to aid schools implementing effective organizational and instructional practices. The guide provides "research-informed, field-tested guidance and tools that support schools in coordinating and building upon evidence-based SEL practices and programs to achieve systemic implementation" (CASEL, 2021b, p. 1). These practices are coordinated to promote outcomes directly related to the five competencies of SEL—self-awareness, self-management, social awareness, relationship skills, and responsible decision making (CASEL, 2021b). The guide is organized into four focus areas and ten indicators of effective programming. Contained within the four focus areas are the development of schoolwide goals and establishing a plan and a strong focus on student and staff social-emotional development; all of which are encompassed within a continuous improvement cycle focused on data gathering and analysis (CASEL, 2021b).

To achieve implementation fidelity, schools are guided to create SEL goals and priorities aligned to the school's existing school improvement goals and priorities (CASEL, 2021b). In addition, the establishment of a SEL team, with a vision aligned to the school's vision, is paramount for reviewing school data (CASEL, 2021b). In conjunction with the establishment of a SEL team, a strong emphasis is placed on the social-emotional competencies of staff members (CASEL, 2021b). To more effectively integrate SEL practices into school culture, staff must receive professional development on "learning, collaboration and modeling of SEL," with these practices incorporated into staff and grade level meetings (CASEL, 2021b, pp. 34-39).

To effectively impact school culture for implementation, CASEL promotes developing school norms to guide the implementation of SEL programming (CASEL, 2021b). These norms guide the delivery of explicit SEL instruction guidelines, as well as integrating SEL concepts into curricular concepts across content areas (CASEL, 2021b). Additionally, school staff develop partnerships with students, staff, and community stakeholders to identify key priorities and needs, which will ultimately inform selecting an

Schools in Crisis

evidence-based SEL curricular program that ensures support for implementation throughout the community (CASEL, 2021b).

Lastly, for implementation fidelity, schools must review data related to implementation with a focus on continued growth and improvement of SEL implementation. CASEL's (2021b) implementation guide recommends utilizing walkthroughs to gather data on classroom instruction, teacher use of resources, professional learning coaching, and integration into curricular content. Additionally, schools should seek to connect the lived experiences that inform the data through perception surveys from a variety of stakeholders, as well as assessments of student competencies throughout the year. The data should then be utilized to measure progress toward goals, as well as implications for future work.

Barriers to Effective Implementation

Many barriers that impact the implementation of SEL curriculum within schools have been identified within the research base. Barriers include: a lack of consistent guidelines for implementation, limited resources for implementing SEL curriculum, a lack of metrics to measure success of implementation activities, and a lack of accountability for implementing SEL curriculum (Council of Chief State School Officers, 2019).

The development of clear guidelines must be established and communicated to all implementers (Jones & Bouffard, 2012). Implementation inconsistencies are often associated with a lack of clear, concrete, communicated expectations for implementers to follow (Durlak et al., 2011; Jones & Bouffard, 2012; Mahoney et al., 2018). Without clear expectations, long-term benefits and outcomes are not likely to be achieved (Durlak et al., 2011). Numerous meta-analyses indicate professional learning for SEL implementation is limited in most schools (Durlak et al., 2011; Jones & Bouffard, 2012; Mahoney et al., 2018). In most cases, training if it does exist, is inconsistent with limited coaching and follow-up to provide long-term support. Durlak et al., (2011) indicated that for program implementation to be successful, the components of training and clearly established goals and expectations must be present.

The lack of accountability systems and metrics of success is a barrier to SEL implementation. Without effective measures for success, teachers are unable to determine the efficacy of their instructional practices and to effectively plan for improvement (Durlak et al., 2011; Jones & Bouffard, 2012; Mahoney et al., 2018). In a standards-driven era, the lack of SEL standards serves as a barrier to designing, assessing, and implementing SEL curriculum. SEL standards would "provide guidance for schools in the kinds of SEL skills students should have, how to align academic and SEL goals, and how to make SEL a core part of their mission" (Jones & Bouffard, 2012, pp. 18).

These barriers serve as an impediment to teachers developing comfort and commitment to implementing SEL curriculum within their classrooms. Additionally, without clear guidance and proper support for staff to develop necessary skills for teaching SEL curriculum, a culture conducive to developing SEL skills is difficult to achieve. These barriers directly impact the core components impacting teacher perceptions around SEL curriculum—comfort, commitment, and culture.

Comfort

The focus of SEL is on nurturing the social and emotional awareness and skills of students (CASEL, 2013; Payton et al., 2008). Collie et al., (2012) found that a teacher's comfort with teaching SEL was directly correlated with their own personal social-emotional competencies. Jones et al., (2013) found that a teacher's own self-awareness of their social-emotional competencies directly impacted their ability to infuse SEL into their classrooms.

Additionally, Collie (2012) found that as focus on students' social-emotional well-being and associated learning have gained more focus among parents, media, and governmental leaders, there has also been an increase of "the pressure on teachers to implement SEL effectively and stress among teachers who do not feel that they have the appropriate SEL skills" (p. 1197). Jones and Bouffard (2012) assert that "it is difficult, if not impossible, for adults to help students build skills that they themselves do not possess" (p. 14). Without appropriate training, coaching, and support, teachers develop a negative perception of their skills, and by extension the associated SEL curriculum (Brackett et al., 2009; Brackett et al., 2012).

Schonert-Reichl et al., (2017) found that preparation programs for teachers often fail to train their students on how to implement SEL curricula and strategies, which requires teachers to learn on their own while implementing the curriculum. The researchers learned that these circumstances often led to teacher stress, which negatively impacts students, as well as teacher attrition issues, requiring new staff to be hired and trained. The study involved 246 students in grades 4 to 7 (aged 9-12 years) from six public schools in Vancouver, Canada (Schonert-Reichl, 2010). While the student population matches the current research proposal, the setting is a major metropolitan area, highlighting the need to conduct additional research on rural populations with typically fewer resources and less access to care.

Commitment

Teacher commitment to the implementation of SEL programming has been found to have a direct and substantial impact on the outcomes achieved (Brackett et al., 2012). This commitment manifests in: i) professional learning about the components and tenets of SEL, ii) how to integrate components of SEL into the curricula currently being implemented, and iii) integrating SEL interventions for specific needs identified within the student population (Brackett et al., 2009; Brackett et al., 2012; Devaney et al., 2006; McCormick et al., 1995).

Teacher commitment also manifests in their perceptions of student needs for SEL interventions. In a 2021 survey, McGraw-Hill found 84% of educators surveyed indicated that implementing SEL curriculum has become more important to address student needs since the COVID-19 pandemic. Additionally, in Houghton Mifflin Harcourt's *2021 Educator's Confidence Report*, 72% of educators surveyed identified social-emotional needs as a top concern. Fifty-six percent of educators surveyed identified resources to support SEL implementation as a major need. Additionally, 87% of educators believe a well-crafted, fully integrated approach to SEL would have a moderate to significant impact on student achievement (Houghton Mifflin Harcourt, 2022).

Culture

Research indicates that teacher perceptions around whether the school culture, and by extension, leaders within the school and district, support the implementation of SEL programs directly affects the overall results achieved (Fullan et al., 1980; Kam, et al., 2003; Ransford et al., 2009). Jones and Kahn (2017) found that effective implementation of SEL programming had to occur in environments that were supportive. This support includes features that promote positive norms and expectations, and that help students and staff feel safe, connected, and engaged. Zolkokski et al., (2021) found that when teachers perceived the school climate to be positive and supportive, they were more likely to be early adopters of an SEL curriculum.

Schonert-Reichl (2017) identified the learning context as integral for SEL implementation, noting that skill development associated with SEL must occur in an environment that is safe, supportive, and well-managed, in addition to allowing for the practice of developing skills (Schonert-Reichl, 2017). These types of environments are critical to the development of relationships among all groups within schools. These relationships are critical components for the development of self-regulation skills taught within the SEL curriculum, which is foundational to many other SEL skills (Eisenberg et al., 2010; Sameroff, 2010; Shonkoff & Phillips, 2000).

SEL in Middle School

Neth et al., (2020) found that "adolescence can be a particularly difficult time for youth as they experience the physical, social, and academic changes that accompany maturation" (p. 1). As a result, middle schools face the particularly difficult challenge of "teaching adolescent students positive social and emotional skills, which are crucial for them to succeed academically and emotionally" (Neth et al., 2020, p. 1). After a review of SEL programs, designed specifically for middle school students, Main and O'Neil (2018) found that "many of the competencies such as resilience, a sense of self-worth, decision-making self-control, and relationship building could be proactively embedded within daily classroom learning experiences and linked directly with self-regulated learning to enhance educational outcomes" (p. 161).

Research has shown that SEL implementation in middle schools can lead to positive outcomes for students, including improved academic performance, increased social and emotional competencies, and decreased behavioral problems (Durlak et al., 2011). In addition, SEL implementation has been shown to lead to positive outcomes for teachers, including increased job satisfaction and decreased burnout (Jennings & Greenberg, 2009). These benefits have led many middle schools to adopt SEL programs and strategies.

One effective SEL program that has been implemented in middle schools is the Second Step program. Second Step is a research based SEL program that focuses on improving social and emotional competencies through a variety of methods, including classroom instruction, role-playing, and group discussions (CASEL, 2020b). Research has shown the Second Step program can lead to positive outcomes for students, including improved social and emotional competencies, increased academic performances, and decreased behavioral problems (Durlak et al., 2011).

Another effective SEL program that has been implemented in middle schools is the Responsive Classroom approach. The Responsive Classroom approach is research-based, focusing on creating a positive and engaging classroom environment through a variety of methods, including morning meetings, classroom rules, and positive teacher language (CASEL, 2020b). Research has shown that the Responsive Classroom approach can lead to positive outcomes for students, including improved social and emotional competencies, increased academic performances, and decreased behavioral problems (Durlak et al., 2011).

In addition to implementing SEL programs, many middle schools have also implemented other SEL strategies, such as mindfulness practices and peer mentoring programs. Mindfulness practices, such as meditation and deep breathing, have been shown to improve social and emotional competencies in students (Schonert-Reichl & Lawlor, 2010). Peer mentoring programs, in which older students mentor younger students, have been shown to improve social and emotional competencies in both mentors and mentees (Hurd et al., 2011).

Effective SEL implementation in middle schools requires a coordinated effort among school administrators, teachers, and parents. School administrators must provide the necessary resources and support for SEL implementation, including professional development for teachers and funding for SEL programs and strategies (Kendziora & Yoder, 2016). Teachers must be trained in SEL instruction and be provided with the necessary materials and resources to implement SEL strategies in the classroom. Parents must be informed and engaged in SEL implementation, including being provided with information about the benefits of SEL and how they can support SEL development at home (Zins et al., 2004).

One challenge to SEL implementation in middle schools is the lack of standardized assessments for social and emotional competencies (Rosenblatt & Elias, 2008). While academic performances can be measured through standardized tests, social and emotional competencies are more difficult to measure due to the lack of standardized assessment tools. However, there are a variety of assessment tools available for measuring social and emotional competencies, including self-report surveys and teacher assessments (Zins et al., 2004).

Another challenge to SEL implementation in middle schools is the lack of time and resources (Romasz et al., 2004). Teachers may feel overwhelmed with the demands of academic instruction and may not have the time or resources to implement SEL strategies in the classroom. However, research has shown that SEL implementation can actually lead to improved academic performance, which may help alleviate some of these concerns (Durlak et al., 2011).

An additional challenge to SEL implementation in middle schools is the lack of teacher training and support (Albright et al., 2019). Some teachers may not feel comfortable with SEL instruction and may not have the necessary training or resources to implement SEL strategies in the classroom. School administrators can help address this challenge by providing professional development opportunities for teachers, as well as providing ongoing coaching, support, and feedback (Zins et al., 2004).

SEL in Rural Schools

SEL is an essential part of education that teaches students to manage their emotions, develop healthy relationships, and make responsible decisions (Zins et al., 2004). SEL implementation in rural schools is critical because students in these schools often face unique challenges such as lack of resources, poverty, and isolation. According to a report by the National Rural Education Association (2016), rural students often face poverty, limited access to healthcare, and fewer job opportunities than their urban counterparts. SEL can help students develop the resilience and coping skills needed to overcome these challenges (Chadwick, 2014).

Teacher training is an essential part of successful SEL implementation in rural schools. Teachers need to be trained on the principles of SEL and how to incorporate them into the curriculum. According to Durlak et al., (2011), teacher training is critical because it helps teachers understand the importance of SEL and how to teach it effectively. A well-designed SEL curriculum is critical for successful implementation in rural schools. The curriculum should be evidence-based and include activities that promote self-awareness, self-management, social awareness, relationship skills, and responsible decision-making. According to the Collaborative for Academic, Social, and Emotional Learning (CASEL, 2020b), a well-designed SEL curriculum can improve academic performances, reduce behavioral problems, and increase positive attitudes towards school. Community partnerships can also support SEL implementation in rural schools. Partnerships with local organizations, such as mental health providers and youth programs, can provide additional resources and support for students. According to the Rural School and Community Trust (2014), community partnerships can also help schools address the unique challenges faced by rural students.

Parental involvement is a critical factor in the successful implementation of social and emotional learning (SEL) programs in rural schools. When parents are involved in their children's education, they can reinforce the skills learned in school and model positive behaviors at home, which can enhance student social and emotional competencies (Lerner & Galambos, 2016). This can be especially important in rural areas, where students may have limited access to community resources and support systems outside of school.

The Rural School and Community Trust (2014) emphasizes building stronger partnerships between schools and communities through activities such as parent-teacher conferences, volunteering, and community events that promote SEL and positive youth development. This type of engagement has been shown to yield positive impacts on student academic achievement, as well as their social and emotional well-being (Epstein, 2011). However, in rural areas, parental involvement may face unique challenges due to geographic isolation, limited resources, and cultural differences (Gibson & Astor, 2017). However, schools can take steps to overcome these barriers by actively engaging parents and providing opportunities for them to participate in their children's education. This can include providing transportation and child care for parents who may have limited mobility or resources, offering flexible scheduling for parent-teacher conferences, and using technology to facilitate communication between teachers and parents (Baker, 2018).

SEL and COVID-19 Pandemic

The COVID-19 pandemic has intensified the urgency for reinforcing SEL in schools, especially in rural middle schools, with unique considerations given the varied impacts of the pandemic on different communities. The widespread stress, anxiety, and trauma induced by the pandemic have accentuated the significance of SEL in helping students, particularly in rural areas, to develop resilience and cope with these adversities (CASEL, 2020c). Rural middle schools, nested within close-knit communities, experienced unique challenges, including limited access to resources and increased isolation, necessitating an emphasis on contextualized, community-driven SEL approaches to address the multifaceted needs arising during and post-pandemic (Durlak et al., 2020; Hamilton & Ercikan, 2022).

Amidst these challenges, there lies an opportunity to refine and tailor SEL programs to be more responsive and inclusive to the varied needs exacerbated by the pandemic. For rural middle schools, the specific need is to develop and implement SEL strategies that are aligned with cultural norms and values of communities, thereby fostering a sense of belonging and connection amid pandemic disruptions (Durlak et al., 2020). By integrating voices and perspectives of community members, educators can ensure SEL programs are not only relevant but also reflect shared aspirations and experiences of students and their families during these unprecedented times (Stewart-Brown et al., 2000).

Furthermore, the post-pandemic landscape offers a conducive environment to prioritize and engrain SEL within the educational systems to facilitate academic success and holistic well-being. By leveraging locally available resources and community partnerships, rural middle schools can create supportive learning environments that are inclusive and resonant with the communal ethos, thus promoting students' social, emotional, and academic development in tandem (Hamilton & Ercikan, 2022). The integration of community-based learning and activities can further enhance the relevance and applicability of SEL programs in addressing the unique needs and experiences of rural students during the pandemic.

In the pursuit of fostering social and emotional well-being post-COVID-19, equity and inclusion stand as pivotal pillars. It is paramount for rural middle schools to ensure SEL programs are equitable and accessible to all students, addressing systemic disparities and barriers that may impede students' social and emotional development (CASEL, 2020c; Stewart-Brown et al., 2000). Addressing underlying issues such as socioeconomic disparities and limited access to mental health resources is crucial in delivering comprehensive and equitable SEL support to all students, acknowledging the diverse experiences and challenges encountered during the pandemic.

The post-pandemic era underscores the indispensability of SEL in fostering resilience and holistic well-being among students in rural middle schools. Prioritizing community engagement, teacher training, culturally relevant pedagogy, assessment, and evaluation, rural middle schools can actualize a harmonious and inclusive learning environment that is reflective of the communal values and experiences disrupted by the pandemic. By embedding equity and inclusivity in SEL implementation, schools can navigate the complexities of the post-pandemic world to nurture socially and emotionally resilient students.

Conclusion

The importance of SEL in rural middle schools cannot be overstated. SEL skills and competencies enable students to establish and maintain healthy relationships and effectively manage their emotions, leading to improved academic achievement and social competencies. However, rural communities and schools face significant challenges in addressing the social-emotional needs of students due to limited resources and other factors. Middle school is a critical period when students often encounter social-emotional challenges, making SEL even more essential. The alarming statistics regarding student well-being, such as feelings of sadness, hopelessness, and engaging in risky behaviors, highlight the urgent need for effective SEL programming in rural schools.

Implementing SEL effectively in rural middle schools necessitates a careful consideration of the unique cultural and communal attributes of rural communities. Rather than following a step-by-step approach, a holistic strategy, involving collaboration between administrators, educators, and stakeholders, is critical to developing culturally relevant and community-supported SEL programs (CASEL, 2022). By actively engaging with community members and families, schools can ensure that SEL curricula resonate with the students and are sustainable and adaptable to the changing needs and aspirations of the rural communities they serve.

Professional development for educators is pivotal for the effective integration of SEL strategies into teaching methodologies. Continuous training ensures that educators are well-equipped with the requisite skills and knowledge to deliver SEL programs that are in harmony with the values and beliefs of the community (Durlak et al., 2011). Emphasizing culturally relevant pedagogy within these training sessions is essential to ensure the seamless incorporation of SEL components without conflicting with prevailing cultural norms of the rural settings.

Furthermore, embedding SEL within the existing academic curriculum makes the learning experience more relevant and contextual for students. Incorporating community-based projects and activities reflective of community values enables students to develop social-emotional skills concurrently with academic skills (Schonert-Reichl et al., 2017). This integrated approach not only fosters a supportive learning environment but also contributes to better academic and social outcomes for students in rural middle schools.

Evaluative frameworks are essential in monitoring and optimizing the impact of SEL programs. Regular feedback and assessments and incorporating local knowledge and resources provide insights into the effectiveness of these programs and areas needing refinement (Taylor et al., 2017). A continual process of evaluation and feedback in rural settings involving students, parents, and community members, ensure SEL programs remain culturally relevant and adaptable to evolving needs of the community.

Building and maintaining strong relationships with families and the larger community are crucial for the successful implementation of SEL. By fostering partnerships and maintaining open communication with the community, schools can co-construct SEL goals and values that align with the expectations and aspirations of the community (Mapp & Kuttner, 2013). In closely knit rural communities, leveraging community engagements and parental involvement helps in aligning home and school learning environments and reinforcing a holistic and community-supported approach to SEL.

Understanding the history of SEL provides valuable insights into its evolution and its connection to educational philosophies and theories. The work of pioneers like John Dewey and Daniel Goleman, as well as organizations like CASEL, have contributed to the development and promotion of SEL as an essential component of education. Effective SEL programming involves the coordination of evidence-based practices, the establishment of school-wide goals, and a focus on continuous improvement through data analysis. Prioritizing social-emotional learning in rural middle schools is crucial for addressing the current crisis. By equipping students with SEL skills, providing necessary resources and support to educators, and implementing evidence-based practices, we can create a positive and conducive learning environment that promotes the well-being and success of students in rural communities. It is essential that we recognize the importance of SEL and take concrete steps to integrate it into the fabric of education in rural middle schools.

References

Allbright, T. N., Marsh, J. A., Kennedy, K. E., Hough, H. J., & McKibben, S. (2019). Social-emotional learning practices: Insights from outlier schools. *Journal of Research in Innovative Teaching & Learning, 12*(1), 35-52.

Baker, J. A. (2018). Parent involvement in rural education. In M. W. Berends, M. G. Springer, & D. Ballou (Eds.), *Handbook of research on school choice* (pp. 378-391). Routledge.

Bowen, S. J., & Graham, I. D. (2013). From knowledge translation to engaged scholarship: Promoting research relevance and utilization. *Archives of Physical Medicine and Rehabilitation, 94*(1), 3–8. https://doi.org/10.1016/j.apmr.2012.04.037

Brackett, M. A., Patti, J., Stern, R., Rivers, S. E., Elbertson, N. A., Chisholm, C., & Salovey, P. (2009). A sustainable, skill-based approach to building emotionally literate schools. In M. Hughes, H. L. Thompson, & J. B. Terrell (Eds.), *Handbook for developing emotional and social intelligence: Best practices, case studies, and strategies* (pp. 329-358). Pfeiffer/John Wiley.

Brackett, M. A., Reyes, M. R., Rivers, S. E., Elbertson, N. A., & Salovey, P. (2012). Assessing teachers' beliefs about social and emotional learning. *Journal of*

Psychoeducational Assessment, 30(3), 219-236.

Bridgeland, J., Bruce, M., & Hariharan, M. (2013). *The missing piece: A national teacher survey on how social and emotional learning can empower children and transform schools* (ED558068). ERIC. https://eric.ed.gov/?id=ED558068

Buchanan, R., Gueldner, B. A., Tran, O. K., & Merrell, K. W. (2009). Social and emotional learning in classrooms: A survey of teachers' knowledge, perceptions, and practices. *Journal of Applied School Psychology, 25*, 187–203. doi: 10.1080/15377900802487078

Chadwick, S. (2014). *Impacts of cyberbullying, building social and emotional resilience in schools*. Springer International.

Collaborative for Academic, Social, and Emotional Learning (CASEL) (2013). *The CASEL guide: Effective social and emotional learning programs*. https://schoolguide.casel.org/uploads/sites/2/2019/09/2021.6.15_School-Guide-Essentials.pdf

Collaborative for Academic, Social, and Emotional Learning (CASEL) (2020b). *What is SEL? Collaborative for Academic, Social, and Emotional Learning*. https://casel.org/what-is-sel/

Collaborative for Academic, Social, and Emotional Learning (CASEL) (2020c). *SEL amid COVID-19*. https://casel.org/sel-amid-covid-19/

Collaborative for Social, Academic, and Emotional Learning (2021a, September 9). *Our history*. https://casel.org/about-us/our-history/

Collaborative for Academic, Social, and Emotional Learning (CASEL) (2021b). *CASEL Guide to Schoolwide SEL Essentials*. https://schoolguide.casel.org/uploads/sites/2/2019/09/2021.6.15_School-Guide-Essentials.pdf

Collaborative for Academic, Social, and Emotional Learning. (2022). *Core SEL Competencies*. https://casel.org/fundamentals-of-sel/what-is-the-casel-framework/

Collie, R. J., Shapka, J. D., & Perry, N. E. (2012). School climate and social–emotional learning: Predicting teacher stress, job satisfaction, and teaching efficacy. *Journal of educational psychology, 104*(4), 1189.

Council of Chief State School Officers (April, 2019). *Measuring the school climate and social and emotional development: A navigation guide for states and districts*. https://ccsso.org/sites/default/files/2019-04/EC_CCSSO%20ESSA%20SEL%20Brief-FINAL.pdf

DePaoli, J. L., Atwell, M. N., & Bridgeland, J. (2017). *Ready to lead: A national principal survey on how social and emotional learning can prepare children and transform schools*. Civic Enterprises with Hart Research Associates.

www.aspeninstitute.org/wp-content/uploads/2017/11/ReadyToLead_ES_FINAL_EMBARGOED.pdf

Devaney, E., O'Brien, M. U., Resnik, H., Keister, S., & Weissberg, R. P. (2006). *Sustainable schoolwide social and emotional learning: Implementation guide and toolkit.* Collaborative for Academic, Social, and Emotional Learning (CASEL).

Dewey, J. (1916). *Democracy and education.* Macmillan. https://iwcenglish1.typepad.com/Documents/dewey_democracy_and_education.pdf

Dewey, J. (1933). *How we think.* Heath. http://www.gutenberg.org/ebooks/37423

Durlak, J. A., Domitrovich, C. E., Weissberg, R. P., & Gullotta, T. P. (2020). *Handbook of social and emotional learning: Research and practice.* Guilford Publications.

Durlak, J. A., Weissberg, R., Dymnicki, A. B., Taylor, R. D., & Schellinger, K. (2011). The impact of enhancing students' social and emotional learning: A meta-analysis of school-based universal interventions. *Child Development, 82,* 405-432.

Elias, M. J., & Haynes, N. M. (2008). Social competence, social support, and academic achievement in minority, low-income, urban elementary school children. *School Psychology Quarterly, 23*(4), 474.

Eisenberg, N., Valiente, C., & Eggum, N. D. (2010). Self-regulation and school readiness. *Early education and development, 21*(5), 681-698.

Epstein, J. L. (2011). *School, family, and community enterprise: Preparing educators and improving* schools (2nd ed.). Routledge.

Fullan, M., Miles, M. B., & Taylor, G. (1980). Organization development in schools: The state of the art. *Review of Educational Research,50*(1), 121-183.

Georgia Department of Education. (2022). *Georgia student health survey.* https://app.powerbi.com/view?r=eyJrIjoiY2E1OTI0Y2EtZTc2Yi00OTY2LWE0YTYtZGQ3NGZhN2NhOGE0IiwidCI6IjFhYTU

Gibson, C., & Astor, R. A. (2017). Toward a conceptual framework for understanding rural school-based mental health: A community-partnered research approach. *School Mental Health, 9*(3), 191-203.

Gingiss, P. L., Gottlieb, N. H., & Brink, S. G. (1994). Measuring cognitive characteristics associated with adoption and implementation of health innovations in schools. *American Journal of Health Promotion, 8*(4), 294-301.

Goleman, D. (1996). *Social Intelligence: Why it can matter more than IQ.* Bloomsbury Publishing.

Goleman, D. (2001). An EI-Based Theory of Performance. In C. Cherniss & D. Goleman (Eds.), *The emotionally intelligent workplace* (pp. 27-44). Jossey-Bass.

Hamilton, L. S., & Ercikan, K. (2022). COVID-19 and US schools: Using data to understand and mitigate inequities in instruction and learning. In F. Reimers (Ed.), *Primary and secondary education during COVID-19* (pp. 327-351).

Houghton Mifflin Harcourt. (2021). *Annual Educator Confidence Report (7)*. https://s3.amazonaws.com/prod-hmhco-vmg-craftcms-public/documents/2021-Educator-Confidence-Report.pdf

Houghton Mifflin Harcourt. (2022). *Annual Eductor Confidence Report (8)*. https://s3.amazonaws.com/prod-hmhco-vmg-craftcms-public/documents/2022-Educator-Confidence-Report.pdf

Hurd, N. M., Zimmerman, M. A., & Reischl, T. M. (2011). Role model behavior and youth violence: A study of positive and negative effects. *The Journal of Early Adolescence, 31*(2), 323-354.

Islam, M. H. (2015). Thorndike theory and it's application in learning. *At-Ta'lim: Jurnal Pendidikan, 1*(1), 37-47. https://ejournal.inzah.ac.id/index.php/attalim/article/download/166/139

Jennings, P. A., & Greenberg, M. T. (2009). The prosocial classroom: Teacher social and emotional competence in relation to student and classroom outcomes. *Review of Educational Research, 79*(1), 491-525. doi: 10.3102/0034654308325693

Jones, S. M., & Bouffard, S. M. (2012). Social Policy Report: Social and emotional learning in schools: From programs to strategies. *Society for Research in Child Development, 26*(4).

Jones, S. M., Bouffard, S. M., & Weissbourd, R. (2013) Educators' social and emotional skills vital to learning. *Phi Delta Kappan, 94*(8), 62–65.

Jones, S.M., & Kahn, J. (2017). *The evidence base for how we learn: Supporting students' social, emotional, and academic development—consensus statements of evidence from the Council of Distinguished Scientists*. National Commission on Social, Emotional, and Academic Development, The Aspen Institute.

Kam, C. M., Greenberg, M. T., & Walls, C. T. (2003). Examining the role of implementation quality in school-based prevention using the PATHS curriculum. *Prevention Science, 4*(1), 55-63. doi:10.1023/a:1021786811186

Kendziora, K., & Osher, D. (2016). Promoting children's and adolescents' social and emotional development: District adaptations of a theory of action. *Journal of Clinical Child & Adolescent Psychology, 45*(6), 797-811. https://doi.org/10.

1080/15374416.2016.1197834
Kendziora, K., & Yoder, N. (2016). *When districts support and integrate social and emotional learning (SEL): Findings from an ongoing evaluation of districtwide implementation of SEL*. Education Policy Center at American Institutes for Research.
Lerner, R. M., & Galambos, N. L. (2016). Positive youth development in rural settings. In P. L. Benson, K. J. Pittman, & J. L. Mahoney (Eds.), *Handbook of youth development* (2nd ed., 453-471). Sage.
Mahoney, J. L., Durlak, J. A., & Weissberg, R. (2018). An update on social and emotional learning outcome research. *Phi Delta Kappan, 100* (4), 18-23.
Main, K., & O'Neil, M. A. (2018). Social and emotional learning in the middle grades. In S.B.
Mertens & M. M. Caskey (Eds.), *Literature reviews in support of the middle level research agenda. A volume in the handbook of resources in middle level educa tion* (pp. 155–174). Information Age Publishing.
Mapp, K. L., & Kuttner, P. J. (2013). *Partners in education: A dual-capacity building framework for family-school partnerships*. SEDL (merged with AIR in 2015).
McCormick, L. K., Steckler, A. B., & McLeroy, K. R. (1995). Diffusion of innovations in schools: A study of adoption and implementation of school-based tobacco prevention curricula. *American Journal of Health Promotion, 9*, 210-219.
National Rural Education Association. (2016). *Rural students: Technology, coursework, and extracurricular activities*. https://www.nrea.net/wp-content/uploads/2016/07/Rural-Students-Technology-Coursework-and-Extracurricular-Activities-Report.pdf
Neth, E. L., Caldarella, P., Richardson, M. J., & Heath, M. A. (2020). Social-emotional learning in the middle grades: A mixed-methods evaluation of the Strong Kids Program. *RMLE Online, 43*(1), 1-13.
Payton, J. W., Weissberg, R., Durlak, J. A., Dymnicki, A. B., Taylor, R. D., Pachan, M. (2008). *The positive impact of social and emotional learning for kindergarten to eighth-grade students: Findings from three scientific reviews*. Collaborative for Academic, Social, and Emotional Learning (CASEL). http://casel.org/publications/positive-impact-of-social-and-emotional-learning-for-kindergarten-to-eighth-grade-students-findings-from-three-scientific-reviews
Ransford, C. R., Greenberg, M. T., Domitrovich, C. E., Small, M., & Jacobson, L.

(2009). The role of teachers' psychological experiences and perceptions of curriculum supports on the implementation of a social and emotional learning curriculum. *School Psychology Review, 38*, 510-532.

Romasz, T. E., Kantor, J. H., & Elias, M. J. (2004). Implementation and evaluation of urban school-wide social-emotional learning programs. *Evaluation and Program Planning, 27*(1), 89-103.

Rosenblatt, J. L., & Elias, M. J. (2008). Dosage effects of a preventive social-emotional learning intervention on achievement loss associated with middle school transition. *The Journal of Primary Prevention, 29*, 535-555.

Rural School and Community Trust. (2014). *Engaging rural oarents in their children's education.* https://www.ruraledu.org/user_uploads/file/engaging_rural_parents.pdf

Rural School and Community Trust. (2014). *Rural education and the importance of place: Where we stand.* https://www.ruraledu.org/articles.php?id=3205

Sameroff, A. (2010). Dynamic developmental systems: Chaos and order.

Schonert-Reichl, K. A. (2017). Social and emotional learning and teachers. *The Future of Children, 27*(1), 137-155.

Schonert-Reichl, K. A., Kitil, M. J., & Hanson-Peterson, J. (2017). *To reach the students, teach the teachers: A national scan of teacher preparation and social and emotional learning.* Collaborative for Academic, Social, and Emotional Learning (CASEL).

Schonert-Reichl, K. A., & Lawlor, M. S. (2010). The effects of a mindfulness-based education program on pre- and early adolescents' well-being and social and emotional competence. *Mindfulness, 1*(3), 137-151. doi: 10.1007/s12671-010-0011-8

Shonkoff, J. P., Phillips, D. A., & National Research Council. (2000). The developing brain. In *From neurons to neighborhoods: The science of early childhood development.* National Academies Press (US).

Stewart-Brown, S., Evans, J., Patterson, J., Petersen, S., Doll, H., Balding, J., & Regis, D. (2000). The health of students in institutes of higher education: An important and neglected public health problem? *Journal of Public Health Medicine, 22*(4), 492-499.

Stokes, E. L., Sass, S., Holm, J. M., Miller, G. J., West, E. M., Aguilera, S. E., & Zolkoski, S. M. (2021). Teacher perceptions of skills, knowledge, and resources needed to promote social and emotional learning in rural classrooms. *The Rural Educator,*

41(3), 1-11.

Taylor, R. D., Oberle, E., Durlak, J. A., & Weissberg, R. P. (2017). Promoting positive youth development through school-based social and emotional learning interventions: A meta-analysis of follow-up effects. *Child Development, 88*(4), 1156–1171.

Yeager, D. S. (2017). Social and emotional learning programs for adolescents. *The Future of Children, 27*(1), 73-94. /www.jstor.org/stable/44219022

Zins, J. E., Bloodworth, M. R., Weissberg, R. P., & Walberg, H. J. (2004). The scientific base linking social and emotional learning to school success. *Journal of Educational and Psychological Consultation, 15*(3-4), 313-337. doi: 10.1207/s1532768xjepc1503_5

Zolkoski, S. M., Aguilera, S. E., West, E. M., Miller, G. J., Holm, J. M., Sass, S., & Stokes, E. L. (2021). Teacher perceptions of skills, knowledge, and resources needed to promote social and emotional learning in rural classrooms. *The Rural Educator, 41*(3), 1-11.

CHAPTER 25

The Unique Needs of Generation Z in the Educational Work Environment

NILA BURT AND JOSEPH R. JONES

Introduction

TEACHER ATTRITION IS PROBLEMATIC and is well-documented, with differences in leadership style, school climate, high-stakes testing, and school resources have been noted as the primary reasons for leaving the profession (Owens, 2015; Pelfrey, 2020). Moreover, the loss of new teachers comes at great expense for communities in student educational losses and recruitment and hiring costs. Using the Baccalaureate and Beyond survey, Ingersoll et al., (2018) estimated that 44% of teachers left education within five years. Sutcher et al., (2019) showed a shortage of 64,000 teachers in 2015-2016, which increased to 112,000 by 2018. Ingersoll (2001) emphasized the harmful effects of migration and attrition, resulting in the loss of continuity and affecting the school climate. He described the relationship between teachers' decisions to stay in education or leave as a U-shaped curve; the younger teachers have higher departure rates than those close to retirement (2001). Young teachers remain the most prominent group leaving the profession (Ingersoll, 2004). Ingersoll (2004) noted many teachers leave education for personal and family reasons such as parental duties and retirement. However, a growing number of teachers leave due to job dissatisfaction stemming from a lack of support from administration and student discipline issues. Similarly, Farmer (2020) detailed several critical factors for teachers leaving the profession: high stakes testing, material differentiation for multi-level learners, paperwork, lack of parental involvement, and student discipline and violence.

To address the attrition challenge, the researchers utilized narrative inquiry to explore new teachers' (in or on the cusp of Generation Z) perceptions of the influence of leadership style on school climate. For this discussion, the study focused on two research questions: 1) What impact does relational leadership have on teachers' beliefs concerning their profession, and 2) How does relational leadership influence teachers' beliefs about their pedagogy?

After briefly exploring teacher attrition, it is beneficial to discuss the attributes of Generation Z so that we can provide a sociological framework for this study. In doing so, we aim to provide a greater conceptualization of attrition and its impact on new teachers who identify within these categories.

Generation Z and the Teaching Profession

Most teachers currently entering the teaching profession are considered Millennials, born between 1980 and 1994, or Generation Z, born after 1994 (Bako, 2018). Those entering the teaching profession who went to college directly following high school are in Generation Z. Characteristics of this group of young people and their specific needs are significant in understanding their perceptions of leadership and climate. Dimock (2019) characterized Generation Z as the most culturally and ethnically diverse generation in American history, with the entirety of their lives steeped in technology. Considering the average age of young people completing college in four years is 22, most new teachers are members of this diverse new generation. Stahl (2021) projected that by 2025, Generation Z would constitute 27% of the workforce and this generation would have a values-driven approach to careers, specifically mentioning their ethical concerns. When compared to millennials, she described these young people as more interested in job security, financial stability, employer transparency, and a willingness to work harder.

Schroth (2019) described Generation Z as highly educated, racially diverse, economically astute, and achievement-oriented. Bako (2018) called Generation Z digital natives and depicted them as far more pragmatic and career-focused than the previous generation. Although proficiency with technology as a digital native is beneficial, Schroth (2019) pointed out that the smartphone created a detrimental impact on communicating and interacting face-to-face. Whereas Generation Y (Millennials) prefer collaborative and team efforts, Generation Z is more comfortable with isolation (Bako, 2018). Generation Z has matured in an unsafe culture, resulting in emotional trauma, including increased anxiety and depression, (Schroth, 2019). Schroth also explained the impact of a lifetime of witnessing social justice movements influnce on Generation Z's perceptions. Generation Z is the most diverse and accepting of differences, yet globally unaware, and due to their proclivity toward isolation, they seek leaders who are risk-takers and self-sacrificing (Bako, 2018). Despite racial and ethnic diversity and passion for social justice issues, Schroth (2019) suggested that Generation Z is more likely to support free speech restrictions. The subjectiveness of their feelings and what is "objectively offensive" will drive employers to clarify speech and behaviors within the workplace, according to Schroth (2019). Additionally, the parents of Generation Z similarly provided financial freedom during high school, thus reducing the need for jobs while preparing for higher education (Bako, 2018). Due to the increased economic support from their parents, as they enter the workforce, Schroth (2019) postulated that they would arrive with a lack of work experience. Schroth (2019) anticipated the growing need for leaders to compensate for Generation Z's lack of life skills due to overprotective parents who removed obstacles and only gave positive feedback, thus producing inabilities to cope in the workplace.

For comparative purposes and because a number of new teachers are on the cusp of Generation Z and Millennials, it is beneficial to briefly discuss Millennials. Bako (2018) characterized Millennials as technologically proficient, pragmatic, healthy, and clever, likely not to make the mistakes of previous generations. Dimock (2019) described this generation as growing up in the shadows of the wars in Iraq and Afghanistan, becoming politically active when Obama was elected, and entering the workforce during an economic recession, as the "slow start" generation. Millennials have extensive educational, financial, and personal strengths (Bako, 2018). However, Bako commented that this preparation has often resulted in job dissatisfaction due to unrealistic expectations from leaders and employment responsibilities.

As such, it is important to conceptualize how leadership intersects with Generation Z and Millennials. Panwar and Mehta (2019) described leadership as "crafting a context for invention and inclusion in the face of ambiguity and the unforeseen" (p. 66). They explicitly recommended leaders develop those skills to equip Generation Z. Schroth (2019) echoed the need for leaders to manage expectations for Generation Z as they expect clear targets and positive attitudes from employers. Among the list of leader attributes important to Generation Z, Schroth (2019) listed: providing a checklist, facilitating communication, reinforcing culture, clarifying their specific purpose, explaining the significance of their position, and giving feedback. Both generations expect their ideas to be appreciated and considered (Bako, 2018; Schroth, 2019).

According to Robinson's (2021a) research, the effects of the COVID-19 pandemic resulted in millennials becoming more engaged at work. Robinson (2021a) reported an increase from 35% to 75% in 2020 in work engagement, although he mentions working from home could be part of this causality. Robinson discussed how engagement is measured by delineating five variables: the flexibility of remote work, how employers communicate a plan of action, preparation for remote work, shared information, and well-being. Robinson pointed out millennials want to be in the loop, understand their role and expectations within the organization, and have a knowledgeable sense of its vision. Indeed, employment leadership plays an important role in the professional careers of Generation Z and Millennials.

After briefly examining teacher attrition, Generation Z, and Millennials we will next discuss the methodology utilized in the study, specifically focusing on the demographics of the school community, the participants involved in the study, data collection, analysis, and the theoretical framework that guided the analysis.

A Rationale for Narrative Inquiry

In qualitative research, the researcher is often personally immersed, observing, and gathering data to understand and describe a phenomenon (Creswell, 2014). Jones (2010) suggested researchers use the qualitative research approach to comprehend participants' social settings from their perspectives rather than making predictions or testing hypotheses. Creswell (2014) also discussed choosing a methodology by considering the study's problem, personal experiences, and the audience critiquing the research. Likewise, Patton (2015) defined qualitative research as interpreting humans' meaning-making process with personal experiences. He encourages in-depth, open-ended interviews, direct observations, and written communication to interpret and understand experiences.

In the study, the researchers utilized narrative inquiry, a qualitative approach which "aims at understanding and making meaning of experience through conversations, dialogue, and participants in the ongoing lives of the research participants" (Smit, 2018, p. 79). Narrative inquiry examines human life through a lens that characterizes experiences to illuminate the culture (Patton, 2015). Connelly and Clandinin (1990) suggested that educational research, in particular, should focus on the participants' stories. They claimed that life narratives are the context for making meaning in school scenarios. Carter (1993) posited that stories from teachers capture the complexity of their lived experience and inform others about how to prepare for the profession.

Moreover, narrative inquiry involves a relationship between the researcher and the participant. The researcher's involvement in narrative studies allows a co-construction of events by the researcher and the participants based on the dyadic interpersonal relationship experiences and knowledge of the phenomenon under investigation. The shared experiences during field operations and interviews provide needed constructs for the deep understanding required in qualitative research (Connelly and Clandinin, 1990). In fact, researchers conducting a narrative inquiry must focus on the participants and their stories and be aware of their part of the process (Smit, 2018).

Demographics

This study was conducted in a large public school district in the southern United States with a district population of 31,899 students. The population of the city is 189,296. The district student ethnicity is approximately 58% Black, 26% white, 5% multiracial, 8% Hispanic, and 3% Hawaiian or American Indian. Males comprise 51% of the student population and 79%

receive free or reduced lunch. Special education students make up 12.74% of the student population, with 67.98% of that population male. There are approximately 2,245 full-time teachers (Niche, 2020; U.S. Census Bureau, n.d.). There are similar graduation rates between races, and the district has traditionally higher graduation rates than the state averages.

The city has been declining in population in the last decade. It is adjacent to one of the world's largest military bases, contributing to its diversity. Poverty is a significant factor in the area, with a poverty rate of 21.15%. According to the Niche (2020) website, there is a 16:1 teacher ratio, and teachers have an average salary of $54,200, compared to an average household income of $63,902. The median house value is $141,700, and rent averages $877 monthly. The district spends an average of $11,716 per student, 59% on instruction, 35% on support services, and 6% on other expenses (Niche, 2020; U.S. Census Bureau, n.d.).

Although there are relatively equal numbers of high school graduates among different ethnicities and races, Caucasians are twice as likely to have a bachelor's degree (Niche, 2020; U.S. Census Bureau, n.d.). The city was once rich in cotton mills, which supported a wide middle-class base. It is now home to several large companies and several well-respected private schools which have impacted public schools in the county.

This high school has 92 teachers, 19 paraprofessionals, and four administrators and is the largest of the eight high schools in the district. Seventeen teachers are within their first five years of teaching. Of the 17 teachers, only two of those teachers are from historically underrepresented groups. Eight percent of the teachers at the identified school are African-American, 4% are Hispanic, and 2% are Pacific Islanders. Only 33% of the teachers are males and the administrative staff is White, with two females and two males. According to the local district website, this school's overall performance is higher than 83% of schools in the state and is the highest in the district. The graduation rate is 96%, and 61.5% of graduates are considered college and career-ready. The state's Department of Education calculated climate star rating from the state's student health survey, the state's school personnel survey, the state's parent survey, student discipline data, and attendance records for students, teachers, staff, and administrators. The state assessment score of this school was 86.1 in 2019, with a five-star school climate rating.

Participants

Maxwell (2013) described purposeful sampling as a procedure used to select informative research representatives as experts in an area one is studying. He listed five goals of purposeful selection: achieving representativeness, capturing the heterogeneity in the population, deliberately selecting participants critical to the research theory, establishing comparisons to show reasons for differences between settings or individuals, and selecting participants who will provide a productive relationship, or enable the researcher to answer the research question. Group characteristic sampling was implemented for this study to evaluate "a specific information-rich group that can reveal and illuminate important group patterns" (Patton, 2015, p. 267).

Five teachers at the high school, anonymously named Martinville, who were in their first five years of teaching, participated in the study. The participants provided background information about their experiences during their initial interviews before beginning their teaching careers. Two participants resigned in March 2022 for the following school year, and three continued teaching.

James

James is 26-years-old, is in his fourth year teaching, and is from a mid-sized city in the state. He attended a liberal-arts high school and graduated from the local university. He began college majoring in environmental science, but he changed his major to secondary education. James enjoyed his science classes in college and appreciated his ability to "dabble" in so many classes during his program of study. He has broad-field certification in science, emphasizing earth and space science. After completing his science degree with an alternate math/science certification program, James added his secondary education.

Sam

Sam is in his second year of teaching mathematics and is 24-years-old. He grew up "in the dead middle of the state" and jokingly added that his town would be at the crease if one folded the map of the state both ways. Sam attended college at the local university in the same city as Martinville. Sam and James both attended this college and attained their education degrees through the alternate STEM education preparation program, but they did not attend at the same time, nor did they have the same experience with the program.

Holly

Holly grew up in the city where she now lives and work. She was the only participant who began college, intending to become an educator. Holly is 25-years-old and graduated from Martinville. Many of her immediate and extended family are educators. Holly followed her sister to a state university for a couple of years because her sister had a softball scholarship. She returned home and finished her degree at the local university. She majored in middle grades education, and she gained secondary education certification by passing the state's certification exam.

Sara

Sara is 26 and 12 days shy of being a part of Generation Z. She is a science teacher in her second year, and like James and Sam, she obtained her education degree through an alternate degree program. Sara attended a large state university specializing in science and technology in the Midwest. She began her education as an undetermined engineering major, although she initially applied for physics and secondary education.

Joe

Joe is a 27-year-old special education teacher in his third year of teaching. He attended a liberal arts magnet high school for one year, then transferred as a sophomore to Martinville, where he currently works. Joe went to a small liberal arts college in the state for a year and then transferred to a more prominent religious-based university to complete his undergraduate degree in business administration and play baseball. When Joe graduated, he started applying to large local corporations. The head baseball coach at

Martinville informed Joe of an open coaching position. Joe did not hesitate, and he immediately began his master's degree in special education at a local university.

Theoretical Framework

Smit (2018) credited Ospina and Uhl-Bien (2012) as the pioneers of Relational Leadership Theory (RLT). According to Smit (2018), Ospina and Uhl-Bien identified leadership as a social process of influence through social constructs, or in other words, how communication transpires between leaders and followers based on an accepted list of social norms. Uhl-Bien (2006) defined RLT as "the study of both relationships (interpersonal relationships as outcomes of or as contexts for interactions) and relational dynamics (social interactions, social constructions) of leadership" (p. 667).

Uhl-Bien (2004) argued that RLT moves from hierarchical leadership, a top-down, pyramid-shaped organizational structure, to an influence process between leaders and followers to create dynamic institutional change. Uhl-Bien (2006) theorized relational leadership differs from personal relationships in that it starts with processes that center relational realities rather than people. She also considered leadership in terms of social constructions made through rich connections among members of an organization.

Leaders who practice relational leadership build interpersonal relationships, which increases communication (Uhl-Bien, 2006). Leaders who communicate their vision and are transparent create positive school climates, contributing to a teacher's well-being (Lasater, 2016; Reitman & Karge, 2019; Wigford & Higgins, 2019). Ultimately, new teachers who are fostered emotionally are more likely to remain in the profession (Wigford & Higgins, 2019). These interconnected challenges within schools provide a unique and challenging task for school leaders. It is necessary to examine challenges through a relational theory lens.

Sutcher et al., (2016) revealed that 42% of teachers left the profession because of dissatisfaction with the administration due to a lack of support, input, and control over teacher decisions resulting in unhappiness with working conditions. These researchers reported that administrative support was the most consistent factor associated with teacher attrition. Kraft et al., (2016) surveyed teachers and illustrated how school leadership style predicted teacher retention decisions and leaders who supported teachers influenced retention. They analyzed reciprocal relationships between leadership styles, organizational capacity, teacher practices, and student achievement and found multiple correlations. The Learning Policy Institute (2017) concluded teachers' perceptions of administrators were a dominant factor in career decisions; leaders who set clear expectations, supported and encouraged, and recognized staff increased teacher retention.

Tran and Smith (2020) also examined teachers' needs in different career stages, human resource strategies, and how principals should intentionally support teachers. They showed a need to approach teacher retention differently in the various stages of a teaching career. They summarized that beginning teachers' concerns include day-to-day functional skills and a need for encouragement and recognition.

In addition to meeting the needs of new teachers, providing a positive culture is necessary for the success of all teachers in the building (Jones & Watson, 2017). Branson and Marra (2019) remarked it is essential in today's workplace for leaders "to know more about the people they are leading and not just about what people do at work each day" (p. 100). They further explained that employees need to feel included, valued for their skill diversity, and given opportunities to focus on mental and physical well-being. Teachers interviewed by CooperGibson Research (2018) felt resigned to excessive, unsustainable workloads, feelings of unwarranted scrutiny, and a lack of support from the administration. CooperGibson Research (2018) recommended increasing the level of support from school leaders to "reduce feelings of pressure in terms of scrutiny, accountability, and workload" (p. 5). They suggested principals focus on teacher well-being, including assistance in managing stress, and help with performance and policy procedures (CooperGibson, 2018).

Data Collection and Analysis

The researchers conducted two semi-structured interviews (approximately 60 minutes each) with open-ended questions, allowing for flexibility for the interviewer and interviewee to follow important concepts during the interview process to ensure a more knowledge-producing experience (Denzin & Lincoln, 2017). The participants' stories were coauthored in the dyadic nature of narrative interviewing.

The first interview in this study aimed to clarify the educational background and experiences, concentrate on relationships between teachers and school-based administrators, and discuss professional futures. A variation of Seidman's (2019) three-interview technique was implemented, combining the first and second interviews to clarify educational background and experiences and concentrate on relationships between teachers and school-based administrators. The second interview included discussions about professional futures based on data collected in the previous interview. All interviews were conducted on Zoom; coding included three stages: organizing data and familiarization, reducing data and fracturing into open codes with axial coding for chunking resulting in themes, and finally, connecting the main themes into categories which allow the participants' narratives to be represented holistically with appropriate rich, descriptive detail (Patton, 2015).

Themes and Findings

The data analysis revealed several valuable findings, yet the purpose of this article will focus on results specific to Generation Z and leadership interactions. For these participants, supportive climates and administrative presence and feedback were paramount in creating the positive environment needed to continue in education.

Supportive Climates

Sam and Sara struggled more than the other participants with pedagogical issues and were also the two participants who did not return to the classroom the following year. Despite parent or community influences, Sara struggled with setting expectations and determining how to hold students responsible to academic and behavioral expectations. Sara felt she struggled with classroom management, felt defeated at times, and worried about the rampant cheating, as Sam did. Sara shared, "it's demoralizing when students are not concerned with missing assignments." As a Summa Cum Laude graduate in high school and college, Sara expressed that it was hard to understand a lack of effort from students.

Sam, much like Sara, had difficulties with classroom management.

Sam struggled with enforcing school rules such as allowing students to leave campus, the attendance policy, the dress code policies about hats and hoods, and the cell phone policy. He worried that some rules' enforcement ruin relationships that might keep students from learning. He viewed it as a weakness he needed to work on to be compliant but believes the older guard ("old and crotchety") should reconsider the rules. He lamented:

> If I see a kid who is already bouncing in and out of ISS [in-school suspension], missing lots of class time, who I can see is taking notes or working on a problem, and he has his hat on, and I have to decide between telling him to take his hat off which would disrupt his work, he might retaliate, we might bicker a little, and he might give up for the day or let him work in peace, I am 100% of the time going to let him work. I had a lot of kids, who I know are routine troublemakers, tell me they appreciated me not being on their case for every little thing.

Sam had practica and student teaching experiences in other schools with more stringent rules and felt concerned about students' suspensions for extended periods for behavior offenses. Sam recognized the students' access to apps that solve math problems but felt he could usually outsmart them. He tried to work around it to avoid writing referrals for cheating.

The participants with positive attitudes and experiences returned with excitement about the prospect of a new year. Sara and Sam were the only participants who did not return. Sara struggled with the perception of teaching, frequently mentioning how she primarily had a science degree.

Moreover, participants devised strategies to create successful work/home boundaries. For example, James tries not to take work home, but he struggles with not responding to emails, especially when assignments are due or when he knows the student worked late. He extended his work schedule to Sunday afternoons, as did Sara, to get ready for the next week, modify/improve lesson plans or assessments, or complete necessary grading.

Similarly, Sara did not do well with time management. She adjusted when her husband complained about how stressed she seemed. She captured the tension in the following vignette:

It wasn't working for me and my husband. So I just kind of had to draw the line and say, if I'm not at school, then I'm not going to do schoolwork. And I had to be okay with not grading everything. I kind of had to figure out when it's okay to just put something in the blue filing [not grade it]. I don't know. I still don't think I've got it figured out.

Sam and Holly, the youngest participants, reported the least amount of stress. Their ability to extend themselves is possibly because of their love for the profession. Sam attributed his ability to balance to a peer with whom he student taught:

I learned this from [the cooperating teacher], and he taught me this like my second week there. I don't even know if he remembers telling me this, but he told me, he said, "Look, you get here at 7:30, and you leave to go to practice at 3:45. Your work will be here at 7:00 a.m. You leave it at school. You leave it; you leave it at school. It'll be here. Those papers will get graded, whether today, tomorrow, or the next day. They'll get in before the deadline. But when you're at school, you work.

Sam embraced the words, remembering a manager he had at Starbucks saying, "If you have time to lean, you have time to clean."

Holly struggled with balancing work and stress the previous year with teaching in-person and virtually. However, she admits it may have been because she was also pregnant while obtaining a certification in gifted education. Holly feels as if she is managing better this year. She tries to leave by 4:30 and grades only ten essays each day. Joe has late hours from coaching, but he does not generally bring work home. He values time with family and "makes his weekends his weekends."

The data suggest that participants found meaningful and satisfying work and needed the energy to succeed. They discussed the sense of family, the consistency and application of high standards, opportunities for students to connect, and how they managed stress. Each agreed that Martinville had a supportive culture with a favorable climate and unanimously preferred their experiences at the school over other teaching or practica experiences. The participants accredited the school's climate to the leadership, expectations, and attention to detail in school culture. The school climate provided a working environment that supported their social-emotional needs as well as the needs of their students.

Administrative Presence and Feedback

Coleman (2017) postulated that teachers who received positive feedback from school leaders were less likely to leave the profession. Young teachers, especially those in Generation Z, listed meaningful feedback as one of the most desirable attributes of a leader (Bako, 2018; Schroth, 2019). The participants in this study desired more interactions with leaders and wanted feedback on performance. Thus, administrative presence and feedback frequency emerged from the participants' focus on the disruption COVID-19 played on the infrequency of school leaders' presence in the classroom, interactions with participants, and lack of performance feedback.

The school district in which the high school is located has required modified teacher evaluations for three consecutive school years. Evaluations from administrators have been informal and infrequent. Three of the participants never experienced a complete formal evaluation from the state teacher evaluation system.

James experienced at least one complete evaluation in his first year of teaching and has missed the detail and feedback from leaders in the past few years. He believes having frequent formative assessments from the administration was helpful, and having an administrator in the classroom kept students and teachers "on their toes." Before the pandemic, an administrator's presence in the classroom aided student accountability, leading to improved learning stakes. James enjoyed the moments when administrators would "pop their heads in the classroom" for several reasons. James believed the action made students aware that administrators are "not just this big figurehead to be feared" and that we are "there helping to hold them accountable." Also, students see their teachers being evaluated and held accountable.

Sam enjoyed leaders "bouncing in and out of classes for a little bit" but was worried if he had missed something or if there was a problem.

Sam's evaluator praised him for his job performance, and Sam appreciated it "because kids aren't going to tell me that!" Teachers, Sam noted, reassure students all day and would appreciate the same from leaders "even when we don't need it."

James suggested leaders meet with teachers "frequently and cordially" for a type of check-in. He felt that formal evaluations were "impersonal" since the evaluator acted as if they were "a fly on the wall." Usually, evaluators try not to disturb the learning environment. James reiterated the importance of affirmation and reinforcement to do the best possible in the following anecdote:

> In conjunction with that [the formal evaluation], a personal interview... having a conversation... What's going well? What can we do to, you know, keep supporting you? I would find conversations like that very helpful, just because feedback, whether positive, negative, or neutral, will give you information to work with, but in that context, okay, so how was your year? How did that go? Almost like coaching to get a debrief for how they feel, are they overwhelmed?

James saw informal conversations as a way for teachers to "feel a little more in touch with the administration" and improve interpersonal relationships with the school leaders. Sam agreed with James and suggested that leaders should have one-to-one conversations with teachers, especially new teachers. The gesture would "be cool" if administrators brought a coffee to his classroom during planning, inquired how school and classes were going, and asked how they could offer support without formal observation. Sam shared that he was not aware of what he could ask for as a new teacher and wished the administration would ask him what he needed. Holly agreed with Sam and James that a personal conversation about each observation would be more beneficial to her, rather than receiving only written feedback of her pedagogy.

The participants felt a disconnect with administrators and professional feedback on classroom performance. School leaders spent very little time in the classroom during evaluations. The teachers in this study did not feel they were given significant feedback or assistance in connection with the evaluations. Several participants desired more informal, personal communication from school leaders when discussing administrative feedback. James described the interactions he desired with leaders in addition to evaluations:

> I feel like in conjunction with an evaluation, a personal interview where you know you just kind of having a conversation almost like what we're having like, What's going well? What can we do to, you know, keep supporting you? What do you feel could be added, or what do you feel like? Maybe it doesn't work, and I would find conversations like that very helpful, just because feedback of inequality, whether positive, negative, neutral, will give you information to work with.

Sam also recommended more communication with administrators. He said administrators often enter his room for just a few minutes but do not interact with anyone, including him. When an administrator enters his room, he would appreciate a comment such as, "Hey, you're doing a good job, thanks." He mentioned the expectation for teachers to reassure students regularly and how the same reassurance would also benefit teachers. Similarly, Holly also desires more reassurance.

James believes evaluations assist teachers in avoiding complacency. The anticipation of evaluations causes teachers to be consistently aware of classroom practices due to fear of inadequate assessments in their evaluation. As such, James believes that teacher evaluations are the catalyst that prevents apathetic instruction. Sara wanted more feedback this past year because she was "so new to teaching" and did not feel that she received constructive feedback in her teaching program and that her master's program lacked that same component. Oddly, Sara received more feedback during the "Covid" year than this year. She said, "this year, it seems a little not there." She wondered if feedback might not be necessary because "the things in her classroom are good." Sara, having not experienced a traditional evaluation, did not know how truncated the evaluation times requirements were from pre-Covid years. She yearned for feedback from school leaders and wanted to hear the positive reinforcement that things were going well, which she said would be "nice to hear, I'm a bit of a perfectionist, and I want to be better." Sam added, "the biggest thing about being young is that I don't have enough experience to be sure of myself quite yet. So having a little reassurance helps a lot."

Sam valued the feedback from peers more than school leaders. His peers are dealing with similar issues and better understand his struggles. He believes that talking to younger teachers might be preferable to his department head because, although she is "awesome," he feels as if she has routines in place and has forgotten what "it is like to be dumb." Sam has not had a positive experience concerning discipline practices with the administrator in charge of discipline, whom he feels does not like him, and his department head, whom he described as antiquated. They both have insisted he be "harder" on his kids. Sam believes they might be hard on him because they want him to improve as a teacher. However, Sam "did not have the emotional energy" to deal with those issues.

Holly has only been evaluated twice in the past year. She longs for more care from her leaders. She captured this longing in the following anecdote: "How do you think that went? Do you think that could have been better?" As a teacher, she wants "to evolve and change and get better." Joe received "good and sufficient" feedback. He thought six evaluations were enough, and teachers should strive to meet standards, even overachieve if possible. Ultimately, Joe reflected, it "goes back to making sure we meet the kids' needs," and he argues we have enough feedback to ensure that process.

James had the most experience with the evaluation process and was comfortable with expectations. He feels comfortable with his evaluator, who was previously a science teacher, and stated they had a good rapport. However, Sara had the same evaluator and did not share the same experience as James. Sara does not see the value in the evaluation she received. She said:

> But I don't want to call him out... especially this year. Last year it was better. He seemed really distracted. When he was in my room for my evaluation, I was like, "Am I being evaluated or not?" He came in, he did not pick up my lesson plans, and I'm like, I put those together. Can you at least pretend to look at them? And then he sat in the back, and he just did not seem like he was paying attention. But, yeah, it's one of those things where I wish I could

get a little bit more constructive feedback. I appreciate the positive reviews, but I do want to know what I can do better or how I can do things, or even if it's just like, hey, I saw this happen.

Sam's evaluator is a new assistant principal who previously taught science and mathematics at Martinville. She was helpful to Sara but "scares the begizzes" out of Sam. He does not know why his anxiety level increases when she enters his classroom. The evaluator tells Sam to "continue doing what you're doing." Sam wishes the administration would be more specific, give suggestions, evaluate more frequently, and interact with him during evaluations. Holly mirrored Sam's thoughts and was disappointed that the evaluator did not return after she found out the class was only reading silently. She wanted feedback from a more critical rather than surface-level instruction. Holly and Sam think administrators do not have much time to work with them. Joe was not sure who evaluated him.

Implications and Discussion

The findings in this study offer implications that we posit are important to consider when preparing future school administrators and providing professional development for current school administrators.

First, a transformative shift in administrative training requires professional development or college preparation in relational leadership. The participants described relationships with peers, students, and school leaders as critical to the culture and climate of a positive working environment. Leaders who provide opportunities for growth in this area and maintain high expectations for students and staff are effective. Second, Generation Z teachers lack internal reflective tools and construct meaning from external reassurance and feedback about their pedagogy. Participants desired frequent feedback on classroom performance, discussions about professional goals, and individual attention from school leaders. Indeed, the relational aspects of schools is incredibly important (Jones, 2020). Furthermore, Holly, Sara, and Sam mentioned wanting immediate reassurance from administrators during evaluations. James and Sam suggested informal conversations with administrators to check-in and support throughout the school year.

These requests mirrored the leadership needs Schroth (2019) and Panwar and Mehta (2019) recommended for Generation Z. These researchers noted how leaders would need to manage expectations and craft "a context for invention and inclusion in the face of ambiguity and the unforeseen" (p. 66) to facilitate this generations' employment journey.

Conclusion

Based on findings from this study, administrators should consider providing thoughtful, genuine commentary on pedagogical performance. New teachers need to know they are valued, and their job is essential. It is also necessary to consider the specific needs of Generation Z. They are dedicated to their profession and classroom practices, but they need informal feedback, formal evaluations, and frequent reassurance from school leaders. Administrators should consider visiting classrooms regularly and rotate, so each leader visits classrooms other than the teachers they evaluate; in doing so, teachers receive feedback from multiple sources, which is important to this generation of new teachers. Listening to the ideas of young teachers in this generation can benefit school leaders while giving them a voice in school decision-making to which they feel entitled. The participants desired a more personal relationship with the school leaders and valued their input. Where research showed teacher evaluation as a fearful experience throughout the state, these teachers wanted more interaction and constructive feedback from evaluations.

After analyzing the data, the most poignant discovery in this study was the desire of young teachers to be known personally by their administrators, which is antithetical to the belief of an older school leader. Generation Z explicitly expects this level of personal affiliation with supervisors. Every participant shared that they desired a school leader who was invested in learning about teachers' personal and professional background. For these participants, relationships are the cornerstone of their professional journeys.

***This chapter first appeared in the *Journal of Educational Leadership and Policy Studies*.

Burt, N. J., & Jones, J. R. (2023). The Unique Needs of Generation Z in the Educational Work Environment. *Journal of Educational Leadership and Policy Studies*, 7(1).

References

Bako, M. (2018). Different leadership style choices, different generations. *Prizren Social Science Journal, 2*(2), 127-143. https://bit.ly/2VV3FG8

Branson, C. M., & Marra, M. (2019). Leadership as a relational phenomenon: What this means in practice. *Research in Educational Administration & Leadership, 4*(1), 81-108. https://doi.org/10.30828/real/2019.1.4

Carter, K. (1993). The place of story in the study of teaching and teacher education. *Educational Researcher, 22*(1), 5-12, http://www.jstor.org/stable/1177300

Casey, K. (1995). The new narrative research in education. *Review of Research in Education, 21*, 211-253. http://www.jstor.org/stable/116782

Coleman, S. S. (2017). *Examining public school educators' perceptions of variables studied in correlation to teacher attrition issues within a select rural school district in the state of Mississippi: Implications for teacher retention*. Semantic Scholar. https://radar.auctr.edu/islandora/object/cau.td:2017_coleman_shawonna_s

Connelly, F. M., & Clandinin, D. J. (1990). Stories of Experience and Narrative Inquiry. *Educational Researcher, 19*(5), 2-14. https://doi.org/10.3102/0013189X019005002

CooperGibson Research. (2018). *Factors affecting teacher retention: Qualitative investigation*. Department for Education: Brentwood, England. https://bit.ly/3ulwnNp

Creswell, J. W. (2014). *Research Design: Qualitative, Quantitative and Mixed Methods Approaches* (4th ed.). Sage.

Denzin, N. K., & Lincoln, Y. S. (2017). *The Sage handbook of qualitative research* (5th ed.). Sage Publications. ISBN-13: 978-1483349800

Dimock, M. (2019). *Defining generations: Where millennials end and generation z begins*. Pew Research Center. https://pewrsr.ch/3xV6MLJ

Farmer, D. (2020). Teacher attrition: The impacts of stress. *Delta Kappa Gamma Bulletin, 87*(1), 41-50.

Ingersoll, R. (2001). Teacher turnover and teacher shortages: An organizational analysis. *American Educational Research Journal, 38*(3), 499-534. https://www.jstor.org/stable/3202489

Ingersoll, R. (2004). Four myths about America's teacher quality problem. *Yearbook of the National Society for the Study of Education, 103*(1), 1-33. https://bit.ly/3o9dxb7

Ingersoll, R., Merrill, L., & May, H. (2012). Retaining teachers: How preparation matters. *Educational Leadership, 69*(8), 30-34. https://bit.ly/2XLyQVc

Ingersoll, R., Merrill, L., & Stuckey, D. (2018). *Seven trends: The transformation of the teaching force*. (ED593467). ERIC. https://eric.ed.gov/?id=ED593467

Jones, D., & Watson, S. B. (2017). The relationship between administrative leadership behaviors and teacher retention in Christian schools. *Journal of Research on Christian Education, 26*(1), 44-55. https://doi.org/10.1080/10656219.2017.1282903

Jones, J. R. (2010) *Homophobia in Secondary Schools: An Investigation of Teachers' Perceptions of Homophobia Through a Collaborative Professional Development Program*. University of Rochester. https://bit.ly/3Pa9KW1

Jones, J. (2020). A Virus, Remote Learning, and Educational Leaders: How Relational Pedagogy Informs My Leadership during a Crisis. *Teachers College Record.*

Kraft, M. A., Marinell, W. H., & Shen-Wei Yee, D. (2016). School organizational contexts, teacher turnover, and student achievement: Evidence from panel data. *American Educational Research Journal, 53*(5), 1411-1449. https://www.jstor.org/stable/44245351?seq=1#metadata_info_tab_contents

Kreiner, G. E., Hollensbe, E. C., & Sheep, M. L. (2009). Balancing borders and bridges: Negotiating the work-home interface via boundary work tactics. *Academy of Management Journal, 52*, 704–730.

Lasater, K. (2016). School leader relationships: The need for explicit training on rapport, trust, and communication. *Journal of School Administration Research and Development, 1*(2), 19-26.

Learning Policy Institute. (2017). *The role of principals in addressing teacher shortages*. https://bit.ly/3AVZlFW

Maxwell, J. A. (2013). *Qualitative research design: An interactive approach* (3rd ed.). Sage. ISBN13: 9781412981194

Merriam, S. B., & Grenier, R. S. (2019). *Qualitative research in practice: Examples for discussion and analysis*. Jossey-Bass.

Mishler, E. G. (1995). Models of narrative analysis: A typology. *Journal of Narrative and Life History, 5*(2), 87-123.

Niche. (2020). *Muscogee county schools*. Niche.

Ospina, S., & Uhl-Bien, M. (2012). *Advancing Relational Leadership Research: A Dialogue Among Perspectives*. Information Age Publishing.

Owens, S. J. (2015). *Georgia's teacher dropout crisis*. Georgia Department of Education. https://bit.ly/3jMqiDy

Panwar, S., & Mehta, A. (2019). Fostering Leadership in Generation Z: Onus on Whom? *IUP Journal of Soft Skills, 13*(3), 65-70. https://www.proquest.com/scholarly-journals/fostering-leadership-generation-z-onus-on-whom/docview/2311514156/se-2?accountid=14800

Patton, M. Q. (2015). *Qualitative research and evaluation methods* (4th ed.). Sage.

Pelfrey, R. (2020). *2020 Georgia K-12 teacher and leader workforce executive summary*. The Governor's Office of Student Achievement. https://bit.ly/3yog6bq

Reitman, G. C., & Karge, B. D. (2019). Investing in teacher support leads to teacher retention: Six supports administrators should consider for new teachers. *Multicultural Education, 27*(1), 7-18.

Robinson, J. (2021a). *What disruption reveals about engaging millennial employees*. Gallop Workplace. https://bit.ly/3iiqGdB

Schroth, H. (2019). Are You Ready for Gen Z in the Workplace? *California Management Review, 61*(3), 5–18. https://doi.org/10.1177/0008125619841006

Seidman, I. (2019). *Interviewing as qualitative research: A guide for researchers in education and the social sciences* (5th ed.). Teachers College Press.

Smit, B. (2018). Expanding educational leadership theories through qualitative relational methodologies. *Magis, Revista Internacional de Investigación en Educatión, 11*(22),75-86. https://doi:10.11144/Javeriana.m11-22.eeit

Stahl, A. (2021). *How gen-z is bringing a fresh perspective to the world of work*. Forbes. https://bit.ly/3diTsJj

Sutcher, L., Darling-Hammond, L., & Carver-Thomas, D. (2016). *A coming crisis in teaching? Teacher supply, demand, and shortages in the U.S.* Learning Policy Institute. https://eric.ed.gov/?id=ED606666

Sutcher, L., Darling-Hammond, L., & Carver-Thomas, D. (2019). Understanding teacher shortages: An analysis of teacher supply and demand in the United States. *Education Policy Analysis Archives, 27*(35), 1-39. https://eric.ed.gov/?id=EJ1213618

Tran, H., & Smith, D. A. (2020). Designing an employee experience approach to teacher retention in hard-to-staff schools. *NASSP Bulletin, 104*(2), 85-109. https://doi.org/10.1177/0192636520927092

Uhl-Bien, M. (2004). Relational leadership approaches. In G. R. Goethals, G. J. Sorenson, & J. M. Burns (Eds.), *Encyclopedia of Leadership 3* (pp. 1304-1307). Sage.

Uhl-Bien, M. (2006). Relational leadership theory: Exploring the social processes of leadership and organizing. *The Leadership Quarterly, 17,* 654-676. https://

digitalcommons.unl.edu/leadershipfacpub/19/

U.S. Census Bureau. (n.d.). *Quick facts columbus city, Georgia*. U.S. Department of Commerce, Retrieved November 10, 2020, from https://bit.ly/38Itei0

Wigford, A., & Higgins, A. (2019). Well-being in international schools: Teachers' perceptions. *Educational & Child Psychology, 36*(4), 46-64.

ABOUT THE AUTHORS

Editors

Joseph R. Jones, PhD is a Professor of Education and qualitative researcher whose research resides within a critical theory paradigm. His research primarily examines inclusivity within educational environments, specifically heteronormativity. He is the recipient of several awards including the 2017 *Stonewall Service Award* from CCCC/NCTE. He is also the recipient of the Georgia Council of Teachers of English 2020 *Teacher of the Year Award*.

Anna Dunlap Higgins-Harrell, PhD has a master's degree in English with Teacher Preparation and a PhD in English. Her research focus began with Emily Dickinson, then moved to Appalachian Studies. For the last decade, her scholarship efforts have centered on excellence in teaching and learning.

Julie Little, EdD is an Associate Professor of Education. She spent 20 years as a K-12 educator in Special and General Education; she now teaches Special Education courses to teacher candidates. Julie's research interests include ungrading, relational pedagogy, service learning, and utilizing the Principles of Universal Design (UD) for Learning in higher education.

Contributors

Erinn Bentley, PhD is a professor and program coordinator of an English education in a teacher preparation program. Prior to joining higher education, she taught English language arts and ESOL in Michigan and Japan.

Randall Brookins, MEd worked in elementary education for over 26 years serving as a fourth-grade general education teacher, second-grade general education teacher, and K-5 literacy specialist. He is currently a lecturer of education in a teacher preparation program.

Nila Burt, EdD is a high school principal. She taught high school French and mathematics for 20 years and transitioned into administration, where she has remained for 17 years.

Adam Dovico, EdD currently works in higher education administration and is a former principal. He has been recognized by organizations such as the Japan Fulbright Memorial Fund, Learning for Justice, and the Atlanta Falcons for his leadership and teaching. He continues to work for greater equity in schools through his culturally responsive pedagogy.

Rebecca Doyle is a teacher candidate in an elementary education program. She will complete her program in May 2024.

Fran Dundore, EdS is a doctoral student in Curriculum Studies. She is a former high school English teacher, principal, curriculum director, and assistant superintendent for teaching and learning. Currently, she leads the Governor's Honors Program through her work at the Governor's Office of Student Achievement for the state of Georgia.

Lindsay Tisdale Harrell has a bachelor's degree in elementary education, and is currently working on her master's degree in education. She taught 12 years at the elementary level, primarily in 3rd and 4th grades. Named *Teacher of the Year* in 2011 and 2021, she's currently a member of her school's leadership team and an ELA representative from her school at the county level.

Noah Lawton Harrell, MEd is a high school assistant principal. He earned a MEd in Educational Leadership and a bachelor's in social science with an emphasis in history. For 14 years, he taught social studies in high school. While teaching, he also coached multiple sports such as basketball, golf, soccer, and baseball. In 2021, he transitioned to a leadership position as an assistant principal.

Kraig Howell, EdS is a K-12 administrator whose career centers around special education, positive behavior supports, social-emotional learning, professional learning, and assessment. He's currently researching social-emotional learning within educational institutions, specifically in rural communities.

About the Author

Michael Jeffcoat has been working in education for eight years, and is currently completing a bachelor's degree in elementary and special education.

Jennifer Medgull, EdS holds bachelor's degrees in mathematics and Christianity, a Master of Arts teaching mathematics, and is a specialist in teacher leadership. She has taught math at every level from sixth grade through college, but her passion is serving teachers and students through instructional coaching.

Amy Morgan, EdD is an 18-year Title 1 veteran teacher. After having had most of her experiences in middle grades, she changed to elementary grades in her 18th year. She is also an adjunct professor in a teacher education program.

Jadziah Ogletree is enrolled in a dual certification program in elementary education and special education. She hopes to work with students with special needs when she graduates May 2024.

Forrest R Parker III, PhD has worked in education for the past 13 years. He served as a special education teacher for students with severe behavioral and emotional disorders. He currently serves as a Lecturer of Education teaching classes in educational psychology, child development, and classroom management.

Tenecia Powe, MEd is a former research and development chemist and spent eight years teaching science before becoming a Digital Learning Specialist for a school district, where she currently serves as Coordinator of Innovation and Redesign.

Stephen Raynie, PhD is a Professor of English and a college Dean. His scholarship ranges from Renaissance and 18th-century British literature to student success and issues in education. He's a strong proponent of studies in the humanities and helping students transitioning to college understand the relationship between quantitative and qualitative reasoning.

Emily Salmon, EdS has been an educator for 31 years. She has served as a library media specialist in all school levels, with extensive classroom experience teaching English. In addition to teaching high school students, she's an adjunct college professor in a teacher preparation program.

Jessica Traylor, EdD was a school psychologist for over a decade before entering higher education. Her research interests include mental health literacy, deliberative pedagogy, adverse childhood experiences, resilience, service-learning, and civic engagement. She enjoys teaching courses in Psychology of Adjustment, Human Growth & Development, and Trauma & Resilience.

INDEX

504 plans, 21, 22, 75

A
accountability, 23, 201
ADHD, 19
administration, xi, 19, 31, 35, 63, 78, 90, 233, 243
advanced placement, 21, 28
alternative certification, 43
anxiety, 19, 34, 45, 131, 221
assistant principal, 19,

B
behavior, xiii, 7, 24, 27, 30, 39, 71, 90, 151, 163, 183, 210, 239, 245
bullying, 153, 157, 170
burnout, 93, 95, 100

C
Career, Technical, and Agricultural Education, 137
ChatGPT, 45
Chromebooks, xiii, 15, 17, 39
classroom management, 9, 24, 58, 87, 229, 245
cognitive, 17, 135, 184, 244
collaborative planning, 191
communication, 8,
community, 3, 82, 135, 152, 165, 169
conflict resolution, 168
COVID, 20, 47, 125, 203, 208, 222, 232, 234
credit recovery, 24
critical pedagogy, 144
culture, 79, 82, 98, 114, 120, 135, 164, 169, 178, 200, 202, 221, 231
cyberbullying, 153, 159, 170

D
depression, 34, 40, 41, 46, 50, 161, 221
differentiation, 77, 220
digital citizenship, 168
discipline, 31, 36, 55, 60, 79, 89, 114, 132, 220, 235
discrimination, 46, 121, 164, 177
diversity, xiv, 114, 136, 164, 178, 221, 224, 229
dress code, 36

E
early intervention, 168
elementary, 6, 15, 17, 33, 44, 111, 175, 184, 243, 244
Eliot, T. S, 141, 142, 147
Emotional Behavior Disorder, 7
equity, 48, 97, 141, 178, 209, 244
exceptional student education, 6, 36

F
federal mandates, 30, 167
Freire, Paulo, 144
Frost, Robert, 146
foundations of education, 3
funding, 25

G
gay, 44, 46, 105, 108, 114, 116, 119, 140
Generation Z, 45, 219, 220, 237
Greene, Maxine, 145
Gorman, Amanda, 141
grading, 24, 72, 75, 81, 127, 130, 23, 243

H
high school, xiv, 1, 19, 24, 43, 44, 53, 75, 111, 127, 158, 162, 179, 221, 225
high stakes testing, 96, 133, 184, 219

I
inclusivity, 105, 117, 165, 171, 178, 243
identity, 115
individual education plan, 6, 21
inequity, 182
instruction, 112
instructional coaches, 87
instructional strategies, 135

K
K-12, xi, 33, 69, 122, 125, 127, 179, 191, 243

L
lesbian, 109, 116
Lexile, 85
LGBTQ+, 105, 113, 121, 165
lockdown, 2,

M
marginalized identities, 5, 44, 46, 175
mental health, 20, 34, 45, 50, 152, 156, 164, 167, 170, 207, 246
mentor, xi, 90, 98, 125, 127, 133, 170, 205
methods, 3
middle school, xiv, 6, 10, 24, 33, 34, 59, 82, 110, 111, 128, 175, 197
millennials, 220
motivation, 21, 31, 78, 186
multi-tiered system of support, 7

N
narrative inquiry, 222
neurodivergent, 5
No Child Left Behind, 22, 95

O
Oliver, Mary, 142

P
pandemic, 17, 30, 34, 45, 95, 99, 125, 132, 161, 203, 208
paraprofessionals, 27, 185, 224
parents, 5, 7, 10, 15, 28, 30, 47, 57
parent teacher association, 34
pedagogy, 15, 37, 53, 79, 108, 112, 113, 120, 141, 183, 209, 220, 233
peer mediation, 168
poetic inquiry, 141, 143, 148
political mandates, 30
Positive Behavioral Inventions and Support, 59, 169
principal, 96
privilege, 55
professional development, 12, 49, 64, 69, 165, 209, 236
professional learning, 10, 69, 70, 89, 194

Q
qualitative research, 222, 243
queer theory, 109

R
racism, 110, 122, 175, 177
Read180, 77
reading, 13, 15, 76, 85, 95, 113, 130, 146, 236
resource officer, 2, 3, 4
relationships, 2, 30, 60, 175, 209, 223, 227
relational pedagogy, 3, 37, 58, 243
restorative justice, 168
rural communities, 197, 206

S
salaries, 53, 56, 101, 180
scaffold, 80
school psychologist, 49
school shootings, xi, 1, 3, 151, 161
school violence, 153, 156, 163
secondary, 3, 34, 54, 104, 106, 109, 120, 125, 144, 225
Social Emotional Learning, 169, 197, 209, 243
social intelligence, 199, 212
social media, 20, 34, 152, 159
special education, 2, 21
standards, 23, 31, 70, 82, 95, 178, 202, 231, 236
standardized testing, 19, 22, 23, 35, 37, 77, 206
state mandate, 25,
STEM, 44
stigma, 53
student achievement, 23
student teachers, 125, 133
superintendent, 24, 48, 51,

T
Teacher Alternative Preparation Program, 43
teacher attrition, 219, 222
teacher candidates, 3, 16, 175, 184, 243
teacher preparation, 3, 105, 186, 243
teacher shortage, 26, 29, 179
technology, 15, 34, 39, 152, 159, 221
threat assessment, 168

Title-1, 16, 20, 33, 39, 93, 102, 245
Tik Tok, 27, 34
trauma, 9, 10, 22, 51, 170, 221
trauma-informed teaching, 9, 12, 169

V
veteran teachers, 19, 31, 91
violence, 151

W
writing, 15, 32, 53, 60, 78, 81, 144